If
Only

If Only

How to Turn Regret into Opportunity

Neal Roese, Ph.D.

Broadway Books
New York

PRINTED IN THE UNITED STATES OF AMERICA

BROADWAY BOOKS and its logo, a letter B bisected on the diagonal, are trademarks of Random House, Inc.

Visit our website at www.broadwaybooks.com

Verse: from *Happy Birthday to You!* by Dr. Seuss, copyright TM & copyright © by Dr. Seuss Enterprises, L.P. 1959, renewed 1987. Used by permission of Random House Children's Books, a division of Random House, Inc.

First edition published 2005

Book design by Donna Sinisgalli

Library of Congress Cataloging-in-Publication Data
Roese, Neal J.
If only : how to turn regret into opportunity / Neal Roese.—1st ed.
p. cm.
ISBN 0-7679-1577-1 (alk. paper)
1. Regret. 2. Counterfactuals (Logic) 3. Self-actualization (Psychology)
I. Title.

BF575.R33R64 2005
155.2'4—dc22
2004050251

1 3 5 7 9 10 8 6 4 2

For Emma
and Annie

Contents

Acknowledgments

With a book called *If Only,* you can be sure that I am well aware of the many ways the project might have gone differently, were it not for the contributions of several key individuals. Indeed, this book project would probably not have begun at all if not for my agent, Eileen Cope, of Lowenstein-Yost Associates. Over the years I had kicked around the idea of writing a book on counterfactual thinking, but I'd never quite gotten serious about it until Eileen contacted me out of the blue and suggested it. Eileen discovered me by way of a research news website that I've maintained for nearly a decade (counterfactual.net) and urged me to write the book sooner rather than later. Eileen was instrumental in helping me assemble a sellable proposal. Kris Puopolo has been my editor at Broadway Books; and again, the book probably would not have happened without her. She gave the early drafts an exceptionally sharp review, pushing me to make important changes that improved and clarified the final manuscript tremendously. From the start, Kris keenly understood the essence of my ideas, on some occasions better than I myself did. I feel enormously lucky to have had the good fortune of working with Kris.

Throughout the writing process, I have deeply appreciated the enthusiasm and support of my wife, Karen. She is the only person to have waded through the entirety of the overly long first draft. She then not only corrected the silly mistakes but also suggested many a new interesting avenue to explore in subsequent writing. Although my daughters, Emma and Annie, were too young to quite realize what it was that Daddy was doing on the computer for so many months, their joyous spirit and energy pervade this book. Indeed, the book is dedicated to them, and I look forward to a time in the future when they can read it for themselves and tell me how I might have written it better.

I wrote this book during my first year on the faculty at the University of Illinois. During that time of adjustment, it was a continuing delight to work among such an extraordinarily talented group of scientists. I especially want to thank professors Ed Diener and Justin Kruger for their incisive discussions of recent research findings.

I am grateful to the following scholars who answered my questions about their own and others' research: Renée Baillargeon, John Bargh, Ruth Byrne, Adam Galinsky, Dan Gilbert, Paul Harris, Sheena Iyengar, Ned Lebow, Keith Markman, Michael Morris, Dave Piercey, Barry Schwartz, Jeff Sherman, Phil Tetlock, Kate White, Carsten Wrosch, Maia Young, and Marcel Zeelenberg. I very much appreciate the feedback on specific chapters offered by the following individuals: Galen Bodenhausen, Larry Sanna, and Steve Wiseman. The following people lent me various bits of additional assistance during my time of writing: Richard Corley, Kemberly Crummet, Beth Haymaker, Jeff Kuban, Vuk Vuksanović, and Michelle Zimmerman. And from the very beginning, I have treasured the kind words of support offered by my sister, Tanis, uncle Gary, and mom, Geraldine.

Finally, I would like to thank Jim Olson, my academic mentor, longtime collaborator, and friend. Without his kind encouragement and keen insight over many years of joint projects, this book could not have been written.

If
Only

Introduction

Take an ordinary coin and flip it. As it arcs through the air, it has two possible futures, two potential outcomes. Heads or tails. It lands and one side is facing up, the other down. At the moment of landing, those two potential outcomes vanish to be replaced by a single factual outcome. This time, heads is up. Heads is the factual outcome. It is what *is*: factuality, actuality, reality. Tails is the outcome that did not occur. But it could have occurred. It might have been. The coin is fair, and so there was an even chance that tails might have come up. But that's not what happened. Tails is a *counterfactual* outcome.

Counterfactual means, literally, contrary to the facts. Counterfactual thoughts are thoughts of what might have been, of what could have happened had some detail, or action, or outcome been different in the past. Whenever we say "if only" or "almost," or use words like "could," "would," or "should," we may be expressing a counterfactual thought: *If only I were taller . . . I almost won that hand . . . I could have been a contender . . . I would have caught that ball, if not for the sun in my eyes.*

You might think that counterfactuals are examples of mere fantasy, of our brain engaged in unproductive navel-gazing and time-wasting. Maybe you agree with the main character in Norman Rush's novel, *Mating,* who muses to herself: "Nothing is more profitless than going back over what interventions might have changed the shape of things. . . . I want to scream at myself when I do that." For years psychologists agreed with this sentiment, that counterfactual thinking is at best pointless, at worst an impediment to sound reasoning and wise decision-making. New research tells a different story.[1]

"If only" thinking is good for you. Counterfactual thinking, along with regret, its emotional offspring, plays a vital role in learning, insight, and improvement. From counterfactuals comes recognition of possibilities, out of regret comes hope for the future, and the essence of human cognition is a set of interlocking mechanisms designed to identify, understand, and fix the problems, both big and small, that appear constantly along the road of life. Regret feels bad, but it is utterly essential for healthy living. Understanding and harnessing your own regrets can make you better.

The positive value of regret is emblematic of a recent revolution in how scientists view emotions. It was once widely believed that emotions are the enemy of rational thought and that to be successful you must stifle your feelings. Many self-help books teach you to avoid negativity. But it turns out that emotions in general, and negative emotions in particular, are a crucial component of rational thought. They are essential to effective performance, whatever the task may be. Regret is an example of a negative emotion that spurs people to problem-solving and personal betterment. This books explains why and shows how you can harness regret for your own benefit.

Along the way, we'll gain a new appreciation for the magnificent power of the human brain. We'll see how a silent set of protective brain mechanisms—what might be called a *psychological immune system*—stand ready to manage regret and console us after misfortune. Most people are unaware of how powerfully these brain mechanisms work. This is a shame, for it can be an enormously liberating feeling to realize that no matter which way you decide things, your own brain stands ready to reconcile you in the end to that decision.

〜

There are many kinds of thoughts, and this book is about just one of them, the counterfactual thought. Now, thoughts are tough things to nail down: they are fleeting, they are ephemeral, they lack concrete form. Indeed, if you were a scientific psychologist in the first half of the twentieth century, you would have thought it ludicrous to even consider measuring something so insubstantial as thought. Yet after about 1950, a curious change overcame scientific psychology, something called the cognitive revolution, in which more and more psychologists realized that it was not only possible to measure thought, but utterly essential to measure thought, as thought is nearly synonymous with human nature.[2] One of the founding fathers of American scientific psychology, William James, said over a century ago that "thinking is for doing," which means that thinking is best understood as a biological tool designed for ensuring survival. The theme of this book updates James's ideas with a new adage: *Counterfactuals are for betterment.*[3]

New research into counterfactual thinking reveals a fascinating spectrum of insights about our everyday experiences, from coping with misfortune to enjoying a good movie. Here is a preview:

• *If only I had told her I love her!* The aching remorse of actions left undone, of better possibilities left unattained, is an emotion common to all people. This emotion is called regret, and it is the most poignant face of counterfactual thinking. New research provides fresh insight into the experience of regret: where it comes from, how it unfolds over time, which aspects of life it tends to envelop. And how to use it to your advantage. When the various life regrets voiced by Americans are tabulated, the same four regrets are consistently at the top of the list. The number one regret centers on education: *I should have studied harder, should have stayed in school longer. . . .* See Chapter 2 for the rest of Americans' biggest regrets.

• *If only I had said something sooner, I could have prevented the accident. It's all my fault.* Counterfactuals and blame go hand in hand. When we say we could have done something to have avoided an accident, we are in essence saying that we are responsible, that we had a role in causing the accident, that we can be blamed. Counterfactuals are a key means by which we express our beliefs about guilt, responsibility, blame, causation, and punishment. Sometimes blame is unwarranted, as in the well-documented "blaming the victim" bias, and in Chapter 4 we'll see how misplaced counterfactuals contribute to this bias.

• *If only I had sold my Enron stock earlier!* Every decision we make, from investing in stocks to buying a new car, is influenced by counterfactuals—that is, by our past history of decisions and foregone alternatives. Once the decision is made, the decision itself unleashes new counterfactual thinking—about the alternative that might have been chosen instead. Unwary investors who feel the sting of regret ("If only I'd sold last month I'd be ahead 20 percent now!") tend to buy and sell too often, losing more money than they otherwise would had they been wary of the biasing effects of regret. Skilled salespeople know how to use your counterfactuals against you, and so understanding how your own mental machinery works can protect you from needless purchases. In Chapter 5 we'll explore the basics of deciding and buying, and learn not only the tricks that sellers use but also new tricks for how best to buy.

• *What if Nazi Germany had won the Second World War?* Historians are drawn to critical moments in history to ask how the world might have been different if events had unfolded differently. But historians are not the only ones: many storytellers use counterfactuals to create great fiction. Sometimes called "alternate history," these stories engage readers with thought-provoking explorations of times and places that might have been. What if the South had won the Civil War? What if the Soviet Union had conquered America? In Chapter 6 we'll see two reasons why these stories are popular. They push readers into further reveries of creative thought, encouraging our minds to roam where they otherwise would not have gone. And in skillfully combining oddity with familiarity, they come across as just odd enough to be interesting, yet still familiar enough to remain inviting.

• *He leaped from the car just before it went over the cliff!* Counterfactual thinking makes movies into thrillers. "What if he hadn't been able to get the door open in time?" "If only he had thought to grab the gold before he jumped!" The cinematic "close call" is so effective because it evokes counterfactual thinking and its emotional offshoots, such as relief or regret. Chapter 6 shows how all successful storytellers, whether they realize it or not, rely on counterfactuals to create feelings of tension and drama.

So, you may ask, are counterfactuals *everywhere*? This morning I took a break from work to have a coffee. I ordered an Americano from the little coffeehouse that sits across the street from the psychology building where I work at the University of Illinois. I sat for a moment at a small table by the window, watching the constant rush of students braving the January cold. Mere moments after taking my first sip, I was second-guessing my decision. I should have had tea. Coffee is what I always have, it's boring and gives me bad breath, I thought to myself. Some exotic green tea, with its purported health benefits and light, clean flavor, seemed at this moment vastly preferable. For a moment I experienced a dull, aching feeling, a sort of mourning for the loss of what might have been. A moment later the feeling was gone.

Had I not been writing a book on the topic, this feeling would have been forgotten forever.

For a split second I second-guessed a decision and thought about how I should have made a different decision. When you think about how often this happens, how automatically it takes place, how purely reflexive it is, you begin to realize the magnificent hugeness of this thought process. Hardly a moment goes by before another counterfactual comes along, sometimes consciously considered, but many other times *unconscious* and out of mental sight. These momentary counterfactuals represent the tip of the iceberg of our relevant memories, activated and brought to mind by experience itself. As bits of memory are retrieved, they give context to current experience. Chapter 1 shows how, moment by moment, counterfactuals help us make sense of our lives.

Where counterfactuals go, regret follows. Regret is an emotion built from counterfactuals. It's the aching feeling you get when you realize you could have done something differently and could have made things better. And speaking from experience, it can be a very painful emotion.

In pursuing challenging careers, my wife and I waited until we were both in our thirties before trying to start a family. With a string of miscarriages, the experience of parenthood was proving ominously elusive. The pain of infertility is one of emptiness, a gnawing, hollowed-out absence of something deeply longed for. Bad situations make counterfactual thinking, and therefore regret, more active. The worse the situation, the more you try to see ways that you could have bypassed it, could have escaped it. The trouble is that once you feel regret, it makes an already bad situation feel even worse. *If only we had tried to start a family earlier* is a regret my wife and I painfully shared. We both knew that a woman's fertility declines with age, and the rate of decline accelerates after age thirty. But when we were graduate students in our twenties, we were far more concerned with advancing our own careers than with starting a new family. When faced with infertility less than a decade later, we recognized that we easily could have started a family while attending graduate school. Indeed, for the generation older than us, starting a family while struggling financially through the twenty-something years was the rule rather than the exception.

For severely traumatic experiences, regrets can gush as though from a fountain. The more painful the experience, the more intense the regret. We can begin to understand a bit more of the nature of depression by examining the most severe regrets that people feel. But even as severe regret can be debilitating, psychologists now recognize that regret in its more moderate and common form is essential to healthy living. Neglecting the messages of your own emotions can mean persisting in counterproductive behaviors and missing unique opportunities for growth and renewal. There seems to be an ideal amount of regret, neither too much nor too little, that is experienced by the most mentally healthy of individuals.

My own story does have a happy ending, because after several years of in vitro fertilization attempts, we became parents of two healthy daughters, Emma and Annie. We were lucky. Strangely enough, the counterfactual realization that this family might never have been, that these two children were almost never conceived, somehow makes them all the more precious. Chapter 7 shows how life experiences gain new meaning when benchmarked against alternatives that might have been. And Chapter 8 provides strategies to help you regret just enough and not too much, for maximum happiness.

In the pages ahead, we will see that counterfactual thinking is an essential component of the quest for personal betterment. Moreover, counterfactuals bring us a sense of wonder, an awe of the magnificent set of improbable circumstances that conspired to create this universe, this world, and the particular life we personally inhabit. "If only" thinking, we will find, has the power to shape the very meaning we give our lives.

Part I

How Counterfactuals Work

Chapter 1

Benchmarking Reality

～

Terry Malloy, the Marlon Brando character in the 1954 film *On the Waterfront*, is a former boxer obsessed with a fight he deliberately lost because of mob pressure. If he hadn't taken a dive, he "could have been a contender," so he says in the film's signature line, "instead of a bum, which is what I am." Malloy's very identity hinges on a fork in the road and a particular road not taken, defined on the surface by a boxing victory but more deeply by a commitment to personal integrity that could have been, and yet may still possibly come to be. In short, Malloy defines the entirety of his life by the contrast to what he might have been. Of course, this makes for personal anguish, but the film also illuminates how a singular life-defining counterfactual can motivate positive change—by the end of the film, Malloy has risked his life to make a stand against mob influence at the dock where he works. Counterfactuals can be a defining aspect of personal identity. And as we'll see throughout this book, counterfactuals, even if painful, hold within them the power to push *individuals* toward regeneration and renewal.

Counterfactual thoughts provide benchmarks for reality. By offering standards of comparison (*this* happened instead of *that*), they place the factual events of our lives into context. An experience feels all the more precious, or all the more poignant, if it very nearly never happened. At the broadest level, people's sense of identity and personality can be shaped by forks in the road, by the lives they might have lived, the riches and disasters that might have been. At the unconscious level, each event in our lives gains meaning via a silent comparison to an alternative, counterfactual event that might have taken place instead. And at the level of our most passionate feelings, counterfactuals (along with other kinds of commonly drawn comparisons) sculpt the contours of our emotions, making us feel worse or better depending on what exactly might have been. On every level, thinking about what might have been shapes the very meaning we see in life.

∾

Counterfactuals are a product of what might commonly be called imagination, but they are also much more. Certainly both counterfactual and imagination refer to creative, generative thought processes: thoughts that go boldly where no thoughts have gone before. But there are at least two important ways that counterfactuals stand apart from imagination.

First, we often assume that some people have a good imagination, say Walt Disney or Steven Spielberg, whereas many more of us possess at best mediocre imaginations, and some (a couple of my high school teachers come to mind at this point) little or none at all. But *everyone* generates counterfactuals. All of us, young and old, every day, with little difficulty. Counterfactuals are an automatic product of the normal operation of human brains.

Second, we tend to think of imagination as boundless, unrestrained, unrealistic. Maybe even silly. By contrast, counterfactuals are quite realistic. They are disciplined, in a way that preserves the essential fabric of reality while altering just one or a few elements. Of the numerous counterfactuals that you generate on a daily basis, nearly all are grounded in fact: *What if I had driven a different route to work? I should have remembered to pack a lunch rather than having to spend money at the cafeteria. I shouldn't have had that piece of cake for dessert.* Seen in this light, it is clear that rather few of our daily counterfactuals are bizarre: *What if I attended a college on another planet? What if I had a flying car like on* The Jetsons? *It would be great if I had eight arms.* Of course, we *could* imagine such things, if we put our minds to it, but the point is that we don't. At least not very often. Such bizarre creations require effort, whereas the typical counterfactual thoughts of everyday life are effortless. They appear so easily that we might even compare them to a reflex, like jerking your hand away from a hot stove. Counterfactuals are *reflexive imagination*. And most counterfactual thoughts are useful precisely because they are disciplined, realistic, and effortlessly efficient.[1] But when counterfactuals do require effort, that is, when they are spun into elaborate stories and speculations, they can have very different effects, useful for different purposes.

What if Kennedy had survived? We all know what actually happened: On November 22, 1963, President John F. Kennedy was killed by two rifle bullets as he was riding in a slow-moving open limousine through the streets of Dallas. But what if he had lived? What if the bullets had just grazed him? What if he had been rushed to Parkland Memorial Hospital only to be given a couple of Band-Aids before returning to the White House and his presidency? Now, just mention these ideas at a party. You're sure to start a lively conversation. Sure, it's all speculative, for no one can know for sure what truly would have happened, but the conversation gets animated because counterfactuals fuel new insights, new points of view, new ways of looking at old facts.

If Kennedy had survived, America might have been a much different place. Maybe the urban riots and violent student protests could have been avoided. And what about Vietnam? Many people continue to this day to believe that had Kennedy been president a little bit longer, some fifty thousand American soldiers might not have died in Vietnam, that Kennedy would have found a way to steer America clear of that divisive war. Whenever we think about such counterfactual possibilities, we accept a tantalizing invitation to explore further and to follow a road of continuing assessment that may take us to new understandings we might not have achieved otherwise. Counterfactuals are cognigenic. This capacity of counterfactual thinking to launch us into further reveries of thought is one of several reasons why counterfactual stories are so entertaining—an idea to which we'll return in Chapter 6.

Avoiding Mishaps

How do you keep bad things from happening?

On July 25, 2000, a supersonic Concorde airliner crashed shortly after takeoff in Paris, killing all 109 people aboard and four more on the ground. Witnesses saw fire spewing from the plane's engines as it took off. It then sank from view. Not long after, horrific images of fire and wrecked metal filled television screens around the world, vividly reminding us all that air travel remains an inherently risky venture that can, occasionally, incinerate us beyond all recognition.

Immediately after the crash, investigators descended on the scene of the accident and began to examine, assess, and formulate working hypotheses about the cause of the crash. There is nothing unique about this. The same thing happens whenever there is a serious accident. Teams of specialists collect information with the specific goal of answering the question *why*. Why did this accident happen at this point in time, relative to other points in time that were accident-free?

This is a question of causation. And like any question of causation, it can be rephrased in counterfactual terms: *How might the accident have been avoided?*[2]

Causation is the Excalibur sword of science. In the tale of King Arthur, the magic sword Excalibur rendered its user all-powerful. In the same way, any person armed with an understanding of causation has the power to change, alter, repair, and control. Causal knowledge is the essential tool for changing the world for the better. This wisdom is contained in the medical adage of treating not merely the symptoms but the underlying cause: treat the cause and you defeat the illness, defeat the illness and you conclusively restore health. Accident investigators try to find the causes of accidents because such knowledge holds the power to prevent future accidents.

And so it was with the Concorde. Investigators compiled their evidence and concluded that a small piece of metal left on the runway from another jet was the ultimate cause of the accident. That tiny piece of metal punctured one of the plane's tires, which flung debris that ruptured a fuel tank, which ignited a fire that blocked the engines from producing the thrust needed to keep the plane in the air. So the plane fell. This is the causal explanation, a map detailing a chain of small events connected together, and it was immediately funneled into a series of engineering fixes that improved the remaining Concordes so that when they started flying commercially again in November 2001, they were even safer than before.[3]

This process—in which an accident triggers causal analysis which results in fixes that prevent future mishap—is one of the most important, basic, and automatic functions of human brains. Our brains do this constantly, and counterfactuals are a prominent marker of this process. The craving to undo a tragic event is a simple expression of our most basic urge toward survival, toward self-preservation. If we see danger ahead of us, we move out of its way. We try to *avoid* it. But when danger has already produced tragedy, we still try to avoid it, reflexively imagining how the tragedy might have been avoided. Along the way, such counterfactual musings on the past can prepare us to avoid similar tragedy in the future. That counterfactuals help us see the world more clearly by illuminating causation and avoidance is the first example of how counterfactuals are for betterment.[4]

Counterfactuals Shape Emotions

You might have noticed that there are two distinctly different kinds of counterfactuals. One makes us feel bad, the other makes us feel grateful. The kind that makes us feel bad is called an *upward* counterfactual. By upward, we mean that a comparison is made between a factual situation and something better, something more desirable, something that you would much prefer to have happen. Wishing that you'd ordered a more delicious meal, avoided a car accident, or married a richer spouse are all examples of upward counterfactuals. They are called upward because we look up to things desirable, such as a role model that we admire, and down on things undesirable. Accordingly, *downward* counterfactuals are thoughts about how things might have been worse.

When Terry Malloy said that he could have been a contender, he was expressing an upward counterfactual. And he felt bad. When an accident victim realizes that she is lucky to be alive, that she might have been killed, she is focusing on a downward counterfactual. And for this she feels relief, even gratefulness. You might be thinking that there are two kinds of people, those who see the glass as half full (optimists) and those who see the glass as half empty (pessimists). It would seem straightforward then to say that optimists see the past in terms of how it might have been worse (lucky things turned out as they did) whereas pessimists see how things could have been better. But the story is more complicated than that.[5]

For one thing, optimists are excited by the expectation of positive future events, and it is the tendency to generate upward rather than downward counterfactuals about the past that is most clearly linked to this sort of hopefulness (With a little more training, I know I could have finished that marathon; *next time,* I'll finish it for sure . . .). And for most people, optimists or pessimists, research shows that upward counterfactuals come to mind far more often than downward counterfactuals.[6] Upward counterfactuals are common; downward counterfactuals are rare. To understand the emotional offshoots of these two kinds of thoughts, it helps to recognize a basic principle of psychology: the contrast effect.

Have you ever had a sip of hot tea immediately after eating ice cream? Probably the tea felt especially hot. Have you ever jumped into a swimming pool immediately after soaking in a hot tub? Probably the pool felt peculiarly cold, as though someone had forgotten to turn on the heat. These are all examples of one of the most basic of brain mechanisms involved in perception—the contrast effect. The experience that came just before alters the perception of what comes next—pushing it in the opposite, contrasting direction. In reality, the tea and the pool are the same as ever, they just *feel* hotter or colder because of the directly preceding experience.

Contrast effects occur everywhere, for all of our senses. Some of the earliest experiments beginning a hundred years ago used sets of weights, from a few ounces to several pounds. A one-pound weight feels light if you have just hefted a five-pound weight, but heavier if you've just palmed a one-ounce weight. The same effect occurs for light and dark, as you probably noticed the last time you walked out into a summer afternoon from a dark matinee movie theater—*it sure is bright out!* Perhaps more surprising, the same effect also occurs for value. How much we are willing to pay for a good or service depends quite a bit on context. Widely known to salespeople, for example, is that you are more likely to buy a small item—a handkerchief for $20, let's say—if you have just spent a much larger amount on a big-ticket item, like a $400 jacket. Compared to the $400 you've just blown, after all, what's an extra twenty bucks? But if you are in the store without any need for a new jacket, that $20 feels like quite a bit more, and you are much less likely to part with it.

Contrast effects are one reason why counterfactuals influence emotions. Counterfactuals alter our emotions, push them this way and that, by juxtaposing what is against what might have been. Just as the tea feels hotter next to ice cream, Terry Malloy's life as it is now seems pallid when positioned next to the life he might have led—a contender's—had he not taken a fall.

Contrast effects can alter our feelings of satisfaction in surprising ways. Take, for example, the emotional reactions of Olympic athletes who have just won medals. There they are on the medal stand, basking in the warmth of worldwide applause. And of course, the accolades are color-coded: Gold is best, the winner, the absolute champion. Silver is second-best: obviously talented enough to beat everyone save one. Bronze is third-best. And after that comes everyone else, medal-less. We all understand that these medals correspond to clear rankings of value, and certainly this understanding is clearest of all to the athletes themselves. Why then are bronze medalists more satisfied than silver medalists?

It took a team of social psychologists led by Vicki Medvec, working out of Cornell University, to even notice in the first place that bronze medalists are happier than silver medalists, but their research went even further in linking this curious fact both to counterfactual thinking and also to contrast effects. In one of their studies, they began by videotaping television coverage of the 1992 Olympic games held in Barcelona, Spain. They edited this video coverage down to a series of clips showing both the athletes' immediate reactions to their performances and also their participation in the medal stand ceremony (when the three medalists stand on boxes of varying height). They then showed these videotapes to a group of research participants, whose job was to evaluate each of the athletes' emotional reactions—selecting a number ranging from 1 (complete agony) to 10 (complete ecstasy). All participants had declared themselves uninterested in sports or Olympics at the outset, thus ensuring a relatively unbiased set of judgments. Sure enough, for both immediate reactions right after the winner was announced, and also for those delayed reactions on display during the medal ceremony, observers found the emotional expressions to be more ecstatic for the bronze than silver medalists. So far so good—this piece of evidence establishes the existence of a puzzle: bronze medalists are happier with an objectively poorer outcome. But it does not yet tell us why.[7]

To answer this deeper question, the researchers needed to assess counterfactual thinking directly. They needed to get inside the athletes' heads, not rely on the observations of others. The 1994 Empire State Games, an annual amateur meet in New York state, provided just such an opportunity. Medvec descended on the games, tracking down athletes individually after they had completed their events. The athletes completed a simple rating of their current thoughts corresponding to the distinction between upward and downward counterfactuals. They used a number between 1 and 10 to express how much they were thinking things along the lines of "I almost" (upward) versus "at least" (downward). Sure enough, silver medalists were more focused on the upward possibilities *(I could easily have had the gold!)*, whereas the bronze medalists were more focused on downward prospects *(I could easily have missed getting a medal entirely)*.

Counterfactuals are more likely to come to mind when something almost falls into a different category or almost crosses a boundary. In athletics as well as in many parts of our lives, we can see categories of performance that have clear boundaries. One powerful boundary separates just two types of people, winners and losers. The gold medalist is best, and everyone else is the rest. To the silver medalist, this boundary is the most compelling. He or she is the one who came closest to that boundary and missed out. To the bronze medalist, however, this boundary is further away, and so not as compelling a candidate for something that might have happened. But to the silver medalist, this boundary powerfully lures counterfactual thoughts, ensuring that they are upward. *If only I had poured it on in the last seconds. . . . If only I had kissed my lucky charm a second time . . . that gold medal would have been mine.*

Another way of categorizing athletic performance is to contrast medal winners to non-medal winners. This is a completely different boundary, this time separating those with and without precious metal dangling from their necks. Though not quite as potent, it nevertheless is quite meaningful to the athletes—it is better to have some metal than no metal at all. And in this case, it is the bronze and not the silver medalist who is closest to this boundary. And notice also that this boundary is in the other direction, representing a "worse than" cutoff. For all three medal winners it constitutes a downward comparison—aimed in the direction of how lousy it would have been to win no medal at all. The bronze medalist, being closest to this boundary, feels his or her thoughts lured in this direction. *If I had blinked, I would have missed out on this medal and been left with nothing at all.*

Counterfactuals get their basic emotional power by placing two events—one real and one imagined—side by side for direct comparison. This contrast effect explains a great deal, and in the chapters ahead we will see it at work in a variety of situations. In the next section we'll see how such contrasts happen all the time without our ever realizing it.

Pop-Up Benchmarks

Counterfactuals can be vivid, "in your face" thoughts. When they are obvious thoughts, thoughts that you know you are having, psychologists call them *explicit* cognitions. But the majority of our brain operations take place without awareness. Thoughts that are hidden from conscious view but that may be shown nevertheless to exert an effect on ongoing behavior are called *implicit* cognitions. Freud had the pioneering notion a century ago that much of our thinking is hidden from conscious view. But whereas the Freudian conception of the unconscious mind resembled a soap opera, replete with outlandish secrets, untamed desires, and shocking betrayals, cognitive scientists now view the unconscious mind as more akin to a modern factory filled with robot machinists, continually, reliably, perhaps even *boringly* churning out product after product with little drama yet tremendous efficiency. Social psychologist Tim Wilson explained: "The adaptive unconscious does an excellent job of sizing up the world, warning people of danger, setting goals, and initiating action in a sophisticated and efficient manner. It is a necessary and extensive part of a highly efficient mind and not just the demanding child of the mental family and the defenses that have developed to keep this child in check."[8]

Like the rest of our thought processes, most counterfactual thinking is unconscious, silently automatic. Counterfactual ideas commonly come to mind and then disappear without our ever realizing it. Yet, as they do so, they are a crucial component of our mental navigation system. They guide us from moment to moment, imbuing events with meaning, underscoring our effortless ability to make sense of what's going on around us.

How does this mental navigation system work? Although there is variation in the amount of mental effort various activities require (say, doing a crossword puzzle versus watching TV), the important thing to remember is that the brain is *always* working, in that it is always retrieving information from memory in light of the current situation, always providing insight, commentary, annotation. Speaking of TV, on the VH1 cable channel I sometimes see something called *Pop-Up Videos*. The show consists of "old" popular music videos overlaid with "new" humorous commentary in the form of pop-up balloons containing brief written anecdotes about the action in the video itself.

Singer Celine Dion had a huge hit in 1998 with the song "My Heart Will Go On," which appeared in the film *Titanic*. The music video of the song featured scenes of Dion intercut with scenes from the film. When the video for this song appeared on *Pop-Up Videos*, thirty-six pop-up balloons accompanied the song, providing such nuggets of trivia as:

"Celine was filmed singing along to a sped-up version of the song . . . the footage was then slowed down to match the song's pace."

"The director originally wanted Celine to appear as if she were in the movie."

"Celine's high school nickname: Vampire Queen."

"A soup served on the set was mysteriously spiked with PCP."[9]

This basic format, with bits of trivia popping up at the exact moment of relevance to an ongoing flow of events, is a remarkably tidy metaphor of how implicit counterfactual thinking assists the brain's on-going attempt to assign contextual meaning to reality.

The one big difference is that you are rarely aware of this continuous mental popping. Every moment, every glance, every interaction is accompanied by a running stream of mental pop-up notes, concepts, and ideas that are retrieved from memory and available for use. Your memory is a collection of tiny individual bits of information, and sets of bits are pulled out, assembled into standards, guidelines, and expectations, to operate as benchmarks against which the meaning of *Now* is established.

Say you're driving down the street. You see a pair of golden arches. This is a restaurant called McDonald's. Popping into mind, silently and automatically, are various bits of information regarding McDonald's—the signs are yellow and red, the food is inexpensive, the fries are delicious yet bad for my diet. Myriad other facts arise, too, basic and minimal, mere locations, spatial positionings, lighting effects due to time of day. You don't necessarily experience these as full-blown thoughts, but the information is ready, at your mental fingertips. These implicit thoughts establish context. They establish familiarity. You've seen these things before. Memories of past relevant experiences, activated by this current experience, match what you are now seeing, and this informational match results in the feeling that the situation is normal.

Drive farther and you see another pair of golden arches. These are not gently curved arches, but sharp, angular arches, basically two straight lines meeting at a sharp angle. These arches are similar enough to the McDonald's arches that they bring to mind, if only briefly, mental images of McDonald's. But this establishment is not McDonald's, it's part of a different restaurant chain called In-N-Out Burger, and their angular arches are a common sight along the streets of Los Angeles. Implicitly, a mismatch has occurred, in that these arches are not the same as the arches that are most easily recalled from memory. This makes for a momentary feeling of surprise—those arches are *almost* like the ones at McDonald's!—but not quite.

Advertisers and marketing experts are adept at playing on our expectations like this. If you have a new chain of restaurants, a new brand of shoes, even a new song, it pays to make it highly similar to another chain, another brand, or another song that is highly familiar to the average person. This guarantees a cognitive reaction, a feeling of vague surprise, and most important a few moments of extra thought dedicated to the new chain, brand, or song.

You're driving a bit farther and you witness an accident. An SUV impales a minivan. Metal crumples and plastic shatters, gasoline drenches the street. Airbags inflate and no one is hurt. At this moment, yet again we have information popping up from memory, information that now takes the form of a mix—a blend of information related to past accidents that you've witnessed, heard about from others, seen on TV, along with information about the way driving usually goes, the way this driving experience would normally, typically have proceeded. And naturally . . . how it should have been. These bits of information coming to mind about how traffic usually proceeds are the raw ingredients of a counterfactual—how things might have been had they gone normally. This particular situation is not normal, and your brain recognizes this instantly because specific bits of information drawn from past experience are right there, at your mental fingertips.

These silent thoughts establish the benchmarks of experience. What is normal versus abnormal? We are all like grade-schoolers with encyclopedias in our laps, constantly thumbing and retrieving informative commentary on current experience. Usually, it is only when things go very oddly or very badly that these thoughts swim into conscious view, dramatically illustrating how a particular event has deviated from what normally occurs. In other words, counterfactual thoughts typically become vivid to us when the current situation deviates substantially from what is normal.

I've just been summarizing some of the ideas contained in "Norm Theory," a landmark scientific paper published in 1986 by two pioneers of the science of counterfactual thinking, Daniel Kahneman and Dale Miller.[10] Professor Kahneman is a cognitive psychologist from Princeton University who in the fall of 2002 became the first psychologist to win the Nobel Prize. (They don't offer Nobel Prizes in psychology; he won his in economics.) Professor Miller is at Stanford University and has been active in the study of counterfactual thinking for two decades now. Their insights about how counterfactuals are part of an automatic system of benchmarking reality, and thereby provide the basic meaning of all experience, continue to have a huge influence on the fields of social and cognitive psychology.[11]

Three Kinds of Comparisons

As we have seen, the counterfactual comparison is one way that we place things in context. Of course, we compare things all the time—an expensive jacket to a cheap jacket, an apple pie to a chocolate cheesecake, even our mother to our father. We can compare things along any number of features—how good they look, how fattening they are, how much love they showed us. But regardless of how many features we think about, it usually boils down to a summary evaluation: an overall opinion of how good or bad something is. Psychologists use the term *valence* to refer to amounts of goodness versus badness.

Valence is the fundamental basis not only of comparisons, but of quite a lot of our thought processes, from categorization to intention. The reason is simple. Valence information is the ticket to survival. Being able to classify something as good or bad, and to do so as quickly as possible, can spell the difference between life and death. I'm out on a hike in the forest, and I see a yummy-looking mushroom over there, but should I eat it? It might kill me. Now, I can take my time with this one, because the mushroom isn't going anywhere. I can take a few minutes to look it up in my field guide to wild mushrooms. But if in this same forest I come across a black bear, I don't have this same luxury to ponder carefully what to do next. It's running straight at me NOW!

What the brain does in this case is remarkable, if we stop for a moment to appreciate it. A blob of color activates a certain pattern of nerves inside the eye. They fire a set of signals to the back of the brain, where the pattern is further processed and assembled into a more complicated pattern of information. This more complicated pattern is then compared to stored patterns of information in memory, which furnish the basis for categorizing the blob into a meaningful idea (bear!) AND assigning it valence (bad!). This all happens in less than a tenth of a second.

This is the simplest case of comparison: taking something right in front of your eyes and matching it to summary information stored in memory. But even in this simplest case, valence is the key question. Is it good or bad? How good? . . . or how bad?

Social psychologists have identified three main types of comparison that we make on a daily basis that provide context to our lives. These three are the *counterfactual* comparison, the *social* comparison, and the *temporal* comparison. The counterfactual comparison, as we have already seen, involves comparison between what was (or is) to what might have been. The social comparison involves the comparison of you to other people. The temporal comparison is between the way things are now to the way they used to be (or may one day become). These three kinds of comparisons have been the focus of thousands of research experiments since the 1950s, yet it is only recently that they have been glimpsed in the same light and seen to share many underlying psychological mechanisms.[12]

We've already seen lots of examples of counterfactuals. Here's an example of social comparison. In the late 1990s it seemed that every second magazine or newspaper article was profiling the latest dot-com millionaire. Here's a 20-year-old who wrote a piece of software that helps people buy shoes on the Internet . . . and she's a millionaire.

Here's someone else who invented a cheaper way to manage a factory using computer software . . . and he's a millionaire, too. One millionaire has a fabulous beachfront mansion near Monterey, another has a stunning penthouse in Manhattan. I remember the conversations with friends about these stories. We'd all feel a little glum, a little bit *inadequate,* after comparing our modest lives to these fabulous success stories. This is social comparison at work, and although human beings have probably always compared themselves to their neighbors, it is an entirely modern experience that we all should have *so much* social comparison information available, with popular media like television, movies, and magazines inundating us constantly with an overwhelming array of successful individuals. With the crash of the technology economy in the early 2000s, these dot-com millionaire stories vanished, much to the relief of my friends and me! Even so, there will never be a shortage of others to whom we compare ourselves, either in daily life or in the media.

Remember a few pages back when I drew the distinction between upward and downward counterfactuals? We can use precisely this same distinction to describe social comparisons. An upward social comparison occurs when you compare yourself to someone better off, someone like a dot-com millionaire. A downward social comparison occurs when you compare yourself to someone worse off. As we'll see in a moment, this distinction is enormously useful for describing the reasons we engage in comparisons in the first place.

A temporal comparison occurs when you compare yourself to how you used to be at some point in the past. What were you like seven years ago? Can you visualize this slightly younger version of yourself? This person probably feels distant, a person who is not really "you" as you now define yourself. Research by social psychologists Anne Wilson and Michael Ross at the University of Waterloo indicates that, roughly speaking, five years is the approximate period of time that includes the current you. More than five years in the past, your previous self begins to feel more and more distant, less and less like the real you. Most people tend to be a bit flattering as they think of themselves of long ago, imagining a continuous upward progression toward personal betterment. You might think, *I used to be a loser in high school, I'm okay now, but I'll be great in the future.* You can see that this downward temporal comparison to some past version of yourself, subjective and unverifiable as it is, can be comforting. But upward temporal comparisons are also possible; for example, you might think: *I was a vastly better athlete twenty years ago than today.* Again, temporal comparisons also may be downward or upward, and can make you feel better or worse as a consequence.[13]

Of these three kinds of comparisons—counterfactual, social, and temporal—which do we rely upon the most? That's hard to say, because the necessary research is incomplete and still coming in from labs around the world. In research published in 2000, Wilson and Ross looked only at social and temporal comparison, and discovered that as people describe themselves, they use temporal comparisons most. In my own research, I have looked at all three comparisons, using the approach of asking people to speculate how often they use each in everyday life. This strategy must be taken with a grain of salt, because people's beliefs about their own behavior are not always accurate. Nevertheless, when college students are asked, they say that they compare themselves to their future hoped-for self most often (future-temporal). Counterfactual comparisons come second, past-temporal comparisons come third, and social comparisons come last. You probably see now why this ranking should be taken with a grain of salt: The average person probably hesitates to admit how much he or she likes to gossip. Although we are still awaiting the next generation of research that will decisively answer the "how often" question, I suspect that social comparisons are actually the most common of all.

It's worthwhile to reflect for a moment on the observation that the human brain naturally and spontaneously seeks out three kinds of comparison information in order to make sense out of ongoing events and circumstances. This would seem to offer a simple suggestion to journalists regarding how to clarify news stories. I don't know how many times I've come across stories in which a single, isolated number is given. The mayor's budget for the new task force is set at $98,000; the ombudsman's personal staff numbers 25; the new hydroelectric dam will produce 860 giga-doodles of power. What on earth do these numbers mean? With no benchmarks, I haven't the foggiest idea of what to make of them. Journalists should feel obligated to provide those benchmarks, and basic research in psychology suggests a road map of *which* benchmarks will be most useful: counterfactual (what the ideal task force budget ought to have been), social (the average ombudsman has a staff of 12), or temporal (dams of twenty years ago produced an average of 500 giga-doodles of power). You don't need to provide all three benchmarks in each case to make sense, but you definitely need at least one.

Why are these comparisons so important to our psychology? Counterfactual, social, and temporal comparisons each represent a fundamental facet of the brain's standard response to trouble. There are really just two main ways to react to a problem. Change the situation or change your mind. If you change the situation, it means you take active steps to fix the problem, and end up changing the objective situation for the better. If that doesn't work, you can just change your mind, reconstruing the situation so that it seems not so bad after all. These two main kinds of reaction have been written about in various ways, labeled with dozens of different pieces of jargon, but the underlying meaning remains the same. One focuses on behavior and action, the other on mind and emotion.

We've seen three kinds of comparisons (counterfactual, social, and temporal) and two forms of each comparison (upward and downward). Here's how they all come together. The upward comparison tends to be the starting point for fixing the actual situation, whereas the downward comparison tends to be the starting point for changing your mind about the situation. Upward comparisons spur us to action and betterment; downward comparisons console us.[14]

Here's an example. Betty has been dating a man much older and with vastly different interests than herself. He abruptly breaks up with her and she is devastated. She can react with an upward or a downward counterfactual comparison.

First take the upward comparison. *Maybe if Betty had been dating someone closer to her own age, someone who had similar interests, the relationship would have been more durable.* To the extent that she is able to act on these insights, to go out now and find someone who IS closer to her age and DOES share the same interests, she may forge a more enduring relationship in the months to come. This is the essence of the upward counterfactual—although directed at the past, it spells out how improvement might be achieved in the future. The upward counterfactual is a recipe for betterment. Notice that exactly the same insight can come from an upward social comparison (Maybe I should do what my friend Wilma does, as she's had more luck dating than me) or from an upward temporal comparison (I used to be luckier in love; I know I can be that way again). Upward comparisons, be they counterfactual, social, or temporal, are recipes for betterment, blueprints for future action.

Now take the downward comparison. Betty could have been dating someone even worse, or she might never have had a boyfriend at all. Now, this counterfactual comparison does not so much tell you how to make things better. It tells you how to keep things from getting any worse than they already are. Preventing deterioration has its uses, to be sure, but it's not the same as fixing a problem and improving the situation. The main value of the downward comparison is that it can make Betty feel better. The contrast to a worse alternative makes the current state of affairs feel slightly more tolerable. The downward comparison feels good. Notice that exactly the same consoling feeling can come from downward social comparisons (My friend Julie was dating a *real* loser; I'm much better off than she is . . .) and from temporal comparisons (I dated such losers in high school; compared to that I'm now way better off).

People use upward comparisons to achieve the goal of betterment, and they use downward comparisons to achieve the goal of consolation. But notice also that although upward counterfactuals can be useful for assembling plans for improvement, they at the very same time create negative feelings. By way of the logic of the contrast effect, it hurts to realize that things might have gone better in the past. Selecting between upward and downward comparisons therefore involves a trade-off between performance and emotion. You can better your performance at the expense of feeling bad, or forsake performance so as to feel better. A trade-off means a calibrated balance between cost and benefit, and as we shall see repeatedly in this book, human beings have an uncanny knack for making this trade-off to their overall advantage.[15]

It turns out that most counterfactual thoughts are upward (Things might have been better), and the same holds for future temporal comparisons (I expect to get better). Past temporal comparisons are nearly always downward (I used to be worse). Social comparisons involve a nearly even mix of upward and downward (Some are better off, some are worse off). This tells us about how each type of comparison tends to be used. Counterfactual comparisons as well as future temporal comparisons seem to be reflections mainly of desires for betterment. Past temporal comparisons are mainly about emotional consolation. Social comparisons are flexibly used to achieve both.[16]

Downward comparison as a means of feeling better about a bad situation is really just the tip of the iceberg. Harvard social psychologist Dan Gilbert recently coined the phrase *psychological immune system* to describe the numerous mental tricks people use to change their mind, to sweeten an interpretation of a bad situation, even to deliberately distort the facts. The old fable of "Sour Grapes" perfectly captures this "after-the-fact" distortion. The hungry fox tries to reach some delicious grapes growing high on a vine, but is unable to jump high enough. In short order, he changes his mind: "They were sour anyway. I never *really* wanted them."

People are surprisingly good at finding silver linings, inventing comforting consolations, and seeing the world in overly flattering ways. Early in the twentieth century, writers in the Freudian tradition used the term *rationalization* to describe how people recast their own past to justify the present. By midcentury, social psychologists were using the term *cognitive dissonance reduction* to describe the more general process of changing one's mind so as to maintain consistency among beliefs, particularly in ways that justify recent behavior. This conception spearheaded an explosion in research from the 1960s onward that has quantified and classified the numerous ways that people go about reshaping their construal of reality in a manner that is emotionally comforting.

The metaphor of a psychological immune system is an apt one, and I'll use it throughout the book. Our body's physiological immune system constitutes a defense against invading microorganisms. It silently stands guard, constantly vigilant against infection. And yet it is not a single system, but embraces numerous interlocking mechanisms, like the B lymphocytes, the T lymphocytes, and the complement components. In the same way, the psychological immune system consists of an abundant variety of mental tricks. Skillful creation of downward comparison targets is one example, and in the chapters ahead we'll encounter still more. And as the body's immune system works efficiently in the background beyond our conscious awareness, so too does the psychological immune system operate with graceful precision largely without our ever realizing it.[17]

Redemption Stories

The famous line from *On the Waterfront*, "I could have been a contender," is a life-defining counterfactual. In that film, Terry Malloy walked around with this gigantic counterfactual in his head, and it colored his view of his entire life. In surveys of younger Americans, particularly college students, few seem to embrace this sort of life-defining counterfactual. But with advancing age, people become more likely to define their existence by reference to what might have been. For a recognizable minority of older adults, a single life-defining counterfactual becomes the seed of a story of transformation. Rather than feeling miserable about the road not taken, a big regret for these people is instead converted into a positive narrative called a *redemption story*.

Dan McAdams, a psychologist at Northwestern University, is an expert on personality development over the life span, and for several years he has studied the stories that people tell about their lives. Such stories are one way of encapsulating personality. How we explain our lives both to ourselves and to others is a powerful ongoing effort, like writing a novel, and by examining these stories carefully, we open a profound window into personality. Redemption stories are those in which a tragic event is framed in terms of a later transformation to a better, more positive situation. An alcoholic, after years of abuse of this substance, makes a decision to give up drinking, then decides to deploy those years of abuse to a better end by becoming an addiction counselor. According to McAdams, in a redemption story, "the bad is redeemed, salvaged, mitigated, or made better in light of the ensuing good."[18]

In their investigations, McAdams and his team collected life stories from adults, either in face-to-face interviews or in written questionnaires. Respondents were encouraged to get into a lot of detail, to provide a full account of particular experiences, including who was involved, what started it all, what they were thinking at the time, and what overall the experiences say about their lives. After all these stories were collected, members of the research team pored over them, dissecting them into smaller parts and assigning those parts to standard categories. Whether or not a story fit the definition of redemption story is one of several categorizations that were drawn. Not everyone defines their life in terms of a redemption story, but those who do were also those most likely to be emotionally healthy, to cope successfully with adversity flung their way, and, most important, to be most interested in nurturing the ambitions of younger people, lending a helping hand to those in the next generation. Adults with redemption stories were more likely to volunteer at community centers, spend time in after-school programs, and contribute to youth-oriented charities. Wrapping a life-threatening counterfactual in the cloak of the redemption they've found is the signature of individuals actively engaged in their communities.

Lessons from Research

Counterfactual thoughts provide individuals with benchmarks against which reality is compared and more deeply understood. As Douglas Hofstadter wrote in 1979, "We compare what is real with what we perceive as *almost* real. In so doing, what we gain is some intangible kind of perspective on reality."[19] We have reviewed a lot of basic principles and basic research in scientific psychology, but what does all of this mean to you personally? Below are some quick tips for making use of the insights reviewed in this chapter.

Don't Overreact. Maybe you have noticed a lot of counterfactual thoughts in your own head. Even if you are the sort of person who declares that they have "no regrets," you may still notice a lot of regrets, which of course you are actively denying or fleeing. The overall message of this chapter is that it is all perfectly normal. Don't overreact. Reacting to a negative situation with imaginings of how it might have gone better is a nearly reflexive operation of the normal human brain. Such imaginings are a crucial component of how the brain establishes context and meaning. So don't fight them. Sometimes people react to a regrettable situation by becoming cautious and conservative, taking fewer chances and missing out on new opportunities. Try not to stave off counterfactual thoughts by becoming overly cautious. To eradicate the counterfactuals themselves from ever appearing is futile. So relax and enjoy the mental ride.

Think Downward. Downward counterfactuals are constructed by the mind all the time, yet they leave little trace in consciousness.

Whereas upward counterfactuals tend to be more obvious and "in your face," downward counterfactuals are mostly automatic and hidden from conscious view. If they are hidden from consciousness, they can do little to make you feel better at a conscious level. This means that it is not a bad idea to consider occasionally those downward alternatives. How could a bad situation have gone even worse? Maybe you didn't get the job you wanted, but at least you didn't get into a car accident on the way to the interview. Although downward counterfactuals can seem false and even comical, they need not be. Focusing for a moment on how things could have been worse brings, by way of a contrast effect, a momentary burst of relief, maybe even of pleasure.

This turns out to be one of many examples of something your mother might have known that is confirmed by contemporary psychological science. She might have told you to look on the bright side, at least you're not dead! You might have reacted with a groan, but to take it to heart is to bring a momentary appreciation for all the good things that might otherwise be taken for granted. Pondering for a moment ways in which your life might be a lot worse clarifies aspects of value and worth as they truly exist now. Best of all, downward counterfactuals do nothing to interfere with performance. In studies in which people are pushed to consider either upward or downward counterfactual versions of their own past performance (on academic skills tasks), upward counterfactuals help them improve. Downward counterfactuals don't help (compared to another group of participants who were not asked specifically to think of counterfactuals), but they don't get in the way either. They just feel good.[20]

Chapter 2

How Regret Serves Us

~

If matters had fallen out differently, she wondered, might she not have met some other man? She tried to picture to herself the things that might have been—that different life, that unknown husband. He might have been handsome, intelligent, distinguished, attractive. . . .

—*Flaubert*, Madame Bovary

Madame Bovary, the heroine of Flaubert's great novel,[1] was trapped in a dull marriage, her days filled with boredom, and she longed for something better, something she might have had . . . *if only* "matters had fallen out differently." The painful longing for an alternative that might have been better is called regret. The aching, nagging feeling that you should have acted differently, should have seized an opportunity, should have seen it coming, is the most familiar face of counterfactual thinking. Whereas the full range of mental processes involving counterfactual thinking remains largely hidden from view, unconscious, regret is the loud, glaring offspring we all know and dread.

You might take this to mean that regret is bad, something to be avoided at all costs. But this conclusion is wrong. Regret in particular and counterfactual thinking more generally have both a dark and a light side. This chapter is all about how the light outweighs the dark. Regret is good for you. Indeed, regret is essential for healthy living, as it offers a sharp signal that tells you when you've got to change your strategy, alter your course of action, and start thinking outside the box. Indeed, what made Flaubert's novel so entertaining was the boldness with which Madame Bovary channeled her deep regret into attempts to find a new and more fulfilling romantic relationship. To harness regret is to seize upon the natural creativity that is a normal part of brain functioning. But too much regret, regret that is severe or long-lasting, can be so bad as to sow the seeds of depression, a major mental disorder. To be useful, regret must hurt then disappear quickly, a spur to action that does not compromise that action through distraction and depression. New research has begun to shed light on this middle ground of just enough but not too much regret, and which sorts of regrets tend to linger beyond their welcome.

The positive value of regret is where we'll begin, and the most useful of regrets are precisely those that hurt bad but disappear fast. These are the regrets we tend to not remember much. Mild regret, short-lived and useful for spurring new action, abounds in daily life. Just how common is it? Psychologist Susan Shimanoff found out in a 1984 study in which she tape-recorded conversations between husbands and wives, then counted the instances in which the discussion involved expression of particular emotions. Regret came in at number two. In other words, regret was the second most frequently discussed emotion. Encouragingly, love came in at number one![2] Regret is just as complicated, multifaceted, and mysterious an emotion as love, yet it is only recently that psychological research has thrown a spotlight on this misunderstood emotion.

Regret Helps

Regret is the most prominent form of counterfactual thinking, and it is easy to see how regret, which feels so awful, can be dismissed as an unnecessary evil of mental life. Early research on counterfactual thinking agreed, showing that it could interfere with decision-making and thwart effective coping with misfortune. True enough, but the wider context is essential. In the same way that a single traffic accident hardly means that you should give up driving, an unpleasant yet rare mental by-product by no means indicates that regret overall is bad. New research shows how regret and counterfactual thinking are essential to an exquisitely effective set of brain mechanisms responsible for the coordination of all behavior, from learning to working to playing to loving.

Counterfactuals most often center on how a problem could have been avoided. By spelling out past alternatives that would have been effective, these insights prompt people to engage in proactive measures that may prevent similar problems in the future. To take athletics as an example, a boy stands at the plate and swings his bat as the baseball sails past. The ball is in the catcher's mitt; the boy swung and missed. Over practice, over many repeated attempts, the boy will surely learn to hit the ball. But this first miss will create sharp feelings of disappointment, sorrow, even anger. At the same time, the coach might call out "Swing sooner" or "Bend your knees a bit more." Now, the goal is to hit the ball, but the boy has missed, and the coach sees instantly the gap between the factual and the counterfactual, the miss and the hit, and suggests behavior changes that will narrow this gap and turn future swings into hits. Eventually the boy will learn to hit nearly every ball. Without our realizing it, there is a coach in the back of our head telling us which behaviors would have brought us closer to past goals, and many of these goal-oriented counterfactuals flow unconsciously to coordinate silently the process of learning from experience.

Beginning with research I first published in 1994, psychologists have found evidence for this and other kinds of benefits born of regret and counterfactual thinking. My own studies showed that encouraging research participants to engage in certain sorts of counterfactual thinking (upward, and focused on specific and novel solutions) produced improvement in academic performance. The improvement came because participants channeled the insights they'd made from scrutiny of their own past performance back into their next attempts. In short, counterfactuals helped them learn faster. Counterfactuals also create a mental environment in which new alternatives, new options, new creative solutions are more actively considered, as revealed in one recent study in which counterfactual thinking was found to improve the quality of decisions made by work groups and teams. In other research, reports of aviation near-accidents were combed for mention of counterfactuals. Pilots who emphasized how their own actions might have averted the near-accident were also more likely to emphasize the lessons they had learned and intended to put into practice in future flying. When the regrets of midlife women were tabulated in yet another research project, it was discovered that women were more likely to act effectively on their regrets to produce positive life change when they spent little time dwelling or ruminating on past mistakes. Regrets that were sharp and short-lived as opposed to those that lingered were most useful. These and other recent studies confirm the overall psychological benefit of regret.[3]

Besides problem-solving and short-term performance improvement, counterfactual thinking also confers a greater sense of control over life, which in turn fortifies us, gives us the confidence to work longer and harder despite adversity. By seeing that we personally *could have* acted, we see a higher and brighter picture of ourselves as doers, as active agents, capable of effectively handling our own affairs.

Research conducted by Suzanne Nasco and Kerry Marsh at the University of Notre Dame vividly affirms this message. They tracked 293 college students for a month, measuring their thoughts and reactions to exam scores, then comparing these to exam scores a month later. Immediately after receiving grades on a test early in the semester, students were asked to write down any counterfactual thoughts that came to mind. Specifically, they were asked: "Please list any things that might have occurred differently that would have resulted in a different grade on the test." Students also described how much they felt they had control over the test situation. Test scores a month later were then collected. A week before taking this final test, students completed another measure, which assessed how much their study habits had changed since the last test. Nasco and Marsh looked at these measures in several ways, testing several alternative patterns by which they might be interconnected. What they discovered was dramatic. The more that students thought about how their just-completed test might have gone better (counterfactual thinking), the more they took action to improve their situation (changed study habits). These actions corresponded in turn to greater feelings of personal control. Finally, personal control corresponded to higher scores on the next test.[4]

This body of new research dramatically reveals the positive value of counterfactuals and regret. With this positive value of regret setting the stage, we can now take a closer look at the nature and essence of this emotion. Useful regret appears and disappears rapidly. But why do some regrets last longer, haunt us for years? To answer this question, we'll first take a closer look at which regrets haunt Americans most.

What We Regret Most

In the 1978 film *Superman*, the caped superhero uses his power, after the death of Lois Lane, to turn time back, relive the moment of her death, but this time prevent her death from happening. Stories of time travel abound in popular culture, in no small part because time travel, if it were possible, permits the time traveler to go back and right wrongs and make things better. A time machine can convert what you wished had happened into what actually happens; it makes a counterfactual come true. *If only we actually had time machines. . . .*

To go back in time, to live part of your life over again, and with the benefit of hindsight to fix your mistakes, grab those opportunities, make things right . . . who would not jump at this chance? But alas, there are no time machines, just regrets.

In a fascinating series of studies conducted by independent researchers and published between 1989 and 2003, adults of all ages were asked questions just like this. If you could go back and live your life over again, what would you do differently? What parts of your life would you change? Combining the results of these similar studies (eleven in all), the following ranking appears. The percentage indicates the proportion of adults voicing a regret that can be placed into that category.[5]

1. Education — 32%
2. Career — 22%
3. Intimacy — 15%
4. Parenting — 11%

These four regrets appear consistently at the top in study after study, in just this same order of priority. If we look further down the list, there is less consistency across studies. It's still possible to summarize based on the averages, but the actual rank order is less meaningful, so take it with a grain of salt.

5. Self-Improvement — 5.4%
6. Leisure — 2.5%
7. Finance — 2.5%
8. Relatives and In-Laws — 1.7%
9. Health — 1.5%
10. Friends — 1.5%

11. Spirituality — 1.3%
12. Community — 1%

Here we have life lessons refined into bite-size chunks: the collective wisdom of thousands of adults condensed into one simple list. A word of caution is in order, however. By focusing on regrets, we might get an overall picture of dissatisfaction and sadness in the general population, but this would be wrong. The overall context of life regrets is that most people are mostly happy with life. Ed Diener, a colleague of mine at the University of Illinois and one of the world's foremost experts on the psychology of happiness, has discovered this in numerous studies conducted around the world. "About 80 to 85 percent of Americans are above neutral," Diener says. "They feel more positive than negative, at least half of the time." This certainly contradicts the thrust of so many doom-and-gloom self-help books, which assume that the average American is miserable. The title of one of Diener's scientific papers says it all: "Most people are happy." Sure, there is always room for improvement, and that is what the regrets below focus on, but be sure to read these within the context of widespread satisfaction with life.[6]

Education. Said one survey respondent: "My one and true regret is that I did not apply myself in school, in so much as to not fulfill my dream in life. Instead, I followed my friends in what was 'cool' and acceptable in life. If, way back when, I followed my dream, I would not be stuck in a middle of the road job in a grocery store, without a college education, trying at 46 to eke out a living. With a better education, I know I could have done better if only I had applied myself."[7]

At first glance it may seem surprising that education comes first among the regrets of Americans rather than love, relationships, or family issues. But on second glance, the reason for its prominence becomes clear. Education is a gateway. It is a juncture from which many diverging roads of life might be traveled. It represents one set of actions that can spell the difference for innumerable other aspects of life.

Take money, for starters. It is a recognizable fact of modern life that the more education you have, on average, the more money you make. Certainly there are many exceptions, as in the case of the self-made millionaire who never completed high school and the unemployed Ph.D., but these are rarities next to the vast majority of people whose incomes correspond to the number of years spent in school. So for money reasons alone, it is not surprising to see regrets like those of Mary Ann, age 55: "I regret that I did not obtain more education to enable me to make more money so that I could have given my children more tangible things." Education is a gateway to prosperity.

Education is also a gateway to personal fulfillment, to finding satisfaction with work that involves demands and challenges that are in line with one's talents. Education can get you a more demanding job, offering more numerous challenges, which in turn spell greater opportunity for personal growth, resulting ultimately in greater overall satisfaction with yourself as a person.

Education is a gateway to the next three biggest regrets on the list: career, intimacy, and parenting. The connection of education to career is obvious, as we have seen. The connection of education to intimacy passes through concerns about money. One of the most serious threats to the success of a marriage is financial difficulty, and if education can bring more money, then it is easy to regret not having more education so as to alleviate marital strain. Education can be a source of regret involving parenting concerns for the same reason. The experience of Mary Ann, quoted above, makes this clear. Being able to afford dance classes, swimming lessons, and the inevitably changing fashions of youth is something that a better education might well have enabled.

Another reason why education is the most common life regret is that for nearly everyone, you could always have gotten more schooling, could always have obtained another diploma or degree or certificate, could always have studied harder, could always have done better. If you dropped out of high school, you regret not having that high school diploma. If you attended college, you might regret not putting more time into studying, not achieving the higher grades that would have guaranteed a place in a top firm or a top graduate school. If you attended graduate school, you might think you should have chosen a different path, an MBA instead of a law degree. In my case, I got a Ph.D., supposedly the highest education level attainable, yet more than a few times I have regretted the educational path I took. If only I had gone to medical school, I could have realized my childhood dream of becoming a surgeon. It doesn't matter how little or how much education you have; you always might have done it differently, which in turn would have unlocked a gateway to so many other alternatives in life.

There are several aspects to career . . . money, prestige, power . . . but these tend not to form the basis for the kinds of regrets that stick with people over years. What really gnaws at the soul are missed opportunities to reach one's true calling, to fulfill one's hidden talents and abilities in a challenging and rewarding work experience. Jo, 46, says: "All my life I have loved horses. If I had become an apprentice to a horse trainer when I was just out of high school . . . I could have learned all the ins and outs of horse riding, showing, breeding, training, equine health, etc. By now, I could have been an experienced trainer with a waiting list of people wanting to gain a little knowledge from my vast experience in dealing with horses. I could have owned my own stables, raised a certain breed of horses and had a job I loved and looked forward to each day." Clearly, career can be a way of fulfilling inner personality needs and defining who you are as a person. Failing to live up to those needs and yearnings creates the longest-lasting of regrets.[8]

Less frequent are cases where people have attained a career that they find challenging and fulfilling, yet they put so much time into it that they regret missing out on other things in life. Rick, 43, says: "I regret spending so many hours at work and not taking time to stop and celebrate the really important things in life—family, friends, hobbies, etc." Pretty much the same lament is echoed by Michelle, 30: "My largest regret by any means is my desire to work and to become the first female sales manager in my field. I neglected my children and my own personal life. I have said my apologies to my family, but how do I ever get back their first steps and all of the little hugs I missed?"[9]

And so we have an interesting pattern here. Whereas regrets of education nearly always focus on wanting more education, regrets of career sometimes focus on having a better career, but other times focus simply on spending less time on the career. When people wish they had spent less time on their career, it is nearly always because they felt they missed out on the next two areas of regret, intimacy and parenting.

Intimacy. Long-term romantic relationships reach the very core of our existence. Finding love and romance, and preserving it once it has been found, demands for most of us an enormous amount of thought, time, and energy. In reading through hundreds of intimacy regrets, it's hard for me to break them down into any recognizable pattern. Stretched before me is a maddening cacophony of regrets of all shapes and sizes, from the tragic to the inconsequential, from the bizarre to the hilarious. Here is just a small taste of the regrets men and women voice when talking about their relationships, selected from an Internet survey that I ran last year.

Male, 53: "If only we had discussed goals and long-term plans more. . . ."

Female, 21: "If only I didn't say such an awful thing about him to my friends, I wouldn't feel so guilty and afraid that he would find out what I said eventually."

Male, 22: "If I had a better control on my temper, she would be happier, and our relationship would be happier."

Female, 46: "If I had been clear about needing a significant amount of time to myself to do activities and socialize with other people separately, my partner wouldn't be expecting me to spend so much time with him regardless of whether he's interested in the activities I like to do."

Male, 25: "If only I had chosen a different pair of earrings to give her in honor of our anniversary, she would wear this different pair more often, thereby getting more use and enjoyment from them."

Female, 26: "If only I hadn't laughed in his face when he told me he loved me that very first time. . . . I really thought that he was teasing me . . . and I replied 'ya, uh-huh, you don't love me, you don't even love yourself' and then I laughed. Then . . . he would trust me now with his deep thoughts and feelings and it wouldn't be so difficult for me to get it out of him."[10]

Regrets focusing on romance and relationships are complicated and multifaceted, as these examples make clear. As we turn now to the fourth regret on the list, parenting, a bit more of a pattern emerges.

Parenting. Looking across the various regrets surrounding child-rearing, three main kinds are apparent. First, parents later in life often regret not spending enough time with their children when they were young. Second, older parents sometimes regret having children too soon. A third finding is the near absence of regrets of having children in the first place. Let's look at each of these in turn.

We have already encountered two individuals, Rick and Michelle, who regretted putting too much time into their work and neglecting their family life. This is significant, as this type of parenting regret is shared equally by men and women. Not long ago, of course, men were the sole breadwinners in the typical American family, and so this sort of regret would tend to be theirs alone. But now, at the beginning of the twenty-first century, both parents tend to work, and so both women and men find themselves equally vulnerable to the regret later in life that they neglected their children's upbringing in favor of job concerns.

Many couples have painful disagreements about parenting strategies. One survey respondent simply wished she had put more effort into communicating with her husband about child-rearing earlier in their relationship: "[If we had] talked about our views on child-rearing prior to having children, we would have fewer disagreements."[11] Another respondent said, "I regret saying short, curt things to my children when they were little and I was tired."[12] Put simply, parents take a lot of responsibility for how their kids turn out. When kids get into trouble, this type of regret immediately comes to mind and parents end up blaming themselves.

The second type of parenting regret focuses on having had children too soon. Unlike the "not enough time" regret, this one is experienced mainly by older women. These women talk about how they wished they had put off having a family so that they could have had more time to study, travel, and build their careers. Psychologists Janet Landman and Jean Manis found in their studies, published in 1992, that "it was common for the adult women to imagine having put off marriage in favor of finishing their education and establishing a career."[13]

The third observation is the rarity of regrets focusing on the decision to start a family. It is nice to know how rare it is that parents end up regretting having children in the first place. Even when parents do indeed regret the issue of timing, they hasten to affirm their lack of regret for starting a family, as in the case of Carol, 24: "I regret not staying in school . . . regret rushing into a marriage and a family so young. But I love my kids and wouldn't change that." Gordon, 45, emphasizes his lack of regret at becoming a father by wishing he had started even earlier: "With three beautiful children . . . my big regret is that I didn't start a family until I was thirty-three. If I could have my time over again, I would start a family at eighteen and have ten kids."[14]

How can we make deeper sense of this list of top regrets? Regret is good for spurring action, but when what's done is done, it's best to move on and leave the regret behind. As we'll see shortly, most regret indeed gets swept aside and left behind. But when there is still a chance to make a difference, regret persists. The ranking of Americans' biggest regrets underscores this point clearly. No matter how old, for example, people can always go back to school. No matter how set in their ways, people can study new subjects, receive new certifications, and improve their skills through further studying. Given that education throughout life remains an open opportunity, always an option to be grabbed should one desire it, it is not surprising that it invites the lion's share of regrets. People can also modify their careers and romance throughout life, although much less easily than they can their level of education. The older you get, the harder it is to change jobs and the more costly it is to change spouses. Parenting, though obviously just as important a life goal as education, does not invite the same amount of regret because there is much less elbow room to actually alter the larger realities of child-rearing (it's hard to give your kids back once you've got them!). In short, there is a hopeful message here: *Regret lingers where opportunity knocks.*

Why Some Regrets Last Longer

You have probably heard the adage, we don't regret the things we do, only the things we didn't do. Any nugget of popular wisdom can be either accurate or inaccurate, begging a direct test through psychological research. Several research teams have indeed tested this old adage, and they have discovered that it is largely true . . . sort of. But these new findings are exciting not so much in their scrutiny of an old saying as in their revelation of how the psychological immune system, mentioned in the last chapter, works to eradicate most of our regrets to protect us from emotional harm.

To properly test an adage, it helps considerably to clarify what it means. One way to restate the idea of regretting not what we do but what we didn't do is that we can take deliberate, effortful steps in order to reach our goals, or we can hold back, hesitate, be cautious about not screwing things up worse. We can leap with little looking, or do a lot of looking before we leap. These two behavioral strategies produce two distinct types of regret: regrets of action (wishing you hadn't done something, which means regretting too much leaping without enough looking) versus regrets of inaction (wishing you'd done something, which means regretting too much looking and not enough leaping).

Cornell social psychologists Tom Gilovich and Vicki Medvec discovered that time is the key ingredient that determines whether we focus on action regrets or inaction regrets. Over the short term (say, what happened last week), we tend to regret our actions. But over the longer term (months and years), what haunts us most are regrets of inaction. For example, in one study, people approached at bus stops and Laundromats were asked to report their biggest regret of the past week and also their biggest regret from their entire life. Over the course of a week, action regrets just barely outnumbered inaction regrets (53% vs. 47%). But when gazing across the expanse of an entire life, inaction regrets vastly outnumbered action regrets (84% vs. 16%).[15]

Marcel Zeelenberg found the same pattern in observations of participants on a Dutch reality television show. If you happened to be in the Netherlands in the mid-1990s, you might have caught an episode or two of *I Am Sorry*, in which ordinary people explained (often in excruciating detail) some terrible thing they had done to someone close to them. One guest regretted ignoring a friend during a difficult time, another regretted saying nasty things about a deceased friend at his funeral, still another felt bad about slapping a friend's face. After expressing their regret on television, these participants were then presented with the opportunity to apologize and give flowers to the person who had been wronged. According to Zeelenberg, "This [was] usually followed by emotional scenes with lots of hugging, kisses, and tears accompanied by applause from the audience." Zeelenberg's team collected 82 expressions of regret that appeared on 18 different episodes, then classified these into regrets of inaction or action. They discovered that inaction regrets had been festering three and a half times longer than the action regrets. In short, regrets of action focus on the short term, whereas regrets of inaction focus on the long term.[16]

But why do regrets of inaction last longer? The answer goes a long way to help us see how regrets can be good for us. Overall, many regrets are cleansed quickly from mind by our psychological immune system, leaving only a few to remain long enough to bother us. I mentioned the "Sour Grapes" fable back in Chapter 1, in which the hungry fox declared the grapes to be sour only after he realized he couldn't have them. Like the fox, human beings are marvelously adept at recasting and reframing their earlier actions to make them seem more pleasing by current standards. People change their minds to make themselves feel good. A friend of mine very much wanted a particular job at an ad agency. She interviewed for it, thought she was a shoo-in for it, talked incessantly about how great the job would be, then received a phone call telling her that someone else had got it instead. A few months later she was telling me how relieved she was that she didn't have to be bothered with that job. That's the psychological immune system in action—changing our current view of the past to make it more palatable—and for most of us, it is constantly and silently working to make us feel more contented with our lot, all without our ever realizing it.

But here's the kicker. Regrets of action more effectively activate this psychological immune system than do regrets of inaction. In other words, you are more likely to rationalize actions than inactions. The technical explanation is that these brain mechanisms react primarily to the presence of things, not to the absence of things. Attention shifts toward things that are there while ignoring (the possibility of) things that are not there. Actions are salient; inactions are not. So if we act and the result is negative, the full force of the psychological immune system is brought to bear on minimizing its psychological impact. We feel better rapidly because our brains have reorganized reality to make it seem as though the thing that's negative is not so bad after all. This happens to a far lesser extent for regrets of inaction. They are not so obvious immediately after happening, less likely to recruit our coping mechanisms, and like an unattended infection, slowly fester over time, growing out of all proportion to what originally initiated them. This differential activation of the psychological immune system is one reason why regrets of inaction hurt longer.

Gilovich found evidence for this idea in an elegant experiment patterned after the old TV game show *Let's Make a Deal*. On that show, hosted by Monty Hall, contestants were promised that three prizes lay hidden behind three doors. One of the three prizes was really great (like a new car) while the other two were rather dull (like a wheelbarrow or a can of tuna). In the research version of the game that Gilovich used, the contestants (research participants) faced a similar choice of three hidden prizes (hidden by boxes on a tabletop instead of behind gigantic doors). The participants' first task was to select one of those three boxes. Once selected, however, they weren't allowed to open it, at least not right away. The host—a research assistant—then opened another of the boxes to reveal a not-so-great prize and thus presented participants with the central dramatic dilemma: to stay with the originally selected box or switch to the other box. At this point on the old TV game show, the studio audience erupted in frantic screams of advice: "Keep it!! . . . Take the new one!! . . . Keep it!! . . . Switch to the other one!!" And this brings us to the psychology of action versus inaction—will people regret a decision to switch (act) more or less than a decision to stay (not act)?[17]

What would you do? Stay or switch?

As it turns out, you should always switch. This is the most logical, the most rational decision, the one most likely to reward you with the great prize. Most people think, on first glance, that this can't be right, that your chances of getting the great prize are exactly the same whether you stay or switch. The reason why switching is better hinges entirely on the host's actions. Monty, the host, opens one of the doors (boxes) and shows you a modest prize. Clearly, Monty would *never* select this door at random—he's trying to run an entertaining show here, and if he opened the door to reveal the really great prize, the contestant would face no dramatic dilemma at all. Boring game show. To make the show interesting, Monty *must* reveal one of those two not-so-great prizes. Now, at the very start of the game, the chance that each door is hiding the really great prize is exactly even—33% each. The contestant makes that first selection, and whatever is selected, the chance of winning at that point in time is 33%. But when Monty unveils what's behind one door and *rules it out* as the really great prize contender, nothing has happened to alter the chances that the contestant's chosen door hides the really great prize—it's still 33%. But now there are *only two*, not three, doors to choose from. The one the contestant has selected *still has* a 33% chance of hiding the really great prize. The other door, therefore, *must now have* a 67% chance of hiding the great prize. (Remember, there are at this point only two alternatives, and they have to add up to 100%.) And so we can see that switching doubles your chance of winning the really great prize relative to staying with the original selection.[18]

The logic behind the advantage of switching over staying is not obvious, at least not to most people. In fact, I'm sure there are some readers who still don't believe it, and if you are one of them, be sure to check the endnote at the back of the book that explains this logic in further detail. The subtlety of the logic, however, makes it a perfect task for an experiment in which the choice of switching versus staying is pushed this way or that by way of instructions and advice from the experimenters themselves. Gilovich and his colleagues did this simply by giving a plausible explanation in support of switching to half of the participants, and a different (though equally plausible) explanation in support of staying to the other half. This permitted a straightforward and elegant test of the effect of acting versus not acting on subsequent opinion, which means that the effects of the psychological immune system can be tracked directly. When people rationalize, they alter the subjective value of something. "Sour grapes" means that the quality of the grapes, in the mind of the fox, has dropped, merely because they are out of reach. By the same logic, Gilovich engineered the game so that all research participants got the exact same prize (the not-so-great prize, a Cornell University bumper sticker, worth about $1.10). These participants then told the researchers how valuable they found the prize, by way of giving a price for which they'd be willing to sell it. Sure enough, people who switched wanted more money ($1.58) than those who stayed ($1.11). Remember, those two groups of people ended up with the exact same prize of a bumper sticker, retailing for $1.10 in the campus store. Those who acted rationalized their missing out on the really great prize by inflating the perceived value of what they ended up with. Those who missed out on the really great prize due to inaction showed no such rationalization.

So what was the really great prize in this experiment? I remember watching *Let's Make a Deal* on television when I was a kid, and I vividly recall the exaggerated excitement of the announcer's voice-over when a lucky contestant won the grand prize . . . "A NEW CAR!!" In the Gilovich experiment, the great prize was an "expensive-looking" Cornell T-shirt. Unfortunately, psychological researchers must make do with budgets substantially smaller than those of television shows! Even so, this research dramatically shows how our power of rationalization— our psychological immune system—actively reduces the intensity of regrets of action to a measurably greater extent than regrets of inaction.

A related reason why regrets of inaction last longer centers on the *Zeigarnik effect*. Bluma Zeigarnik, a Russian graduate student working in Germany in the 1920s, discovered that people remember details of tasks that are unfinished, but quickly forget those details when the job is done. Anyone who has worked as a waiter or waitress (as I did when I was a student) will confirm this for you. While patrons are seated at your tables, you can recall easily what each has ordered. The moment the bill is paid, you forget it all. Unfinished business continues to demand our attention and our cognitive resources, but once completed, we can forget about it and free up those precious resources for use elsewhere.[19]

Ken Savitsky found in a 1997 study that regrets of inaction amount to such unfinished business. When something is left undone, you can always fill in more details, more possibilities . . . you can never really know how it might have turned out had you acted. Barbara is the 35-year-old main character in the Harlequin romance novel *What Might Have Been*. She had a chance to act as a teenager, but had been too afraid, too timid. "If only she had let Richard make love to her. How many times had she contemplated the might-have-beens? How many times had she wondered how different her life might have been if she'd had the courage to give herself to him?" Now, years later, she still pines for him, and her brain deftly fills in those unknowable possibilities. "It might have lasted," she thinks to herself. "They might have married, had children, traded shifts comforting teething children in the middle of the night, fought over the family finances, spent winter nights cuddled together under the covers of a king-size bed." And of course, these details just scratch the surface; the possibilities for inaction are virtually limitless . . . almost *anything* could have happened had she acted. By contrast, taking that deliberate action results in tangible outcomes that *are* known. And so they become a closed case that, as we know from the Zeigarnik effect, results in diminishing attention and fading memory.[20]

Regrets of inaction tend to last longer than regrets of action, haunting us for years and echoing through the expanse of our lives. But this raises another intriguing question. How do regrets change as people get older?

Older but Wiser

That list of the biggest regrets of Americans was averaged across a lot of important differences in life circumstance. Some kinds of life circumstance that we might assume matter a lot turn out not to matter much at all. Intelligence is one example. A 1995 study revealed that people with genius-level IQs were no different than the average American in the way they experienced regrets of action and inaction. People living in the Far East and Russia have regrets of action and inaction that do not differ from those of Americans.[21]

One kind of life circumstance that does matter is age. The psychological meaning of regret is very different for the old compared to the young. The most obvious difference is that for the old, there is a whole lot more of life already lived, which means many more personal actions to ponder and many more experiences to reevaluate. For the young, not much life has yet been lived and potentially fewer experiences can stand out as painful life mistakes. As one survey respondent put it: "I've got so much still ahead of me that it feels weird to dwell on the past."

Recall that there are two main reactions to a problem—change the situation or change your mind. At the heart of this distinction is the truism that the circumstances themselves to a large extent dictate which of these coping strategies is most appropriate. If the current situation is fixable, then by all means go ahead and fix it! But if, as in the case of the fox's sour grapes, the current situation poses a challenge beyond one's personal ability to master, then it is better to alter one's construal of the situation; in short, to rationalize.

The key difference between young and old is that for the young, big life problems—such as those involving education, career, and relationships—are still to an extent fixable. There is time enough left to alter their course, to steer life in a new direction. For the elderly, these opportunities have passed. Time and age themselves may be thought of as causing continuous and relentless diminishment of opportunity for major life change. These observations were the starting point for research published by Carsten Wrosch and Jutta Heckhausen in 2002.[22]

Most of the time regrets focus on personal action. This is a direct reflection of our unconscious action-oriented coping strategy. If you regret a particular action in the past, next time a similar circumstance comes around you can change it. If a college student regrets going to a party the night before a midterm exam, then she can take this regret to heart and deliberately refrain from attending a party the night before her final exam. This kind of regret may be painful in the short term, but if it leads directly to useful action, it serves an important and superordinate psychological function: improvement and betterment. If, however, the opportunity to act effectively diminishes with age, regrets focusing on direct personal intervention become less useful. They feel bad but do not carry that psychological benefit of action-oriented betterment. What Wrosch and Heckhausen discovered is that a natural corrective mechanism shifts the focus of regret with age so as to minimize its emotional damage. They examined the regrets reported by young and old citizens of Berlin and found that with increasing age came a tendency for regrets to focus on other people's actions. Now, these regrets are not particularly useful for informing a person about how they might personally improve. They are not well suited for personal betterment, but at the same time, they are not so painful. If anything, they might feel good because they deflect blame away from the self. Thinking *I could have been a contender were it not for my brother* is a lot less painful than *I could have been a contender were it not for my own choices in life.* The second one hurts because it involves self-blame; the first absolves the self while directing blame elsewhere.

The overall message of this research is remarkable. We saw in the last chapter that counterfactuals involve a trade-off between the benefits of life improvement and the costs of emotional pain. This trade-off is often resolved in a way that is optimal for the average person. Here we see an amazing additional aspect, that the trade-off itself gets recalibrated with the shifting life circumstances brought on by aging, so that it remains optimal even into old age.

Women and Men

Much has been written about how different women are from men. A series of books by John Gray, for example, argued that the sexes are so different as to appear to be from different planets. Men are from

Mars, in case you hadn't heard, and women are from Venus. From these and similar arguments, you might expect huge gender differences in the psychology of regret.

It turns out that there are remarkably few differences in the way women and men regret their pasts. Across hundreds of studies, hardly any gender differences have appeared. In terms of the basic psychological underpinnings of attention, memory, and emotion, women and men are nearly the same. Women and men do not differ in the intensity of their regrets, even over long periods of time. For example, I gave a questionnaire to eighty-nine undergraduates at the University of Illinois back in 2003 that included the following six general questions about tendencies to feel regret or engage in counterfactual thinking. Respondents used a number between 1 and 9 to express their degree of agreement with each statement.

- I regret a lot of my actions.
- I wish I could live parts of my life over again.
- I think *if only* a lot.
- I prefer to focus on the future rather than the past.
- I rarely think about what might have been.
- "With no regrets" is how I like to approach life.

In the amount of agreement with *every single one* of these statements, there was no difference at all between women and men. Now, these findings are *general* effects, meaning that people were asked to generalize across many aspects of their lives, perhaps blurring important distinctions regarding the different goals that women and men hold to be important. When we focus more closely on particular aspects of life, some intriguing differences between the sexes begin to appear, as revealed in recent research conducted in my own lab.

To see this gender difference at work, we need to review a little. We have already seen how action regrets versus inaction regrets differ over time. We can now see further implications of this distinction, which center on how people think about and plan for ongoing goals. These goals might be simple ones, like doing the laundry or getting to work in the morning, but also may be important long-term goals like finding a spouse or staying fit.

According to psychologist Tory Higgins of Columbia University, people strive toward two main kinds of goals. *Eagerness goals* focus on trying to get ahead, trying to attain something desirable, trying to reach a good outcome. *Caution goals* focus on being cautious and careful about preventing something undesirable, in other words, trying to stay away from a bad situation. My own research has revealed that eagerness-related problems (like not getting to work on time) evoke inaction regrets (I should have left earlier), whereas caution-related problems (like gaining weight) typically evoke action regrets (I wish I hadn't eaten all that pizza).[23]

Do women and men have the same proportion of action and inaction regrets? When we ask this question in the context of school and job achievement, we see no evidence at all of a gender difference. Both women and men show a greater proportion of inaction regrets when thinking about their time in school and in the workplace. They show the same eagerness to get ahead and equivalent concerns with bettering their own personal performance. This may not always have been so, but in contemporary America, with women now climbing the highest rungs of the corporate ladder, it is not surprising to see a striking similarity in the way women and men think about, plan for, and remember actions on the job.

Where gender differences do appear is in romance and relationships. Men have regrets of romance that look a lot like their regrets of academic achievement: more inaction regrets than action regrets. Not so for women. They express regrets of inaction and action with nearly the same frequency. In other words, they give eagerness goals the same weight as caution goals, demonstrating a balance between moving ahead and preserving what is already there.

This difference in eagerness versus caution finds voice in numerous aspects of relationships, as revealed in a variety of recent studies conducted among college students and also Internet survey respondents from all walks of life. Men regret their lack of action or vigor, focusing on actions that they should have tried out but didn't, like buying flowers or writing poetry. One male respondent said: "If only I had been more forward, then the relationship might have lasted longer." Another said, "If only I was more confident, then I would be more successful." Women regret not having held back, not having exercised more judicious care. A female respondent said: "[If only] I had waited awhile before going out with [this person], then things would not be so awkward between us right now"; another said, "If only I didn't do stupid things at parties, then I wouldn't hurt anyone." But again, when women voice caution in the context of ongoing relationships, they do so in equal measure with eagerness. You might say that when it comes to the kinds of regrets, goals, and priorities of relationships, women are seeking a state of balance.[24]

These are general effects, applying widely to the psychology of women and men in all aspects of their romantic relationships. But perhaps the most striking example, one that we all easily recognize, centers on sexuality. Men actively seek sex with just about anyone; women guard against having sex with the wrong person. Men tend to say things like: "I regret not being more outgoing and I definitely regret that I didn't get enough sex whilst at university!"[25] Even if they are successful at getting sex, men continue to regret not getting even more. Ed, a 48-year-old computer analyst, said, "I have no regrets over those promiscuous three years. . . . I have a pack of great memories. The regret is that I could have had at least a decade's worth more of fantastic memories."[26] Women are more likely to regret going too fast, having sex too soon or too young. One anonymous female survey respondent said that she wished she had "waited to have sex with him a little longer than I did,"[27] and this comment, with minor variations, appears again and again in the regrets voiced by women. It is nearly nonexistent in the comments voiced by men. Michelle, a 22-year-old mother, said: "I regret having sex as a teenager. If I could go back, I would have waited till I was more mature. . . . I would probably still be waiting." In a recent survey in which I asked male and female college students to rate how much they were bothered by each of a set of relationship-oriented regrets, the one regret that showed by far the biggest sex difference was "should have tried harder to sleep with a certain person." Men were vastly more likely than women to say that this bothered them. Indeed, nearly every last woman in this study said that this regret *never* came to mind.[28]

Psychologists can explain such findings using either a socialization theory (it is all due to the learning that goes on early in life) or a biological explanation (it's all in the genes), but it is still too early, with not enough evidence in yet, to decide which of these does a better job of explaining gender differences in regret. In the studies run so far, gender differences in regret occur only for short-term romantic interests and do not occur for other kinds of close relationships, such as those involving friends, siblings, and parents. But the jury is still out as to whether this finding is best explained in terms of socialization or biology.

Emotions: The Teenager in the Ferrari

We've seen how regrets are useful. Regrets are one of the best examples of how important negative emotions are to rational thinking and successful living. This is a new realization for the science of psychology, a product mostly of research that has appeared in only the last two decades. For a long time psychologists thought of emotions as the enemy of rational thought. That's what Freud argued. Earlier still, the British philosopher David Hume proclaimed that "reason is, and ought only to be, the slave of the passions, and can never pretend to any other office than to serve and obey them." Even today most people assume that emotions cloud our mind and make us do things that are unwise, as in crimes of passion, gluttonous overeating, and sexual misadventure.

A *Seinfeld* episode brilliantly caricatured this assumption, when Jerry imagined a game of chess between the forces of reason and the forces of passion.[29]

Jerry: "I have never been so repulsed by someone mentally and so attracted to them physically at the same time. It's like my brain is facing my penis in a chess game. And I'm letting him win!"

George: "You're not letting him win. He wins until you're forty."

Jerry: "Then what?"

George: "He still wins, but it's not a blowout."[30]

But take a moment to imagine what you'd be like without emotion. Devoid of passion, devoid of feeling? To be sure, it doesn't sound like much fun, but would it make you a more efficient worker, a more focused athlete, a more devoted friend? You might imagine the example of Mr. Spock, the emotionless alien character on the first *Star Trek* television series, who was remarkably efficient and effective, just the sort of reliably talented sidekick you'd want should you happen to be seeking out new worlds and new civilizations on a weekly basis. But the truth, it turns out, is much stranger than (science) fiction.

The enormity of the role of emotions in steering us through our social worlds can be illustrated dramatically by those very few individuals whose emotional machinery is broken. Some people experience no emotions at all. Antonio Damasio is a neurologist who studies emotional dysfunction, and in his book *Descartes' Error*, he described a patient named Elliott, who because of a brain tumor experienced no emotions whatever. True!—no emotions! Yet, at the same time, he remained intelligent, coherent, able to recall facts, able to solve mathematical and verbal puzzles. As the tumor grew and his emotions vanished, Elliott was unable to hold a job, pursued a disastrous love affair that ended in ruinous divorce, made fantastically inept financial decisions that bankrupted him, and generally made the sorts of repeated dumb mistakes that the average person would find flabbergasting.[31]

Simply put, emotions are a rapid-response behavioral control system. They alter behavior moment by moment, keeping us out of trouble. We have emotions because they are essential to our survival, both in terms of obvious dangers like falling off cliffs and being eaten by lions, but especially in terms of the complicated and subtle dance that constitutes our social lives. As we interact with myriad individuals from numerous backgrounds in uncountable situations, knowing what to do and what not to do involves vast encyclopedic knowledge, yet most of us do it effortlessly. Subtle emotions, from vague uneasiness to playful pleasure to quickening anxiety, steer us effectively from one situation to the next.

Emotions are immediate feedback as to whether our current actions are good or bad for us. Eat chocolate, and it feels good because sugar is something your body needs to survive. Grab a cactus, and it feels bad because sharp objects breaking into your skin can cause blood loss, infection, and death. Emotions are essential to managing our behavior, moment by moment. Of course, emotions can sometimes signal us to make bad moves, like eating pepperoni pizza at every meal. But it is important to keep this example in context: we have a fantastically efficient drive to consume sufficient nutrients for survival at the moment they are available, which just happens to have been misappropriated by the insane abundance of affordable food in contemporary America. In virtually every environment and society in which human beings have found themselves in previous millennia, it made good sense to eat as much fatty food as was available (because there wasn't that much available!). Emotions represent a general, all-purpose behavioral control system that works remarkably well in numerous diverse circumstances.

We absolutely need our emotions for effective daily functioning. Emotions are a crucial ally, not an enemy, of rational thought. Psychologists speak of two main types of emotions—simple animal emotions versus complex human emotions. The animal emotions are linked to primitive urges like sex, food, and steering clear of predators. They involve simple gratification behaviors (eating) and simple avoidance behaviors (running away). Say you're walking down the street and from nowhere a lion (escaped from a nearby zoo) pounces on you. The stark fear coursing through your body emanates from the lower, "animal" part of your brain. This is the basic housekeeping part of your brain, the part that keeps you breathing and awake but has less to do with higher thought like reasoning, planning, or problem-solving. But vastly more interesting are those uniquely human emotions such as love, envy, ecstasy, and of course regret. These emotions arise by way of an interconnection between that simple animal part of the brain and the higher, neocortical part of the brain, which is the big, thick, wormy upper part that is especially large in the smartest of mammals like apes and whales. This is the center of human thought. And we know now that it is largely in the frontal lobe, that area of the neocortical brain that sits just behind your forehead, where complex human emotions are created. Direct circuits feed into this region from the lower animal brain, bringing those primitive emotions to a mental table where they are examined, imbued with meaning, reorganized, and amplified.

Amplification is the key. Just as a megaphone amplifies your voice, making it louder for those far away to hear, the neocortex amplifies emotions, turning them into bigger, grander mental experiences. Without this amplification, fear would be gone the moment the lion is caught by the pursuing zookeepers—out of sight, out of mind. But amplification by the neocortical brain's frontal lobe means that you can ponder that lion, roll its image over in your mind again and again, gestate the fear, embellish the danger, and ten years later find yourself just a little bit anxious upon walking into a zoo. We might well summarize the human experience overall with regard to a big brain amplifying simple emotions. We live in a constantly churning sea of amplified emotion.

The German philosopher Arthur Schopenhauer realized this a century and a half ago, well before current science confirmed it:

> Since it lacks the faculty of reflection, joys and sorrows cannot accumulate in the animal as they do in man through

memory and anticipation. It is indeed remarkable how, through the mere addition of thought, which the animal lacks, there should have been erected on the same narrow basis of pain and pleasure that the animal possesses so vast and lofty a structure of human happiness and misery, and man should be subjected to such vehement emotions, passions, convulsions that their impress can be read in enduring lines on his face.[32]

This is the essential portrait of negative emotions in general and regret in particular that has emerged in recent years. Negative emotions are essential to our survival. In simplest form, they keep us out of trouble and guide us toward betterment. But the same mental processes that so ably serve our continued survival also condemn us to a fiendish amplification of those emotions. We are more effective as a species than any other both because and in spite of the intensity of our feelings.

Human emotion is a lot like a teenager in a Ferrari. A teenager is a creature of limited experience and unpracticed coordination. A Ferrari is a superbly powerful Italian sports car. Put the two together and you have a comedy of extremes: the vehicle is certainly able to get places fast, but with a teenager at the wheel it does so with repeated lurching, stomach-churning fishtails, and neck-snapping stops. The teenager lacks the experience to control deftly and effectively the magnitude of the power at his fingertips. When it comes to emotions, so too are most of us like teenagers in a Ferrari. Should an emergency arise, we can be confident that our mental machinery can zoom us to safety in seconds. Yet most of the time we find ourselves mentally lurching and fishtailing and careening as our amplified animal emotions ping-pong back and forth in our frontal lobes, embellished, annotated, and finely polished by our oversized neocortical brains. A teenager in a Ferrari is not a particularly elegant sight . . . and neither is the emotional landscape of the average human adult.

From this lofty theoretical vantage point, we much better see how valuable regret can be. The painfulness of regret may make people want only to be rid of it. But much regret comes and goes rapidly, silently spurring us to further action. Other regrets, like those for education, career, romance, and parenting, last longer, but their very longevity is a wake-up call that opportunities still remain. When opportunity shrinks, as when some circumstances become less controllable with advancing age, regrets shift to focus on the actions of others, precluding personal benefit but protecting oneself from further emotional pain. Moreover, the ever-vigilant psychological immune system stands ready to sweep regrets from mind when they are less likely to spur behaviors that bring betterment. Regret is good for us, but negative emotions in general are essential for rational thought and mental health.

Lessons from Research

Many self-help books argue that regret is damaging to mental health and must be avoided. I have argued the opposite, that regret is beneficial, even essential for learning and improvement. What other new insights emerge from the most recent psychological research?

Just Do It. You might have seen the old Nike ads admonishing you to *just do it*. Although occasionally annoying, these ads contained a morsel of insight that extends far beyond athletic endeavors. Psychologists know that our psychological immune system, meaning our powers of rationalization, is extremely effective at washing away regrets of action, dulling their sting over the long haul. If you actually go and do something and it turns out badly, it probably won't still be haunting you a decade down the road. You'll reframe the failure, explain it away, move on, and forget it. Not so with failures to act, with regrets of inaction. For various reasons, these are less effectively assuaged by our psychological immune system, leaving them to fester and grow over time. When we look back at our lives as a whole, we are most haunted by things left undone—romantic opportunities untried, career changes unexplored, friendships left untended.

So the first suggestion is simply to act. Given a choice of barreling ahead versus holding back, just barrel ahead. Of course, this is a very general suggestion, not something to apply mindlessly to all situations. Caution and care have their place, and some actions are plain stupid. Nevertheless, as a very general piece of advice, it makes sense to reduce the looking and increase the leaping.

Remember the List of Regrets. Fifteen years of research were combined into a list of the top four biggest regrets of the average American. The list is essentially a summary of the biggest traps, pitfalls, and mistakes into which people like you might blunder. The list therefore offers a cautionary note, signaling which areas of life in which to exercise the greatest care. Look over the list and try to identify areas of your life that represent the greatest vulnerability to future regret. And act now to avoid regret later.

Tell Me a Story. For several years there was an Internet site called RegretsOnly.com, a forum where people from all over the world could record their biggest regrets in life. From the thousands of responses received in the first couple of years of the site's operation, Barry Cadish compiled the most intriguing into a book called *Damn!* Several of the life regrets you read in this chapter came from Cadish's book. In the introduction to his book, Cadish ponders the fact that some have compared his site to a confessional, but he rejects this description because there is nothing religious about what he does—he is not a priest and has no power of forgiveness.

But like many sacred traditions, the confession ritual possesses psychological advantages that extend beyond its religious significance. The mere act of telling your troubles to another person is good for you. This is a solid conclusion reached after two decades of painstaking research pioneered by psychologist James Pennebaker of the University of Texas at Austin. He discovered that telling another in person, or writing your troubles down (even just typing them into a computer) for as little as fifteen minutes a day brings measurable improvements in emotional and physical health. As long as you go into emotional detail, confronting

your feelings in depth, the sting of life regrets may well be much mitigated. Those who benefit most from writing about their problems tend
to emphasize their positive emotions. They also tend to become more
analytical, going into deeper explanations of why certain events might
have happened as they did. The most successful writers of all put these
together, forging upbeat "spins" of old painful memories.[33]

If this description of the benefits of expressing emotions reminds
you of the "redemption stories" that Dan McAdams has discovered (described in the previous chapter), it should. The construction of personal narratives, of stories of our lives in which the bad is embedded in
a progression toward good, is a sure sign of mental health. If you keep
a diary or tell other people about tragic experiences, try to write your
own redemption story. It may not seem quite right to begin with, but
keep at it. Eventually a redemption story will emerge that is uniquely
you, and you can leave your regrets behind.

Chapter 3

Where Do Counterfactuals Come From?

～

The phone rings and you hear a friend's voice, and she is angry at you. What thoughts come to mind? What emotions? Moment by moment, we have new experiences that evoke new mental responses. When we consider which experiences evoke counterfactual thinking, we find new clues that counterfactual thinking is for betterment. Simply put, counterfactual thinking springs to mind when things go wrong. Whether it's a phone call from an angry friend, a costly car accident, or a squandered opportunity for career advancement, it's those bad moments that are most likely to make us think about what might have been. And tellingly, these counterfactuals tend mainly to focus on how our own personal action might have brought about a better alternative.

Counterfactual thinking also becomes especially active when there is a recognition of *almostness*, as when a lottery ticket is numerically close to the winning ticket (Damn! One digit away from a million bucks!), or when an accident is barely avoided in terms of physical distance (I missed hitting that minivan by less than an inch!) or even in terms of time (I made it onto the plane just seconds before they sealed the door!). Our brains are marvelously adept at picking out these cues to almostness, which in turn set the stage for subsequent counterfactual visions (could have been a millionaire, might have been in an accident, would have missed my flight).

It will soon become clear that there is a deep connection between these two kinds of situations (bad moments and almostness), a connection based on the importance of personal goals. Wishes, dreams, and aspirations are the most essential precursors to counterfactual thinking in everyday life. Put simply, the recognition that some important goal was blocked, thwarted, or in any way impeded is the primary engine driving the production of counterfactual thoughts. Counterfactuals are for betterment, a crucial feedback system constantly monitoring the progress made toward our personal goals.

If counterfactual thinking is so important for human beings, you might think it has a biological basis, that it is innate rather than learned through experience and upbringing. On the other hand, perhaps you are thinking that a thought process as multifaceted as counterfactual thinking must be taught to children. This is the essence of the nature-nurture debate that for many years has generated so much controversy when applied to other kinds of psychological processes (like intelligence). Psychologists are just beginning to assemble the evidence that can shed light on the nature-nurture basis of "if only" thoughts, first by examining the thought patterns of children, and second by surveying thinking styles across different cultures. It is to this question that we turn first.

Children and Counterfactual Thinking

Language is an example of a mental ability widely thought to be innate. Children of all cultures learn to speak with relatively little direct instruction, usually before the age of three. Algebra, on the other hand, is a mental skill that has to be learned. No one can do algebra without teachers, textbooks, and effort. And algebra skill tends to be learned later in life than language, typically among kids older than age ten. Is counterfactual thinking more like language or algebra? By looking at what age kids first start to express counterfactual ideas, we can get a rough idea of the answer to this question: the earlier it begins, the more likely it is to be innate.

Several dozen studies have now tackled this question, and the findings are striking. Children develop a knack for counterfactuals almost as easily as they develop language itself. In other words, as soon as children learn to speak, they express themselves using counterfactual statements.

Harvard developmental psychologist Paul Harris summarized this research in his book *The Work of the Imagination*. Kids at age two were found to use references to counterfactuals, to things that almost happened. Here are some of his transcriptions of what kids actually said: "almost fall down" (age 23 months); "I almost got that squirt" (age 34 months); "you almost broke my arm" (age 44 months). In another experiment, children watched as a toy bear wearing a hat was pushed across a tabletop by an experimenter, who then mentioned a very strong wind, then used her breath to blow at the bear with sufficient force to nearly, *but not quite,* send the hat flying. When asked to describe what had just happened, one child said simply, "It blowed off" (age 28 months); an older child said: "His hat nearly fell off" (age 40 months). From a very young age then, kids use counterfactuals. By five years of age, children can produce grammatically well-formed counterfactuals, as when another child said, "If you had been awake, you would have heard the owl." Echoing the theme that counterfactuals are for betterment, this research reveals that in children, just as in adults, counterfactual thoughts are most likely to emerge when fixing problems and reaching for goals.[1]

If these studies reveal that "if only" thinking develops early in the life of a child, then perhaps learning from parents, teachers, and other members of the surrounding community contributes much less to this ability. In other words, evidence from children suggests that counter-factual thinking is innate. Another way to examine whether it is innate versus learned is to look for differences across cultures. If a mental skill is learned, then the vastly different parental customs, school practices, and societal norms to be found in Asia versus Africa versus South America would likely result in very different patterns of counterfactual thinking within these respective populations. What, then, does cross-cultural research reveal?

Counterfactual Thinking Across Cultures

Back in 1981, Swarthmore psychologist Alfred Bloom argued that the mere ability to reason with counterfactuals, to ask and answer hy-pothetical questions, is deeply linked to culture and especially to lan-guage. In particular, Bloom suggested that native Chinese speakers don't have a lot of counterfactual thoughts because their language holds them back. Their language lacks the basic tool to express the "might-have-been" idea, the grammatical marker called the subjunctive. In English the subjunctive form (as in *If only I had taken out the trash*) is common and easily used, which makes it easy to think of and talk about counterfactuals. Chinese people, lacking this essential tool, just don't do a lot of counterfactual thinking—at least that's the argument Bloom made. We saw in Chapter 2 that counterfactual thinking is the key ingredient of regret, an emotion that is both common and helpful. If Chinese speakers indeed have trouble articulating counterfactual thoughts, they must therefore experience regret only rarely.[2]

This implication bothered Terry Kit-fong Au. A psychology pro-fessor at UCLA, Au told me that when she first came across Bloom's work, she felt insulted. She saw Bloom's work as denying the very hu-manity of Chinese people. Moreover, her personal experience as a na-tive Chinese speaker told her that Chinese people are as likely to experience regret as just about anyone else, American or otherwise. So she set out to explore Bloom's work in greater detail, running her own updated versions of Bloom's experiments, probing further to see if any mistakes had been made.

Au noticed that there were grammatical problems in the translations Bloom used in his original research. These translations were awkward, unusual, and tough to understand. They just didn't *feel* natural. So the first thing she did was to rewrite them so that they came across as more conversational, more easily understood in Chinese. When she used her new, better-written testing materials in her own research, Au found that there was little difference between Americans and Chinese in their basic ability to use counterfactuals to solve logical problems. In other words, Chinese speakers *can* reason counterfactually, as long as they are given a fair test that clearly presents sensible information in a grammatically sound manner.[3] In 1992, Au concluded: "In order to experience emotions such as regret, frustration, gratitude, sympathy, feeling lucky or unlucky, we need to entertain some counterfactual alternatives to reality. These . . . seem to be universal across cultures. How can something so fundamental and pervasive in human thinking be at the mercy of the presence or absence of a distinct counterfactual marker in our languages?"[4] And so there the matter sat for many years, apparently resolved. Case closed.

Until 2003. That's when a research team led by Cornell social psychologist Tom Gilovich returned to the study of counterfactual thinking across cultures. Their approach was, however, quite different.

Whereas the earlier round of research emphasized basic ability in reasoning, Gilovich instead looked at the everyday use and application of these thought processes. This distinction between having an ability versus how the ability is used is an important one. It's a lot like the difference between having something in your house versus actually using it. When I was a kid, my family got as a gift a kitchen appliance called a Hot-Dogger, the sole use of which was to cook hot dogs. You attached each end of the hot dog to an electrode and it cooked basically by electrocution! Although I seemed to eat plenty of hot dogs as a kid, we rarely used the Hot-Dogger to cook them. We had the appliance, in other words, but we never used it. Now on the other hand, we also had a microwave oven, and we used that a lot. The point is simply that whether you have something says nothing about whether or not, *or how*, you use it. Having a particular psychological ability says nothing about how it is applied in everyday life.[5]

Again, whereas the previous generation of research answered the question of whether or not there was a basic ability to reason counter-factually that extends across cultures, the new generation of research has now examined how this ability is used. Gilovich used his earlier research on regrets of action versus inaction as the starting point. As we saw in Chapter 2, over the short term, people are more likely to regret action than inaction. But over the long term, people tend to regret more their failures to act, their inability to take advantage of opportunity or move forward to gain something new. Gilovich wanted to know if this same pattern held across different cultures. It does. In studies conducted in China, Japan, and Russia, with a U.S. sample held up as the benchmark, these psychologists found no difference in the pattern of regrets. As people in all these countries gazed back at their lives as a whole, they tended to emphasize things they should have done rather than things that they should not have done.

Overall, there seems to be a striking similarity in how the peoples of the world think about what might have been. I find this comforting. We often hear of the psychology of difference—of how peoples of different times, places, skin colors, religions, and values are so very different from each other. We hear of tolerance and intolerance, openness and xenophobia, cultural imperialism and melting pots. All too rarely are we reminded of the things that human beings share. It seems that one of those things that people share is the ability, or even desire, to look back at the past, to imagine how things might have been better, to understand that change is indeed possible, and to move forward into

the future armed with new resolve and understanding with which to realize betterment.

Bad Moments

Counterfactuals, at their most basic core, are all about escaping
strife, misery, or disappointment. "I could have done something to
avoid this!!" The more harrowing the experience, the more vivid the
subsequent counterfactual escape attempt. In journalist Nathan Mc-
Call's autobiography, in which he described his adolescent run-ins with
the law, he poignantly recalled the thoughts running through his head
after his arrest for armed robbery, the crime for which he served time
in prison:

> I wish I had listened to my mother. I wish I could rewind
> the last hour of my fucked-up life and reset its course. I wished
> I were someone else, anywhere but riding in a cop car. I wished
> I could vanish, go back to a point in time when life seemed,
> well, hopeful. Strangely, I thought about my third-grade
> spelling bee. I had made it to the competition finals but was
> eliminated after misspelling a word; I think it was "bicycle." If
> I could go back to that night on that school stage, I thought, I
> would spell that word right and straighten out all the other
> things in my life that had since gone wrong.[6]

Just look at how many distinct counterfactuals fill this passage! It
starts with a misspelled word in a spelling bee (if only he had spelled it
correctly). But he also wished he had listened to his mother, had the
power to vanish, to rewind time itself. He wished he were *anywhere* else
but in the back of a police car. This passage vividly reveals the power of
negative experiences to create yearnings for mental escape, *any escape* by

any means. The worse the event, the more intense the desire to escape mentally. The worse the event, the more intense the counterfactual thinking. In this example, we see that with such an intense event, many different kinds of counterfactual escape attempts spring to mind.

You can probably think of many similar examples in your own life. Thoughts of what might have been tend to come as a result of bad work experiences, fights with friends or family, failed romances, poor athletic or scholastic performance, and the like. If you purchase a new shirt and it looks great on you, you give it barely a second thought. If it shrinks after a single wash, you start regretting the purchase, wishing that you'd spent that same money elsewhere.

My own research has revealed the power of negative experiences to evoke counterfactual thinking. For example, in one of these studies, research participants completed word puzzle tasks presented by computer and then received fabricated feedback that they had performed either well or poorly compared to other students. Whether this feedback was positive or negative was determined randomly, by the flip of a coin. This is an essential component of an experiment. Another way we could have done it would be to have participants complete the task and then receive accurate feedback about their true performance. Some would do better than others, due to talent, previous experience, and the like. But notice that this method introduces alternative explanations for any results we might get. If successful people generate more counterfactuals than those who are less successful, does this mean that success causes counterfactual thinking, or that talent causes both counterfactual thinking as well as success? By assigning performance feedback to people randomly, we can assume that these differences due to talent and experience are averaged evenly across positive versus negative feedback, permitting us to make relatively pure conclusions about the role of success versus failure only.[7]

We measured counterfactual thinking using what is called a thought-listing measure. Research participants received a blank piece of paper and could write down whatever came to mind. In our study, the participants completed the thought-listing measure immediately after having received that bogus feedback on their performance. Later, several research assistants read through these written lists of thoughts, counting up the number of instances of counterfactual thinking. The results of this study indeed showed that negative experiences produced more spontaneous mentions of counterfactual thinking than did positive experiences. These counterfactuals nearly all focused on specific actions the participants might have taken to improve their performance (*should have tried X . . . ; should have tried Y . . .*). Children as young as five years of age show the same pattern, in that their counterfactual thinking aims mostly at bad experiences and problems in need of solution.[8]

Breast implants might seem like a good idea at the time, but more than a few women later regret ever getting them. In a 2002 study, Patricia Parker and her colleagues at the University of Texas at Houston studied women experiencing health problems as a result of silicone breast implants. These women completed questionnaires after undergoing MRI (magnetic resonance imaging) scans of their breast implants. These scans are sort of like an improved X-ray test, permitting doctors to peer inside the chest to see whether the implants have ruptured and, if they have, how extensive the leakage has become. Overall, 75 percent of the women reported having regrets in the prior week, wishing they had never had breast implants in the first place and focusing on how much better their lives would be now without persistent health problems. The worse the situation was, the more counterfactuals were reported. The more severe medical cases resulted in litigation against the manufacturer of the silicone implant; those involved in litigation reported more counterfactual thinking than those not engaged in litigation. And those women who had had their implants removed and were therefore feeling better about putting their troubles behind them reported fewer counterfactual thoughts.[9]

These and other studies show that counterfactuals mostly emerge after bad experiences, and that those counterfactuals mostly focus on how things might have been better—upward rather than downward in their direction of comparison. We saw in the last chapter that counterfactual thinking can bring about learning and improvement. Overall, it is now much clearer how counterfactual thinking represents a brain process tuned toward betterment: it's a useful tool for fixing problems, and it is readied for use precisely when problems arise.

Almostness

"I almost got an A on the exam." A student will say this if the cut-off for an A was 80 percent and she got 79 percent. To say that something almost occurred seems like no big deal, especially if we can point to some numbers, to some sort of mathematical basis. A 79 is closer to 80 than is 75, meaning that the difference of 1 is smaller than the difference of 5. Simple arithmetic . . . and no big deal, right?

The story gets more interesting when it comes to gambling. A gambler sits in front of a slot machine at a Las Vegas casino, puts a dollar into the machine, and watches as the wheels spin. As the wheels slow to a stop, they just barely miss lining up for a jackpot of one hundred dollars. In the classic old-style slot machine, you might get a jackpot if the three internal reels lined up with pictures of cherries. Two cherries and a banana *feels* closer to the desired outcome of three cherries than does a banana, a peach, and a plum. *If one wheel had spun a little more, the jackpot would have been mine.* . . . And sure enough, an outcome that is almost a jackpot creates more negative feelings and greater dissatisfaction than a similar loss in which the outcome was more distant from the jackpot. And what happens next? Does a near-win encourage the gambler to blow even more money? We'll come back to gambling in Chapter 5, but for now the point is that we easily recognize situations in which something else almost happened instead. And wherever there are clues to almostness, the brain quickly fills in the rest of the details, fleshing out a full-blown "what if" scenario. Like bad moments, perceptions of almostness invite counterfactual thinking.[10]

There are two main ways real-life experiences can evoke feelings of almostness. One is physical distance, as in the number of inches and miles between two objects. The other is temporal distance, as in the separation over time between two events. Social psychologists Dale Miller and Cathy McFarland demonstrated the role of physical distance in counterfactual thinking by giving research participants a simple test, a description of a tragic plane crash in the frozen north. A lone survivor struggles to reach civilization on foot, but dies trying. Two different versions of this story (each participant saw but one version) were designed to produce shifts in perceptions of almostness. In one version, the survivor died seventy-five miles from the nearest town. In the other version he died just a quarter mile from town. The subsequent emotional reactions of research participants were more intense when the man *almost* made it to safety. In an earlier study, Daniel Kahneman and Amos Tversky gave participants a similar test, this time involving two people, Mr. Crane and Mr. Tees. Both miss an important flight due to traffic delays on the way to the airport. Crane misses his flight by half an hour; Tees misses his by five minutes. As you can guess, emotional reactions to the story were stronger for Tees than for Crane. Tees *almost* made it onto his plane. Crane wasn't even close. Almostness in this example is rooted to temporal distance. And beyond space and time, the mere closeness of numbers creates the same psychological feeling of almostness. Lottery players feel as though they almost won if their number is a digit away from the winning number, even though the definition of a random drawing means that all distinct lottery numbers have an equal chance of winning.[11]

Almostness explains a lot of the drama we feel when watching sports. You can probably recall seeing a basketball game with two closely matched teams, with their scores nearly even, with one team pulling ahead for a while then falling back again, with a very close final score.

This is the essence of an exciting game. The opposite is a blowout, a game in which one team dominates all the way through, with the outcome a near-certainty all the way through. The 1997 NBA finals were close. The Chicago Bulls won the first two games of the best-of-seven series, then the Utah Jazz won two, and then the Chicago Bulls won two more to clinch the championship. In the final game Chicago won by four points; they'd won the previous game by two points. That was an exciting series! I was living in Chicago at the time and I fondly recall watching those games with other very excited Chicago fans at various house parties. The 1993 Super Bowl, on the other hand, in which the Dallas Cowboys beat the Buffalo Bills with a score of 52 to 17, was a blowout. And it was also quite thoroughly boring. I was at a party for that game, too, and by halftime most of us were busy gossiping in the kitchen with the game utterly forgotten. Counterfactuals spawned by perceptions of almostness lie at the heart of the drama and excitement of sports events of all kinds.

Not surprisingly, sportscasters love using counterfactuals to spice up their play-by-play descriptions. Larry Sanna and his research team at the University of North Carolina recorded all sixty-one major league baseball playoff games in 1998 and 1999, then carefully tabulated each instance of counterfactual commentary. "It's a game of inches; if that ball had gotten over his glove, it would have been a double play. . . ," said NBC commentator Joe Morgan; "If Ogea had not deflected O'Neill's bouncer, he'd be sitting in the dugout right now watching his teammates hit already," called Bob Costas. Sanna found that these and other commentators used a counterfactual twice on average per inning, or about once every eight minutes! These counterfactual comments were more common with close scores near the end of the game. Tight games spell almostness, and counterfactual thoughts naturally follow.[12]

Understanding how almostness influences counterfactual thinking can save you money. Without your realizing it, these processes can make for bad financial decisions. Here's a simple example. You are out shopping and you see a great deal on a new shirt, a sale price, marked down 75%. So for just a few dollars you can get a name-brand shirt of superb quality, but there's a huge line at the checkout counter and you're in a rush to meet a friend for lunch. So you pass it up and leave. A few days later you return to the store to find that the sale is over and the shirt is now back to its regular price. Though you still love that shirt, it certainly doesn't seem worth it to pay full price for it, so you wander disappointed through some adjacent aisles and stumble across a pair of pants that are quite fabulous and marked down 50%. What happens next? If you're like most people, you pass this bargain up because, compared to the 75%-off deal you could have gotten, a mere 50% discount doesn't seem as good. But in purely absolute terms, *50% off is still a great deal!* In essence, the counterfactual realization of a different bargain, narrowly but unintentionally missed, *causes* you to miss another (although admittedly smaller) bargain intentionally.

Orit Tykocinski, a social psychologist working at Ben-Gurion University in Israel, has a name for this. She calls it *inaction inertia*, and she has uncovered this pattern in several experiments. Inaction inertia occurs whenever forgoing an attractive opportunity decreases the likelihood that a later action will be taken within that same domain. Having passed up a chance to buy something or make a deal, people become less likely to take advantage of another later deal. Regret is one reason for this. People kick themselves after missing out on an earlier deal, and in an unthinking manner they may then avoid future deals so as to bypass further feelings of regret. Inaction inertia is an example of how anticipating regret can have a big impact on ongoing financial decisions. In a sense, the feeling of almostness can make purchasing behavior less rational. Becoming more aware of how purchasing decisions are influenced by bargains you *almost* got can help you make better decisions. In Chapter 5 we'll delve more deeply into the biasing effects of counterfactual thinking on financial decisions.[13]

Almosts of History

The principle that almostness evokes counterfactual scrutiny applies just as well to the scholarly work of historians and political scientists. As in everyday human cognition, when something seems to have nearly happened, it draws attention, invites further thought, and stimulates attempts to explain what happened. And so it is that a huge volume of academic scholarship focuses on historical events that almost happened, with the greater nearness to having occurred prompting more attention. [14]

The Cuban missile crisis was by most accounts the closest the world has so far come to nuclear war. The United States and the Soviet Union faced each other in a Cold War that lasted forty-five years, during which time no overt battles took place. Yet behind the posturing stood the threat of nuclear war, a threat of force so terrible that it could wipe humanity off the face of the earth. In the fall of 1962, tensions spiked with the discovery that the Soviet Union had been secretly shipping and installing nuclear-capable missiles into the island nation of Cuba, located just ninety miles off the coast of Florida. Missiles such as these could utterly destroy Washington and New York in a matter of minutes, and the Kennedy administration decided quickly that the missiles simply could not stay there.

The joint chiefs advised Kennedy to attack Cuba by air, followed by a land invasion. But if Soviet troops were killed in Cuba, Kennedy feared that the Soviets would retaliate elsewhere in the world, which would then force America to respond further, leading to an escalation that would rapidly turn nuclear. Both the U.S. and the Soviet Union had nuclear weaponry of a scale that would lay waste to much of the planet. Kennedy tried to avoid nuclear escalation by imposing a naval blockade of Cuba along with a direct command to the Soviets to remove the missiles. On October 22, Soviet cargo ships containing nuclear missiles continued to steam toward the American naval armada encircling Cuba. It was on this most dangerous of days, as the ships of the opposing sides neared each other at sea, that the world came closest to all-out nuclear war.

But the Soviet ships stopped and eventually returned home. The nuclear missiles were removed from Cuba. The United States and the Soviet Union reached important agreements lessening the tensions between the two countries within the next year. Nuclear war had been averted. But what would have happened if politicians had not been able to reach an agreement? What was the worst-case scenario? Richard Rhodes, in his 1995 history of the hydrogen bomb called *Dark Sun*, spelled out the following apocalyptic counterfactual:

> The United States would have killed at least 100 million human beings. . . . If the Soviet field commanders in Cuba had launched their missiles as well, more millions of Americans would have been killed. Seven thousand megatons was more than enough fire and brimstone to initiate a lethal nuclear winter over at least the Northern Hemisphere, freezing and starving yet more millions in Europe, Asia, and North America—a phenomenon that scientists had not yet identified. . . . If John Kennedy had followed [his generals'] advice, history would have forgotten the Nazis and their terrible holocaust. Ours would have been the historic omnicide.[15]

Experts will continue to debate the reasons for the Cuban missile crisis for many years to come, and this degree of interest is a testimony to how perceptions of almostness impact scholarly inquiry in the same way that almostness influences the mental processes of ordinary people.

This fascination of the almosts of history makes for entertaining storytelling. What if Nazi Germany had won the Second World War? There is something chillingly disquieting in realizing how much worse the past might have been, a sobering realization in light of the horrors that actually did occur, such as the actual Nazi Holocaust that killed 6

million European Jews. Storytellers are drawn to counterfactuals of the
Second World War, and among the most popular of these are Philip K.
Dick's 1962 novel *The Man in the High Castle* (which takes place in an
America divided between the victorious occupation armies of Nazi
Germany and Imperial Japan), Len Deighton's 1978 detective thriller
SS-GB (which takes place in a Great Britain ruled by a victorious Nazi
Germany), and Robert Harris's 1992 international bestseller *Father-
land* (which takes place in a world dominated by a Cold War rivalry be-
tween America and Nazi Germany). These three examples but scratch
the surface of the many ways that counterfactual thinking can be used
to entertain, a topic to which we'll return in Chapter 6.[16]

Counterfactuals Reloaded

In this chapter we've seen two main kinds of situations that initiate counterfactual thinking: moments that are bad and moments that
came close to almost happening otherwise. Uniting these two kinds of
situations is their common linkage to personal goals. Bad situations are
typically those that involve missing out on something you want or getting stuck with something you don't want. Almostness means coming
close to something you've set your sights on, or narrowly avoiding
something that would be bad for you personally. Counterfactuals on a
moment by moment basis are essentially products, then, of people's ongoing goals and desires.

You can see these ideas at work inside, of all things, video games.
My favorite is the sort of game that simulates a real-world, three-
dimensional environment using a first-person (through-your-own-
eyes) perspective. Games like *Max Payne, Medal of Honor,* and *No One
Lives Forever* put you, the player, inside a narrative stream of events as
gripping as any good novel, but with the essential difference that rather
than passively following along, you actually dictate the flow of events
yourself. Where to go, what to see, whom to talk to . . . all these lie

within your grasp as you manipulate a mouse and keyboard. You see all this through the eyes of a fictional character, and this character is *you*. In *No One Lives Forever 2*, a best-selling game released in 2003, the main character is Cate Archer, a secret agent from the 1960s, essentially a female James Bond. She has a fabulous British accent, an arsenal of slick gadgets, and a vast wardrobe of swinging outfits. And she is on a dangerous mission against an evil organization called H.A.R.M.

So here I am using a mouse and keyboard to control the actions of Cate Archer. Indeed, *I am* Cate Archer, at least for a while. She is silently infiltrating the enemy lair when she is suddenly attacked by a squad of ninjas, and unfortunately I cannot quite move the mouse and play the keyboard fast enough to evade them. Cate Archer suffers repeated blows and dies. I'm looking through her eyes, and what I see is her visual field tilting sickeningly to one side, then slowly fading to black. Obviously the game does not simply end. The game resets itself, restarts the action, with Cate Archer (me!) placed back into the same stream of events, but just a little bit earlier, before my death, so that now I can replay that scene over again, battle those ninjas again, but this time get it right, this time triumph!

One of the most delightful aspects of these games is how easy it is to "save the game" as it progresses. With a simple key press, the player can store in memory all the details of the current moment in time—where Cate is standing, what Cate is looking at, what foes Cate faces. Then at any later moment, simply with another key press, all the details of that earlier saved moment may be restored precisely as they were. This is called reloading the last saved game, and it is a staple of any video game with a narrative plot progression. A savvy player saves the game repeatedly, ideally at points when Cate is healthy, safe, and well hidden from lurking ninjas. When the player next screws up, becomes injured, gets lost, or dies, she simply hits the reload key to return back to the last point where the game was saved. This feature gives gamers the opportunity to replay, or more fittingly *relive*, the last few moments of game life.

In essence, these video games have incorporated counterfactual thinking in the same way that it is used in everyday life, but they have also given players the additional power to *enact* those counterfactuals. A player can think, "Oh, I should have used my crossbow to defeat the ninjas," but rather than save this insight away in memory for the next encounter with ninjas, the player can actually go back and enact that counterfactual, actually use that crossbow, and essentially rewrite history so that it comes out just the way she wants it.[17]

In informal conversations with gamers, I get the sense that the vast majority of reloads take place after bad moves and unsatisfactory scenes; in other words, when players want to play a scene over again so as to improve on the last performance. And that is basically how counterfactual thinking operates in real life: the motive to fix, improve, and make better drives thoughts of what might have been. (The remaining reloads seem to happen mainly because the gamers are having so much fun that they want to do the same thing again and again.)

Wouldn't it be great if real life were the same as the video game, if you could "save" your life at different points, then when things go awry reload it back to the last saved point? For one thing, we'd never die. If I were to be hit by a bus, I'd just reload my body back to the last time I saved it. And I'd never have to live with the permanent consequences of my screwups—I'd just reload my life and do it right the second time. Or third or fourth or fifth time.

Counterfactual thinking rests on the foundation of goals, desires, and ideals. Look at the counterfactual thoughts that come spontaneously to mind on a daily basis and you will see a reflection of your own most basic and intimate desires.

Chapter 4

The Dark Side of "If Only"

〰

It's not your fault. There's nothing you could have done."[1] So goes a line from an old movie, and it could be any movie, or any scene from daily life. When there is nothing a person could have done, it amounts to a denial of a counterfactual, the opposite of "if only." It means that the person was not responsible, cannot be blamed for whatever bad thing has just happened. The flip side is the case in which there *was* something a person could have done, indeed, should have done. In that case the person can be blamed; the person is guilty. Counterfactuals, blame, and guilt are, we'll see, close cousins.

As we saw in Chapter 1, counterfactuals benchmark reality. One result is that they influence our beliefs about how one thing causes another to occur. To say that "If only you hadn't done X, then Y would never have happened" is to say that X caused Y. Counterfactual thoughts are usually useful precisely because they wield this causal information, which in turn illuminates how future betterment may be achieved. But we must concede another dark side to "if only." Blame and guilt are special kinds of causal beliefs, and unfair aspersions cast on others, heartless blaming of victims, and needless self-blame are all the work of the dark side of counterfactual thinking.

Here is how it begins. Blame is accorded to a person who has intentionally done something wrong, something that violates norms, rules, or laws. It usually also means that the person is responsible for having caused an unwanted outcome. This sort of blame is therefore easily and naturally expressed in a counterfactual, which as we have seen is closely connected to causal beliefs. When you have an accused murderer, for instance, another way of conveying belief in the accused's guilt is to say the victim would still be alive were it not for the accused's actions. Causation and blame are summed up in a counterfactual statement. Now this is where it gets dangerous. Because the factors that influence counterfactuals do not necessarily match the criteria necessary for justice, these factors can introduce dangerous bias in our judgments of others. Here's an example.

Dartmouth social psychologist Neil Macrae and his colleagues were among the first to study the biasing impact of counterfactuals on criminal judgment. They presented research participants with case information about a burglary in a house that took place while the family was away on a three-month vacation. Many of the family's most valued possessions were stolen, but police later apprehended the burglar. After reading the case information, participants estimated the overall seriousness of the crime and recommended sentencing for the accused.[2]

Macrae doctored the case information so that some people read that the burglary had happened about halfway through the family vacation. Other people read that the very same burglary happened the night before the family was due to return home. You probably noticed two things about this bit of doctoring. First, Macrae tried to capture the almostness discussed in Chapter 3. Some of the research participants learned that the family was almost home, that they arrived nearly in time to foil the burglar. In this case of *almost*, it is an easier, more compelling realization that the burglary could have easily been prevented. Second, you will note that the time of the burglary, from the standpoint of justice, has absolutely nothing at all to do with the severity of the crime or the punishment it warrants. A crime is a crime is a crime; when it happens ought to be irrelevant.

But it isn't.

Research participants viewed the burglary as more serious when it occurred the night before the family's return than when it happened in the middle of their vacation. These participants recommended harsher punishment for the burglar when the burglary occurred just before the family returned. What's going on here is that counterfactual thoughts can be a shorthand way of expressing blame. Therefore, anything that makes a counterfactual thought more vivid and more obvious—in this case, almostness—in turn exaggerates judgments of blame. Counterfactual thinking has even been shown to play a role in the unfortunate habit many people have of blaming victims for their own misfortune. That is because causation and blame emerge from whatever counterfactual thoughts focus upon, in this case, the behavior of the victim. Our understanding of causation and blame attains greater clarity by taking stock of which aspects of reality lure our counterfactual thoughts; that is, which parts of reality counterfactuals typically shift, cleave, and pull apart. To gain insight into biased judgment, we must therefore begin by asking: Which aspects of reality do counterfactual thoughts typically target?

Shifted Reality

Of all the things that surround us . . . people and animals, cars and houses, trees and grass, sun and moon . . . which are fixed in our own minds, and which shift and slide about, ripe for counterfactual alteration? Which aspects of reality are mental constants and which are mentally alterable? Another way to frame the question is, which aspects of reality do our counterfactual thoughts tend mainly to seize upon for mental mutation?

This is one of the core questions of counterfactuals that first fascinated philosophers. With effort, pretty much everything is mentally changeable, or mutable. In reality, the sky is blue. But I can imagine it as red or green. I can, sure, but usually I don't. In nearly all the "what ifs" that come to mind, the sky stays blue, gravity pulls things down, mother plus father make baby, and pretty much all the essential laws and rules of science remain utterly the same. You might say that these background details are psychologically immutable, but that wouldn't be entirely right because, as I said, I can mentally change them *with effort* anytime I want. A more accurate description is that every concept or category stored in memory can be classified as being more or less mutable. Some things are very mutable, some are moderately mutable, and others are hardly mutable at all.

The first time I came across these ideas was in Douglas Hofstadter's *Gödel, Escher, Bach,* which I read as an undergraduate student in the mid-1980s. This Pulitzer Prize–winning exploration of artificial intelligence wove together examples from mathematics, art, and music to illustrate what computers must do to be considered intelligent. In the work he published in 1979, Hofstadter articulated what became the counterfactual research agenda for psychological researchers of the 1980s. He argued that some counterfactuals simply seem more natural to us, whereas other counterfactuals seem forced, inappropriate, or utterly bizarre. In the opening example of his discussion he laid out a series of counterfactuals ranging from plausible to implausible, establishing for the first time the meaning of mutability:

> Driving down a country road, you run into a swarm of bees. You don't just duly take note of it; the whole situation is immediately placed in perspective by a swarm of "replays" that crowd into your mind.
> —*Sure am lucky my window wasn't open . . .*
> —*Lucky I wasn't on my bike . . .*

—Too bad those bees weren't dollar bills . . .
—Lucky I wasn't the swarm instead of being me . . . [3]

Why are the first two counterfactuals more likely to come to mind? Why do they seem more plausible at face value, more psychologically *real*, than the last two? Back in 1979, Hofstadter could only speculate about the patterns by which counterfactual thoughts dissect reality. A quarter century of subsequent research has identified two primary factors that determine what we perceive as mutable, and therefore where our counterfactual thoughts take us. These two determinants are *agency* and *abnormality*. Agency is simply a more general term for what we've seen so far in this chapter, that counterfactual thinking typically focuses on personal action that is deliberate and purposeful; in a word, *agentic*. Abnormality refers to the notion that counterfactuals tend to gravitate toward features of reality that are unusual or atypical, out of the ordinary or out of character.

When an individual is accused, we all hope that the wheels of justice will turn fairly and result in a fair judgment rooted in evenhanded consideration of the evidence. But if counterfactual thoughts are so closely connected to judgments of blame and responsibility, we gain crucial hints as to where such judgments may go awry, where bias might lead to unfair aspersions and needless self-blame, when we better grasp the main factors that shape counterfactuals themselves. A basic understanding of the importance of agency and abnormality then is of central importance in confronting the problem of biased judgment. [4]

In Control: Personal Agency Shapes Counterfactuals

We all yearn for control over the unfolding of our lives. "I am the master of my fate; I am the captain of my soul" is the commonly quoted line from the William Ernest Henley poem "Invictus." It could well be a mantra for the idealized American life of liberty and empowered personal freedom. Within American culture we are continually admonished to be in charge of our lives, to redirect and reinvent ourselves so as to forge more positive identities and more wondrous futures. And in modern life we are indeed inundated with choice, a point we'll take up in the next chapter.

It is no surprise then that "if only" thoughts tend overwhelmingly to focus on personal agency. Another way of saying this is that counterfactual thoughts zero in on aspects of the situation that we can personally control, alter, or manipulate. On average, we think things like, *If only I'd worn something different. . . . If only I'd picked something else for lunch. . . . If only I'd attended college in a different state,* and NOT *If only my friend had worn something different. . . . If only my mom had picked something else for my lunch. . . . If only my brother had attended college in a different state.*

It's worth pointing out that social psychologists use the word "control" in a rather particular sense. In casual use this word conveys domination, as in the way a dictator controls a totalitarian state (secret police . . . threats of death) or the way a lion tamer controls a lion in a circus ring (with a whip and a chair). Social psychologists use the word "control" in a softer, gentler sense, merely to mean any kind of influence or ability to alter an outcome. In this way you can exert some control over your weight by dieting (and here the meaning becomes clearer, in that few of us can claim to dominate it totally!) or exert some control over a friend's behavior through the judicious use of compliments and gifts (but again, we hardly mean that we rule imperiously over that friend's life). So when I say control, I simply mean influence of a very generic sort.

Social psychologists have long been interested in control for two reasons. First, people exaggerate how much control they have. And second, that bit of exaggeration turns out to be a pretty good thing for both mental and physical well-being. A classic study from 1975 showed that people exaggerate how much influence they have over even obviously random events. People think they are better able to steer themselves toward a win within obviously random gambles, such as dice throws, if they personally throw the dice rather than if someone else throws for them![5] And having real control is beneficial, as in another classic study in which elderly residents of a retirement home, when given some control over their daily routines, enjoyed improvements in health, described themselves as happier, and seemed to others to be zestier. Simply believing that you are in control, even if exaggerated, can bring about these psychological benefits.[6]

In the study by Nasco and Marsh that focused on the role of counterfactual thinking in improvement in academic performance, first discussed in Chapter 2, we saw how counterfactual thinking can be related to subsequent perceptions of control, more active engagement in subsequent tasks, and eventually greater success.[7] But in addition, presumed control influences counterfactual thinking in the first place, in that counterfactuals tend to focus on actions under a person's direct control.

Think about it. The last time you thought *if only*, who or what was the *if only* about? Was it about your own personal actions? Or someone else's? Was it about things you believe that you have the power to influence, like which groceries to buy for dinner, or was it about something over which you have limited power to influence, such as which brands are stocked by your local grocer?

On average, most counterfactual thoughts focus on personal, controllable behaviors. In one study of everyday life regrets, Gilovich and Medvec found that fewer than 5 percent of reported regrets involved circumstances outside of the individual's direct control. Many other studies have shown that the experience of regret is closely connected to perceptions of personal responsibility. Moreover, people's biggest regrets center on aspects of their lives that are personally controllable, like education, career, and romance.[8]

Keith Markman, a social psychologist at Ohio University, provided some of the most convincing evidence of the role of personal control in counterfactual thinking. Markman and his colleagues used a laboratory experiment modeled after the television game show *Wheel of Fortune*, in which participants competed to win lottery tickets. The game was played on computers on which a visual display showed two spinning wheels, each marked into different segments representing different degrees of wins and losses. One segment indicated a jackpot of 75 tickets, another a more modest 10 tickets, another was labeled simply "Bankrupt." Participants were told that the spin of one wheel would determine how many tickets they would win, and the other wheel would determine how many tickets another player would win. So what would happen if your wheel narrowly misses landing on the jackpot and instead lands on the 10-ticket prize? Probably that almostness feeling would kick in and you'd think about how great it would have been to win 75 tickets.[9]

Markman introduced an extra wrinkle into the experiment. He gave some participants control over their own wheel, in that they could decide where the wheel should start and how fast it would spin. Other participants were given control over which of the two wheels determined their payoff. Regardless of what participants did, the game was rigged so that it always resulted in a win of 10 lottery tickets. Participants had no actual control over their gambles, but as we've seen already, many people believe that they have the power to influence, somehow or some way, the outcome of their own gambles (*Hey, let me just blow on those dice first . . .*).

The results of the experiment revealed how counterfactuals gravitated to wherever participants believed they held control. If participants were given control of the spin of their own wheel, their counterfactuals focused on this aspect of the game: *If only I had started my wheel at a different point. . . .* But if participants were given control over which wheel would determine their win, they focused on that other aspect of the game: *If only I had played on the other wheel. . . .* These and other studies confirm that counterfactuals most typically focus on things that the individual has the personal power to alter, manipulate, and control.

That's Odd: Abnormality Shapes Counterfactuals

We just saw how counterfactual thinking focuses on *agency*; we turn now to how counterfactuals also tend to embrace *abnormality*. Another way of saying this is that counterfactual thoughts often target actions that are unusual, abnormal, even odd. Whatever is deemed normal (based on previous experience) moves to the mental background. What stands out, and what seems obvious when we think about what might have been, is action that was in some way exceptional. Counterfactuals embrace the abnormal, converting it back into what is normal.

I know someone (we'll call him Dave) who was once mugged outside a bar in Chicago. Now, if you are asked what caused the mugging, probably your first reaction is: the mugger! Some aspect of the mugger's psychology—depraved nature, financial need—was the ultimate cause of the sordid episode. But there is also an alarming tendency among observers to blame the victim, a tendency explored further a few pages ahead. Such blame can be expressed as a counterfactual, as in: *He shouldn't have been walking in that part of town. He should have been more alert. He should have taken classes in self-defense.* This tendency is increased to the extent that Dave behaved in some manner that was unusual for him. If he were walking on a street he rarely visits, this unusual element becomes prominent in observers' minds. It becomes the basis of the most salient counterfactual—*He should have stuck to more familiar parts of town.* Or, to take another example, maybe Dave was walking on a street that he often visits, but at an unusual time of day. In that case observers will again seize on what was unusual—*He should not have been out at that time of day.* As long as it is Dave doing something unusual, it will be Dave's actions that form the basis of the most salient counterfactual that comes to mind, and this in turn increases the blame directed to Dave.

That counterfactuals embrace the unusual and convert them back into their more normal form *(If only I had been doing what I usually do. . . .)* was first demonstrated by Daniel Kahneman and Amos Tversky. Research participants were presented with a brief story and then asked to write down their "if only" reactions. What exactly was the story? Retracing Kahneman's career path helps frame the story. Professor Kahneman works at Princeton University, but many years earlier he worked at the University of British Columbia. Now, I was an undergraduate at UBC and so I know the place well. UBC is in Vancouver, one of the world's prettiest cities, with its mix of ocean beaches, enormous pine forests, and jagged mountain peaks. UBC sits on a peninsula, which means that if you work at UBC and live in the city, you can drive home in only one direction—east—as the other directions end in saltwater. You'd probably take 4th Avenue most of the time, because it's the quickest. But on a sunny day, with some extra time on your hands, you'd be tempted by the scenic route, Marine Drive's north leg along the grand sandy beach called Spanish Banks with its superb view of ocean, mountainous fiords, and downtown skyline. It's slower but prettier.[10]

So there you are driving along one of these two routes, and *bang!*— you find yourself in a car accident. Would your emotional reaction to the car accident be the same if it happened on 4th Avenue versus Marine Drive? It ought to be. We're talking about the exact same car accident: same degree of damage, same inconvenience, same looming expense. In the Kahneman-Tversky experiment, a similar situation was presented to research participants, who saw either the normal route version or the abnormal route version. Participants then wrote down the *if only* thoughts that came most easily to mind. When the choice of route was normal, people ignored it. But when it was abnormal, they seized on it, saying that *If only they had stuck to the usual route home, the accident would have been avoided.* Counterfactuals gravitate to things unusual, and counterfactual thoughts tend to convert events into their more typical form.[11]

Blame is a causal judgment. When we blame someone, especially if we hold them accountable under the law and hand down punishment as a result, we hope that the means by which we reach causal conclusions are sound. But blame is influenced by counterfactual thinking, and counterfactual thinking is influenced by typicality. Sometimes typicality is informative, as when a factory employee violates standard procedure and the result is an accident on the assembly line. In this sort of case, an action that is out of the ordinary is also a breaking of the rules and a clear indication of guilt and blameworthiness. But at other times, typicality is irrelevant, as when a person is mugged after emerging from a bar he rarely visits, and observers blame him more for his own mugging than if he'd emerged from his habitual watering hole. If blame is influenced by something as potentially irrelevant as whether an action is typical or atypical, then it forces us to assess our own ability to assess others. It serves to caution us in our haste to judge.

Blaming the Victim

The brutal killing of 18-year-old Jennifer Levin transfixed New York City in the fall of 1986. What came to be known as the Preppy Murder Case was at once shocking and titillating, spinning out tale after tale of sexual antics among the wealthy youth of Manhattan. The accused was Robert Chambers, a charismatically beguiling 19-year-old with movie-star good looks. Chambers was eventually convicted of the strangulation murder of Levin, which apparently happened when the two were having rough sex in Central Park. Chambers served time and was released from prison in February 2003.

During the trial, it was a deliberate tactic of Chambers' defense team to smear the reputation of Jennifer Levin so as to make her seem responsible for her own murder. Robert Chambers' side of the story, in fact, was that he was attacked and raped by Levin, and that he accidentally killed her in self-defense. Rumors of Levin's diary, in which her youthful sexual exploits were cataloged in sometimes amusing and occasionally shocking detail, splashed across tabloid headlines. These attempts by the defense team to exploit the image of Levin as a "bad girl who got what she deserved" served as chilling justification for the 1985 law that barred use of a rape victim's sexual history as trial evidence— but unfortunately for Levin, the law did not apply to murder cases. In any case, the tactic did not work and Chambers was convicted. Even so, the attempt to blame Levin for her own murder found a ready audience: many people suspected it beforehand, many more believed it after reading the tabloids.

Social psychologists have long been aware of the tendency to blame victims for their own misfortune. Since the 1960s this tendency has been understood within the framework of the Just World Hypothesis. Essentially, this is a form of rationalization rooted in the operation of the psychological immune system by which people seek to protect themselves from emotional harm by distorting their perception of the world in a self-serving manner. If something terrible happens to an innocent person—someone a bit like *you*—it's threatening to realize that the same thing might happen to you. Moreover, that bad things happen to good people violates a cherished, implicit assumption shared by many, the assumption that the world is—with a few obvious but rare exceptions—mostly fair and mostly just. To preserve that feeling of justness, people blame the victim. In other words, they will seek out character flaws that *set the victim apart* from regular folks like you and me, and in so doing make it seem less likely that harm will ever come to folks like you and me. Now, not everyone has precisely these "just world" beliefs, and not everyone blames victims. But the stronger one's personal belief in the justness of the world (which can be measured with a questionnaire), the more powerful is this tendency to blame the victim. A substantial amount of research over the last forty years backs up the Just World Hypothesis.[12]

Research on counterfactual thinking suggests a further reason be-hind the tendency to blame the victim. Anything that a victim does that heightens the vividness of counterfactual versions of her behavior will invite an exaggerated sense of her personal responsibility for the way things turned out. As we've seen, engaging in any behavior that is abnormal, unusual, or out of character may energize counterfactuals centering on that behavior (*He should have done it the way he normally does it. . . .*), which in turn exaggerates the blame directed to that per-son (*It was all his fault*). Kandi Jo Turley and her colleagues at Wash-ington State University discovered precisely this in a series of studies from 1995. They gave research participants information about a case of rape in which a young woman was attacked on the street while walk-ing home from work. In presenting details of the case to participants, Turley altered the description of the woman's choice of the route she took home from work so that it was either the same route as always or a new route (as always, participants get to see only one of the two ver-sions of the case). Remarkably, participants were much likelier to see the victim as responsible for her own rape when her choice of route home was unusual as opposed to normal![13]

What makes this finding especially unnerving is how automatically it can happen. Our minds have a mind of their own, you might say. In a 2003 study of the role of counterfactual thinking in legal judgments, Steve Goldinger and his colleagues at Arizona State University pre-sented research participants with information about sixteen different cases involving accidents and liability. One case, for example, involved Mark, a basketball season-ticket holder whose foot was broken at a game after a light fixture fell from the arena ceiling. Participants were asked to recommend monetary compensation and estimate how much Mark could be blamed versus how much the arena managers could be blamed for his broken foot.[14]

As in the Turley experiment, Goldinger altered case details so that some actions were normal versus abnormal. For example, some partic-ipants learned that Mark's actions were normal for him: He sat in his own seat as he had all season. But other participants learned that Mark did something unusual: He saw an open seat closer to the action and moved into that new seat. Clearly, shifting seats at a basketball game has nothing at all to do with causing a light to fall, and whether a person is injured in a cheap seat, a seat right on the floor, or while standing in line to buy a hot dog should have no bearing on a legal judgment of liability. And yet the participants in this study were very definitely swayed by whether Mark did something unusual or typical. Unusualness resulted in more blaming of the victim and smaller recommendations for monetary compensation.

But there was an additional and riveting twist to this experiment. Goldinger also introduced a series of distractions that lured participants' attention away from their judgments at various times during the experiment. At the same time that they were reading about these cases, participants were *also* required to memorize nonsense words like *flozick* and *nucade*. This is not terribly difficult in and of itself, but it certainly makes it hard to throw all of your mental faculties into making a fair legal decision. Across all the different cases presented, these distractions caused people to be more biased by irrelevant counterfactuals. When distracted, participants were even more likely to blame the victim if the victim behaved unusually.

The implications of this study are chilling indeed. How many jurors are completely focused at all times on case information presented in court? How many become distracted by the work time they are missing, family problems at home, or the insistent rumblings of their tummies? This problem of incidental yet irrelevant counterfactuals swaying judgments of blame and responsibility clearly gets bigger and more dangerous the longer the trial drags on and the more boringly detailed the evidence becomes.

Unless we are on our guard, savvy trial lawyers can manipulate our interpretation of past events by strategically inserting counterfactuals that dramatize one or another person's acts. In a murder trial like the Robert Chambers case, a defense lawyer might argue that unlike most people her age, the victim liked to go to bars late at night all by herself, *but if only she had gone out with friends, this might never have happened.* Such counterfactuals are sly indeed.

A good rule of thumb is to be on the lookout for influence attempts that not only blatantly paint counterfactual pictures like this, but which push us toward believing them by skillfully setting up those preconditions that make counterfactual thinking more vivid and intense. In this example, making a person's behavior *seem* more unusual, more out of the ordinary, less like what other people do, makes the resulting counterfactual more vivid. Counterfactual thinking is such a common part of everyday conversation that skillful persuaders— lawyers, salespeople, con men—can slip them into casual chatter, yet do so in a way that manipulates the listener without their awareness. The more you know about how counterfactual thinking operates, the more you can defend yourself against others' cunning attempts to manipulate your decisions.

Self-Blame

Because counterfactuals tend to focus on personal action, personal misfortune holds the danger of spinning into self-blame. And self-blame for traumatic misfortune is not only emotionally harrowing, but may also be a first step to depression. Chris Davis examined the thought patterns among a group of patients suffering from spinal cord injuries. These patients, both paraplegic and quadriplegic yet all neurologically intact, were interviewed at Northwestern Memorial Hospital in Chicago within the first week after their injury. Eighty-five percent believed that their accident could have been avoided, and the more they focused on how their own actions might have been different so as to have prevented the accident, the more they blamed themselves for it.[15]

When someone drives while intoxicated, climbs a mountain with little training, or engages in other such obviously dangerous activities of their own free will, then self-blame for any accident suffered is entirely accurate, entirely rational. It is deeply painful for a person to kick himself for needlessly reckless behavior, true, but this hardly amounts to biased thinking. It simply amounts to coming to grips with a bad choice.

It's a very different situation when someone you love is killed in a car accident because the other driver was drunk. Davis and his colleagues studied just such a group of people and found, amazingly, that 55 percent of the counterfactuals voiced focused on the respondents' own actions, even though they were not even in the car at the time. One mother who had lost a teenager in a nighttime car accident said, "I think about the fact that if I had grounded him that night as I wanted to, it might not have happened."[16] These research participants admitted that their own actions were not the main cause of the tragedy. Yet even so, they still blamed themselves, still kicked themselves for things they might have done to prevent it. In these and other studies, counterfactual thoughts about one's own actions that might have prevented tragedy were tightly connected to self-blame.[17]

Self-blame is common. Victims often exaggerate the extent to which they caused their misfortune. More surprisingly, this exaggeration can actually contribute to successful coping, to "moving on" and feeling better about life. The reason is tied to counterfactual thinking and perceived control. Remember Dave, the guy who was mugged in Chicago? He can blame himself by focusing on things he could have done differently. *I should have stayed with my friends as a group rather than wandering off alone,* he might think to himself. By focusing on his own controllable actions, he recognizes that he can take charge in a similar way in the future. *Next time I'll be sure to stick with my friends,* he may then think. *I'm in control, and I have the power to take the necessary steps to protect myself in the future.*[18]

So there are two kinds of self-blame, a good kind and a bad kind. The good kind is behavioral self-blame, and it's good because it helps restore a sense of control after an experience of victimization. The bad kind is *character self-blame*, in which you put down aspects of your core personality, your traits and abilities. The essential difference is that one kind of blame makes reference to aspects of the self that can change and improve, whereas the other focuses on aspects of the self that are static and fixed. If it's bad and you can't fix it, it creates disheartening feelings of hopelessness.[19]

But there is a perplexing wrinkle to these findings. Exaggerated self-blame is by no means the exclusive, inevitable response to tragedy. Social psychologists have long observed the *exact opposite* response as well, an exaggerated tendency to blame others rather than oneself. The standard term for this is *self-serving bias*, and it has been uncovered in people's reactions to academic feedback, sports outcomes, business decisions, and numerous other domains of everyday life. A student got a C on the midterm exam in my social psychology class? She'll tell me the reason for failure was that the test was unfair, and breathe not a word of her own lack of preparation. A deal goes belly up? The ambitious sales associate will tell you that it's a bad economy right now, mentioning nothing of his own decisions. The more a failure threatens a person's feelings of self-worth, the stronger the tendency to be self-serving.[20]

So which is it? Exaggerated self-blame or exaggerated deflection of blame onto others? It can be both, even in the same person, and so the most appropriate question is not *which* but *when* and *under what circumstances*. For one thing, people don't always believe their self-serving pronouncements: sometimes they say them just to look good or to evade the wrath of an apoplectic employer. But self-blame doesn't make you look particularly good, and so most statements of self-blame are probably a bit more accurate as reflections of people's actual beliefs.[21]

Ongoing goals matter a great deal. Remember from Chapter 1, when something bad happens, you can react in either of two ways: change the situation or change your mind. The goal of betterment prompts active attempts to change the situation, whereas the goal of consolation means changing your mind to make yourself feel better about things that you're stuck with. The goal of betterment tends to elicit upward comparisons, and the goal of consolation tends to elicit downward comparisons. This I offered as a "grand connection," but here the connection gets grander still. Self-blame corresponds closely to upward comparisons and promotes goals of betterment and improvement. Downward comparisons and self-serving bias tend to be used for consolation, that is, to manage emotions and improve mood. In other words, both downward comparison and self-serving bias exemplify the psychological immune system in action.[22]

For the average person, these processes stand in an exquisite state of balance, shifting moment by moment according to ongoing experience and acting largely unconsciously. Self-blame tends to be the first, initial reaction to a bad experience. This is a self-focused upward counterfactual specifying actions that the individual could have taken to improve his lot. Soon after, the psychological immune system kicks in and the powers of rationalization converge to make the individual feel better by self-servingly distorting perception into a more positive, more "rosy" view of reality. From studies first reported in the 1960s and confirmed in newer studies, we know that regret over a bad choice can vanish in as little as ten minutes.[23] Indeed, the unconscious psychological work of reducing regret can begin immediately after a decision is made, even before the outcome of that decision becomes known. Certainly regrets can and do last longer, can last a lifetime as we've already seen, but many more missteps disappear from our awareness and are therefore hard to recall later, precisely because the psychological immune system kicked in and spread through consciousness a biased reappraisal of a prior choice that made it seem better, wiser, and prettier than had previously been believed. These rationalized beliefs last a long time. The amazing part of this process is that any useful insights realized in the initial upward counterfactual remain intact, to be called upon and implemented at a later time. But the emotional benefits of self-serving bias also persist, albeit at the expense of a view of reality distorted in a slightly positive direction. As UCLA social psychologist Shelley Taylor has argued from twenty years of careful research, the psychologically healthiest people are not those with a perfectly accurate view of reality, but those who systematically and chronically distort reality so that it appears slightly better than it actually is.[24]

Were it not for the silently slick operation of our psychological immune system, we might all be adrift in a torrential sea of regret and recrimination.

Depression: The Darkest Side of Counterfactuals

Mild regret is the short-lived emotion that is useful for spurring new action, and it abounds in daily life. Severe regret is much rarer, but it can be the first step toward mental illness. It is this severe form of regret that people fear, in part because it often implies self-blame. *You should have known better.* Consider the case of Cheryl, a woman in her mid-thirties. A couple of years back she was pregnant. Sadly, disaster struck in the sixth month of her pregnancy. During a routine check, the doctor failed to detect a heartbeat. The baby was dead. Tragedy of this magnitude unleashes the most awful emotions that we as human beings are capable of experiencing. But as bad as such despair might be, regret makes it even worse. This is a case of severe regret.

Cheryl learned that the baby had died from a lysteria infection. Lysteria is a type of bacteria, producing flu-like symptoms that can be lethal to fetuses and infants. Lysteria is most commonly transmitted by food, especially raw or processed food such as sushi, cold cuts, and unpasteurized cheese. Many women hear warnings about avoiding these high-risk foods during pregnancy. Cheryl, unfortunately, had missed these warnings, learning of them only after it was too late. As the realization grew that her own eating habits had been risky, new anguish accompanied the counterfactual belief that she could have known better and could easily have altered her eating habits. *If only I had avoided the deli counter*, she thought to herself, *my baby would still be alive*. Haunting her for months afterward was the awful belief that she had killed her own baby with food. She could no longer shop at grocery stores much less eat at restaurants.

Tragic events may bring on despair, but the average person is resilient. The death of a loved one would seem to create such unspeakable despair that depression would be the inevitable result. This is certainly the view that seems most apparent in the popular media. And it is true that tragedy can lead to depression, but there are huge variations in how people react to tragedy, and there are many other cases of rapid and successful recovery. Research that systematically charts recovery following tragedy indicates that a majority eventually return to their previous level of happiness and life satisfaction, a clear example of the normal operation of the psychological immune system. In a study published in 2003 that tracked over seventeen hundred widows over fifteen years, most (though, significantly, not all) returned within eight years to the level of happiness that they had enjoyed before their husband's death.[25]

Even so, sometimes counterfactuals, regret, and self-blame do spin out of control, and long-term emotional distress is the result. Depression is a mental disorder that affects over 17 million Americans from all ages and all walks of life. It involves a chronic state of negative emotions like sadness, anger, and despair that may last months. It is accompanied by lack of energy, sleep disturbances, eating difficulties, and inability to complete normal life tasks like working and socializing. A tendency to put oneself down, to see oneself as worthless and unloved is a key component of depression, as is a feeling of hopelessness for the future, a feeling that things can never be good or right again.

Contemporary psychologists explain the genesis of depression in terms of a genetic, biologically mediated predisposition that remains dormant until triggered by traumatic circumstances. In the late 1980s a new generation of substantially more effective antidepression drugs were introduced, drugs like Paxil, Prozac, and Zoloft, and these have revolutionized the treatment of depression, bringing new hope for millions of Americans. Some take this as evidence that depression is a biological disorder as opposed to a disorder of thought or a disorder caused by social circumstances. But this of course misses the point that *all* psychological events, *all* thoughts and feelings, are at root biological, the product of a particular internal organ called the brain. By the same token, all mental disorders must necessarily be biological. Knowing that depression is biological in no way contradicts the observation that depression can be triggered by social situations and by cognitive responses to those situations.

Whatever its precise causes, depression is a severely debilitating medical condition that demands treatment by a medical professional. The favored treatment as of the early twenty-first century involves a blend of drugs plus "talk" therapy, the most prominent of which is cognitive-behavioral therapy. This therapy pays more attention to thought patterns in the "here and now" as opposed to the experiences of one's childhood and targets biased perception of social events that tend to make a person feel worse, such as self-blame and counterfactual thinking.

Several kinds of thoughts therefore may be seen as risk factors for depression and as targets for therapy aimed at lifting the black cloud of depression. Research beginning in the 1980s emphasized a "depressogenic" cognitive style—a way of thinking about and explaining personal events that makes a person feel worse. Part of this style is taking one event (say, some unflattering feedback about job performance) and blowing it out of proportion, generalizing it to the entirety of one's life *(I'm utterly incompetent at everything!)*. Another part of this style is exaggerating the duration of specific bad events. Whereas a psychologically healthy individual might take negative feedback about job performance as an example of a "one-time-only" occurrence, a depressed person would probably see this as a permanent state of affairs *(I'll always be screwing up like this!)*.[26]

Only recently has new research implicated the role of counterfactual thinking as yet another type of depressogenic thought. One recent study revealed that people suffering from mild depression experienced greater regret over the decisions they'd made than those who had no signs of depression. Depression may therefore involve a hyperactive tendency to engage in counterfactual thinking, hyperactive in the sense that such thoughts persist longer than they are needed and unleash more negative emotions than they do in healthy individuals.[27]

Research on the link between counterfactual thinking and depression is only beginning, but this preliminary work has already identified three possible connections. In charting these ways in which the mind can become disordered, we get a glimpse of the majesty of the operation of the healthy mind.

• Counterfactual thoughts typically focus on controllable aspects of life, and this is useful because these represent aspects that we can change for the better. The system is broken when counterfactuals focus mostly on aspects of life that are out of one's ability to control directly.

• Counterfactual thoughts (especially upward ones) typically focus on aspects of life that are recurring, or have the potential to happen again, like buying flowers for a loved one, competing at sports, or completing specific tasks at a job. The system is broken when counterfactual thinking becomes fixated on an event that can never happen again, like the opportunity to prevent the death of a loved one. In this case, nothing useful can be gleaned from counterfactuals, as the event will never happen again, rendering those counterfactuals behaviorally useless sources of misery.

• Counterfactual thoughts pop into mind quickly then dissipate quickly, actively ejected by the psychological immune system. The system is broken when they linger like unwanted house guests. If the psychological immune system is disordered, noxious thoughts can infect a person and result in the misery of chronic rumination.

Unfortunately, the newest research linking counterfactual thinking to depression contains little insight into how best to treat depression. It is worth noting here that no simple rules of thumb or self-help strategies to attempt by yourself at home will be sufficient to combat this dangerous disease. If you or a loved one seems to be suffering from depression, the assistance of a trained mental health professional is a must. In the next section we'll see yet another way that counterfactual thinking can bias perceptions of reality.

I Knew It All Along

There is one final way that counterfactual thinking can bias reality, and for an example we turn to the world of sports. On October 27, 2002, the Anaheim Angels won the World Series, and at that exact moment, a typical baseball fan watching at home on TV stored this finality away in memory. But without his realizing it, inside the fan's brain this information was cross-linked to memories of games watched in the last season, memories of World Series of years past, and still other memories of a wide assortment of trivia accumulated through years of sports spectating. Within moments this fan may well be exaggerating his ability to have predicted the Angels victory before the series started. "Yeah, I knew it would turn out this way," he says. The trouble is, if you'd asked him beforehand, he'd have shown far less certainty.

After events happen, there is often a feeling of inevitability: you knew it all along. Psychologists call this tendency the *hindsight bias*, an exaggerated feeling of having been able to predict an event beforehand, a feeling that comes to mind *after* the event has taken place. In fact, people have trouble remembering what it felt like before an event took place, before a baseball game was played, before the winner won and the loser lost. Hindsight bias is a reflection of how memory updates itself. Once a winner is declared, this knowledge is rapidly connected to and integrated with the vast storehouse of related knowledge.

When you are sitting in your living room watching something unfold, it's hard to notice these shifts in memory taking place. Psychologists on the other hand need only use a few simple experimental tricks to reveal the hindsight bias in action. One trick is a before-and-after study. You ask people to make predictions before a key event, then ask the same people to recall what predictions they'd made earlier. Take the O. J. Simpson criminal trial. In the most notorious court case of the 1990s, former football great O. J. Simpson was accused of murdering his wife, Nicole, and a male companion named Ron Goldman. Month after month, court proceedings aired live on television, transfixing the nation with gruesome details of the murder, many pointing to Simpson's guilt. On October 3, 1995, the jury found Simpson not guilty. Loyola University social psychologists Fred Bryant and Jennifer Brockway could see beforehand that the upcoming verdict would be a great place to look for hindsight bias, so they recruited students in a statistics class and asked them for their predictions just two hours before the verdict was announced. On average, these people estimated that Simpson had a 50% chance of acquittal and a 67% chance for a second-degree murder conviction. (Yes, I know that these two numbers ought to add up to a hundred; the fact that they don't means only that at least some of the research participants bypassed the rules of arithmetic to voice more strongly their gut feelings of certainty.) A week later these same people now estimated that before the verdict was announced the chance for acquittal had been 63%, and the chance of conviction for second-degree murder was just 45%. In short, they had rather dramatically revised their own beliefs about the predictability of the verdict once they knew how it actually turned out.

Hindsight bias plays a big role in judgments of blame and responsibility, and therefore can make a big difference in legal decision-making. Say a woman is injured on an escalator after a child presses the emergency stop button. Jurors tend to see the injury as predictable, almost inevitable. Moreover, they embrace the counterfactual: *The escalator manufacturer should have known better; the designers should have foreseen this kind of accident and designed it so as to prevent it from happening.* But if the same jurors are asked to make predictions, that is, to make judgments in foresight rather than hindsight, they are much less likely to predict such an improbable escalator accident. Correspondingly, jurors who are presented with a one-sided "story" of how an accident occurs tend to fixate on that one explanation. With hindsight, they tend to think the accident was more foreseeable, and that those accused of liability were more negligent.[28]

You may have noticed that an interesting slip happened here somewhere. The slip concerns the relationship between hindsight bias and counterfactual thinking. When you first think about it, it seems like hindsight bias is the opposite of counterfactual thinking. Being more certain about the past means being less certain about ways it might have gone otherwise. You might be thinking, if hindsight bias is so pervasive, then where does this leave counterfactual thinking? After all, being sure that the past had to occur the way it did seems, on the face of it, to foreclose any possibilities for the past occurring otherwise. The more hindsight bias there is, the less counterfactual thinking there is, right?

Wrong.

I was talking to a friend of mine, a big football fan, and whenever he described a game he'd just seen, he was utterly certain that it had to happen that way. The Raiders lost? He'd seen it coming weeks earlier, knew it all along. That's hindsight bias. But at the same time, the same instant, he'd launch into a counterfactual version of the game, elaborating the plays he'd have made had he been coach. Or quarterback, as no doubt by now you've recognized that the catchphrase "Monday morning quarterback" perfectly captures these thought patterns. Knowing that the past happened a certain way *because* of key ingredients, like crucial plays or specific talents of key players, gives you the tools to imagine how it might have been different had any of those things been different.

I ran a study to capture these ideas, and it surveyed college football fans at Northwestern University during their "Cinderella season" of fall 1995. The Northwestern Wildcats, habitually near the bottom of the Big Ten Conference, took the conference title that year and went to the Rose Bowl. (And then promptly lost to the USC Trojans.) During the regular season, my colleagues and I passed out questionnaires before and after three games, played against Wisconsin, Penn State, and Iowa. Northwestern won all three games, and all by more than ten points. The hindsight bias was readily apparent, in that fans interviewed before the games on average gave Northwestern a 14 percent chance of winning by more than ten points, whereas those interviewed after the game and asked to recall exactly what they had thought before the game gave the team a 45 percent chance of winning by ten points. That's hindsight for you![29]

To show that counterfactual thinking can make hindsight bias even bigger, and is therefore a partner rather than foe of hindsight bias, we asked another group of fans to think about how the game they'd seen might have turned out differently, and to write down details of one such counterfactual scenario. For example, some might say, *If Darnell Autry* (the star player that year) *had been injured, we would have lost.* This additional instruction to think counterfactually made people even more certain of victory: They gave Northwestern a 55 percent chance of winning by more than ten points. Counterfactual thinking hadn't reduced hindsight bias; it made it even bigger.

These findings show how counterfactual thinking, hindsight bias, and causal beliefs come together to make blame more extreme. After an outcome becomes known, when clear explanations are possible, people have the gut feeling of grasping the deep meaning of a situation, which fortifies them with the confidence to imagine alternatives that fit and reaffirm their subjective impression of the situation. They may well be wrong, they may be biased, they may be ignorant of important facts, but hindsight bias coupled with counterfactual thinking can breed the sort of overconfidence that is sometimes comically evident in sports fans. *Yeah, I could see that one coming a mile away.*

The danger of this intersection of psychological forces is a tendency to focus on one explanation, one reason why something happened, be it a sports victory, an angry friend, or an inconvenient fender bender. Once a good explanation comes along (good coaching, her family is nuts, the other driver was a maniac . . .), people focus on just that one explanation, fixate on it, and look no further. Other explanations might be just as valid, but if that first explanation clicks, it clicks because it has nestled into a network of compatible ideas stored away in memory, and that neat fit evokes an overall feeling of certainty, of knowing and understanding.

As several legal theorists have recently pointed out, this can be a thorny issue for jurors, particularly in liability cases. In the escalator accident mentioned earlier, if the trial proceedings emphasize mainly one causal explanation, one single way that the accident could have been avoided that implicates liability on the part of the manufacturer (an engineering fix), jurors will fixate on that one explanation, and the result is hindsight bias. Jurors will exaggerate the certainty that the accident had to happen, and they will be especially sure that the manufacturer should have been able to foresee such an accident, should have been able to prevent such an accident. This in turn results in exaggerated punitiveness toward the defendant. A court presentation that is limited to a single, salient explanation will encourage hindsight bias. Is there any way around this? Researchers who examine the psychology of the law have recently experimented with *debiasing*, that is, techniques designed to encourage people to bypass their natural biases to explore a fuller range of ideas and explanations. In the next section we'll see some lessons derived from this debiasing research.[30]

Lessons from Research

Broaden Your Focus. I do this all the time: focus on a tiny aspect of a situation, blow it out of proportion, and use it to disparage the whole situation. There I was, about to move to Champaign, soon to begin a wonderful new job at the University of Illinois, and I was making myself miserable with regret over the decision to move there. I dejectedly surveyed my new house under construction in Champaign, at the edge of the flattest and dullest cornfield plain on the entire planet. Now it should be obvious to everyone, and it certainly is obvious to me right now, that geography is but one tiny aspect behind a decision to move to a new city. But standing there that day, I was focusing on just that one tiny bit and kicking myself for the entire decision.

This became laughably obvious to me later that day as I drove up Prospect Avenue and saw a new Old Navy store under construction. This made me happy because my wife and I usually get good deals on kids' clothes there, and so I was immediately swayed by another counterfactual, a downward counterfactual: this town sure would be less livable with no Old Navy in it! And I remember stopping to laugh right there, an honest, deeply felt laughter at myself and my own silliness in letting such very minor details drive so much second-guessing of a major life decision. It was suddenly clear that the decision to take a job in a new city involves issues of far greater importance than geography or shopping.

Big decisions involve numerous features that are important, but all too often people have a tendency to narrow their focus to one or another tiny aspect. *Focalism* is the term given to this tendency, and it is more common than you might think, influencing not only counterfactuals and regret, but all sorts of comparisons and predictions. For example, what if you lived in California? Would you be happier there? It's warm, the beaches are fabulous, and the sun shines all the time.[31]

You might say to yourself, *Hell yes!* I'd be happier if I lived in California! (If you already live in California, the biasing effect of focalism is probably already apparent to you.) David Schkade and Daniel Kahneman actually asked people how happy they were, that is, people in California versus people in the Midwest. It turned out that people's descriptions of their overall life satisfaction were identical at all these locations! In reality then, people on the West Coast are no happier with their lives than people in the Midwest.

But people in the Midwest nevertheless expected people in California to be happier, even though they clearly weren't. The reason for this mistake was simple: Midwesterners focused on the most obvious and well-known features of California, like beaches and sunshine. But in terms of what life satisfaction really is all about, climate plays a small part. In this same research, people rated career, education, personal safety, and social life as much more important for their overall well-being than climate. Yet when people from the rest of the country imagined life in California, this small aspect of climate swelled to fill their imagination, they focused on it, giving it exaggerated prominence in their predictions about other people and about what they themselves might be feeling if only they lived in California.[32]

Circumventing the focalism bias is tough. It happens without our realizing it, and by our very nature we are creatures sensitive to the moment, to experiences as they happen. It is enormously difficult to step back and construct a view of the "big picture" that is not biased by aspects of our life that are for the moment vivid and obvious. Being aware of focalism, and watching for its subtle operation, is a first step toward reducing its overall impact.

Another Reason? Could there be another reason why? My friend is angry with me and my first thought is that she's in a bad mood, and I see signs that confirm it and I stop right there, think no further about other reasons *(maybe something I said . . .)* that might also account for her anger. This is the natural response of the explaining brain, to stop when the first "good enough" explanation comes along and to ponder no further. As we've seen, hindsight bias can combine with counterfactual thinking to make that first explanation seem particularly vivid and true, even if a better one is perfectly plausible. So a good trick every now and then is to force yourself to think of additional reasons why someone behaved as they did. Maybe there's a better explanation right around the corner.[33]

Beware of Bias. We have seen in this chapter that people can be biased in their assessments of blame, pushed into greater punitiveness by seemingly irrelevant features of the situation. What's more, the brain does this automatically and people often do not recognize that their pronouncements of guilt have fallen prey to bias. Armed with the knowledge that almostness, agency, and abnormality may influence judgments of blame, you can make corrections in your own judgments of others, compensating for these known sources of bias. If your first reaction is to blame someone for their own misfortune, take a second look.

～

Counterfactuals are close cousins of beliefs about causation, blame, and responsibility. They infiltrate legal decisions and can push jurors to overly harsh judgments of the accused. Skilled persuaders, be they lawyers or marketers, can hijack counterfactual thinking and manipulate the "if only" thoughts of unknowing listeners, making them even more biased. Although there is a dark side to "if only" thinking, particularly when self-blame leads to depression, the dark is outweighed by the light. Exactly the same brain process that underlies biased victim-blame and self-blame also produces the main benefits of counterfactual thinking, namely learning from mistakes, improving performance, and feeling in control of one's life. In this next chapter we'll explore more ways that counterfactuals can bias beliefs. The focus, however, is on biased financial decisions, and here some simple knowledge of the workings of counterfactual thinking may save you some money.

Part II

Putting Counterfactuals to Work for You

~

Chapter 5

How Best to Buy

~

Coffee or tea? If you pick coffee, it means you pass on tea. But you *could have* had tea, and it *might have* been better. Mac or PC? If you use a Mac for your personal computing, you might occasionally ponder software you might now be using had you only bought that other kind of computer. To be or not to be? As Shakespeare intuited, choice defines human existence.

Counterfactuals pervade choice, and there has never been a more active chooser in history than the American consumer. Every day we are bombarded by choices, and by messages designed to make us choose a certain way, from clothing to soft drinks to political candidates to automobiles to music to places to live. Choice creates "if onlys" that influence the satisfaction or dissatisfaction we feel. And counterfactuals from previous choices in turn influence our next choice. Understanding the effects of counterfactuals on choice might save you some money.

You walk into a jewelry store with the goal of purchasing a ring for your sweetheart. You have a pretty good idea of what you want—a half-carat ring—and how much you can afford to spend. Now here's an old sales trick. The pleasant gentleman behind the counter shows you several rings within your price range, and you gravitate toward one in particular that appeals to you. At the moment that you seem to be settling on this "best option," the gentleman pulls out a new ring, one of obviously higher quality, "While you're considering this half-carat ring, I just wanted you to see this beautiful one-carat ring. Isn't that workmanship remarkable?" After you express some agreement that it is indeed wonderful, yet clearly beyond your price range, he replaces it back in the showcase and asks you about that ring you'd already eyed as your favorite.

Will you now buy it?

Chances are that you're more likely to buy your first pick after being shown a much more expensive alternative. The trick is a simple but skillful manipulation of your own counterfactual thinking. It is a manipulation of contrast. Compared to that one-carat ring, your favorite half-carat ring now seems, *by contrast*, more affordable. A more expensive alternative is a downward counterfactual—a worse option, at least in terms of cost—and as we know, downward comparisons tend to make current circumstances seem slightly better, slightly more satisfactory.[1]

So here we have *Lesson from Research #1*. We'll call it the *dangled treasure trick*. The best antidote to a salesperson's attempts to interfere with your counterfactual thinking is to disengage. Walk out of the store. Leave the purchase decision for another day. Let your head clear, let all the options and ideas and information relevant to the purchase fade from awareness, and leave the purchase for later. Research shows that it takes less than an hour for minor jumbles of information to fade from awareness and stop influencing decisions. In technical terms, information made temporarily accessible by momentary experience tends, on average, to return to its baseline level of activation in under an hour.

There is a closely related sales trick that I have experienced several times. It is particularly effective in real estate, where for many first-time buyers in inflated markets, the choices seem quite dismal. On an outing with a real estate agent in Chicago a few years ago, I was led through an assortment of abominable houses, each sinking my heart deeper as I imagined living in them, imagined my kids growing up amid their squalor. Near the end of the tour we came across a perfectly delightful bungalow, well within my price range and vastly superior to the houses we had previously seen. The trick is nearly the same, again based on the skillful creation of a downward comparison. All those previous houses were worse in quality, even though priced the same as the current offering. Naturally, this makes the current offering seem, *by contrast*, much more attractive. We'll call this *Lesson from Research #2* the *rotten appetizer trick*.

It might seem that these two tricks are very different, because one involves a much better option, the other a much worse option. But they share the same underlying psychological principle. Price and quality are two essential aspects of purchasing decisions, and the two often (though not always!) go hand in hand: higher quality comes at a higher price. Those two tricks, of dangled treasure and rotten appetizer, both draw their power from a downward counterfactual contrast. The dangled treasure trick emphasizes a downward price comparison (while leaving quality constant), whereas the rotten appetizer trick emphasizes a downward quality comparison (while leaving price constant). Both depend on the force of the downward comparison to make the current, favored option look even better. Savvy salespeople know that the best time to use the dangled treasure trick, then, is when price dominates the choice situation (I'm on a tight budget . . .); that's precisely when a more expensive alternative makes another, more moderately priced option seem better. But when quality dominates the choice situation (I can't stand living in a dump . . .), the rotten appetizer trick is the best bet.

Before buying, it's best to ask yourself, what is the most important factor here, price or quality? Knowing this beforehand alerts you to which trick you are most vulnerable to, allowing you more ably to defend yourself against it.

The Basics

A decision is defined as a choice between alternatives. After one alternative has been selected, the others become might-have-beens, options that could have been selected but weren't. They become counterfactuals. The more similar the options, the tougher the choice. When making the choice, you can predict how much you might kick yourself for not choosing one option over another; this is called *anticipated* regret. Once the choice is made and you think about the possible alternatives, this counterfactual evokes *actual* regret.[2]

A friend of mine, largely happy with a new car purchase (he called it "exquisite"), nevertheless went on in an e-mail message to lament the fact that "it isn't the most powerful or fastest version of the line . . . imagine how much cooler it could get with another hundred horsepower!" In other words, he could have paid a bit more, could have had the top of that product line, king of the heap, and for all the enjoyment he got out of an objectively wonderful automobile, he still could not help imagining how it might be even better had he made a slightly different choice at the dealer's showroom. This of course is the key problem of any choice, the prospect of future disappointment and second-guessing.

Counterfactuals are an inherent component of choice, and the aftermath of every choice is emotion shaped by counterfactual thoughts. All of our choices in life, from finances to friendships to relationships, produce varying degrees of satisfaction and joy that are dependent on the counterfactuals that frame them in our mind.[3]

How Much Choice Is Enough?

The more choice, the better, right? We jokingly remember when the first Ford automobiles went on sale, and Henry Ford quipped that consumers could choose any color they wanted as long as it was black. These days we can have red cars, green cars, azure cars, and cream cars, and the more choices offered, presumably the better able we are to satisfy the exact form of our desire. It sometimes seems as though retailers and service providers are engaged in an arms race of ever greater arrays of offerings; more flavors, more colors, more payment options, all for the simple reason that consumers demand more choice and will gravitate to businesses that can satisfy that demand. More choice spells greater profit, right?

Not so fast. There can indeed be such a thing as too much choice, and too much choice results in consumer apathy and disengagement. And lost sales.

This is a realization stemming from the latest research in social psychology, which for many previous years had largely agreed with the presumption that more choice is better. Social psychologists Sheena Iyengar and Mark Lepper published a series of studies in 2000 that changed that presumption. In one of their studies, for example, they set up a display booth at an upscale California supermarket, offering customers the opportunity to taste some new jams. Every hour they changed the format of their display. One hour there would be lots of choice: 24 different kinds of jam, to be precise. The next hour the choice would be much reduced: just 6 kinds of jam. Over the course of ten hours of total observation, 754 shoppers were tracked. Twenty-four kinds of jam initially lured more customers over to take a look (60%) than just 6 choices (40%). However, of those who stopped to try out some jam, only 3% of those bought jam when selecting from 24 kinds of jam, whereas a whopping 30%—ten times as many!—bought jam after sampling from 6 kinds. Giving customers more choice actually reduced sales.[4]

In a follow-up study of chocolate choices, Iyengar and Lepper found that people both enjoyed having more choice, but also found it to be more frustrating. Most important, those who had lots of choices experienced greater regret—with so many more chocolates that they could have had, it is not surprising that the study participants would have felt this way. Frustration and difficulty with the choice process, and regret over options left unchosen, contribute to disenchantment with the experience of buying. In this chocolate study, like the jam study before it, more choice spelled weaker sales. Participants could take a five-dollar payment for being in the study, or they could take an equivalently valued box of Godiva chocolate. People who had lots of choice took the chocolate 12 percent of the time; people offered a more limited choice took it 48 percent of the time. It seems that too much choice can be *demotivating*, in the sense that exhaustion from the obligation to sample all options and figure out which is best makes a lot of people prefer not to be bothered. They simply avoid the choice situation entirely.

Iyengar, a professor in the business school at Columbia University, has discovered further examples of how too much choice can be demotivating. She noticed the same pattern among employees at large corporations who were being offered 401(k) programs. The more retirement options that employees were offered, the less likely they were to enroll in *any* program at all.[5]

This body of research suggests that too much choice is a bad thing. Fueled in part by regret over the prospect of so many foregone alternatives, too many options cause consumers sometimes to just shut down and avoid the decision entirely. But it is important not to exaggerate this conclusion.

Too much choice can be stressful. But too little choice is also stressful. For each of us, there is a zone of optimal choice, and deviation from that zone with either too much or too little can be equally stressful. I know a couple who moved for a short time to Chicago from Amsterdam, and the average supermarket in Chicago is, to put it mildly, stocked with a vastly greater range of jams, chocolates, yogurts, breads, meats, and liquors than any in Amsterdam. After a simple shopping trip to prepare for dinner, this couple would be frazzled, utterly exhausted by the amount of attention to subtle variation demanded by the enormous variety of brands available. They moved back to Amsterdam after a year, but had they stayed, I am confident that within a couple of years they would have become perfectly satisfied with the level of choice in Chicago. I am confident of this because earlier I had moved to Chicago from the small town of Lompoc, California, and was for a short time also overwhelmed. But soon I became accustomed to the greater range of options available in the big city. Then something funny happened. Six years later, I moved to Vancouver, Canada, and experienced the reverse shock of vastly reduced choice. Canadian supermarkets, like Dutch supermarkets, simply aren't stuffed to the rafters with the degree of choice common to American supermarkets, and my wife and I suffered a kind of "withdrawal" reaction, like chain-smokers stuck on an international flight, anxiously craving not nicotine but variety. Too little choice can be just as stressful as too much choice.

So what is this optimal degree of choice? It's different for each person, and for each domain of choice, be it groceries, clothing, political candidates, or vacation spots. And it all depends on experience. We become accustomed to what we've recently experienced, adapt to it, and expect it without giving it a second thought. This makes it difficult for observers to determine the exact amount of choice that is optimal for satisfaction for any given group of people, and it relegates marketers to a never-ending quest to remeasure and recalibrate this amount for varying market segments, varying products, varying locations, and varying moments in time. For the consumer, perhaps the best advice is to be wary of too much choice as well as too little choice, and not hesitate to back off from the choice situation. There's always another day for spending, another opportunity to consume.

How Best to Buy: Product Lines and Category Boundaries

Earlier I mentioned a friend's car purchase, and his continuing feelings of regret that he didn't buy at the top of the product line. It turns out that substantial research supports the notion that we can all improve our feelings of satisfaction with purchasing decisions by paying attention to product lines and the boundaries between categories.

What do I mean by a product line? Last summer I bought a new bicycle for myself. I have been happy with the bicycle. Without naming brand names, let's just say that this bike manufacturer carries a large product line, including low-end, mid-level, and professional quality bikes. The middle level seemed to suit me. At this level I could choose among four different models: the X30, the X45, the X60, and the X75. Now, I just made these designations up, but you'll immediately recognize this designation scheme as fairly typical of how manufacturers label their goods. Accordingly, the prices rise in a steplike fashion for each of the four models, along with the number of features and overall quality. Pay more, get better quality, no surprise there. But in any purchase decision, the consumer attempts a mental balancing act of quality versus price, aiming for that perfect balance of value for money. Satisfaction comes from value, right?[6]

But here's where a psychologist starts to have some fun. Satisfaction is an emotional judgment, and satisfaction for anything in life, be it consumer products or friendships or relationships, really hinges on two main aspects: the *intrinsic features* and the *comparison frame*. The intrinsic features are the things we are usually aware of and feel we *ought* to be focusing on. In the case of a bicycle, it's things like warranty, quality of construction, weight and strength, and whether the seat hurts your butt on a long ride. The comparison frame, on the other hand, is something we generally ignore, but it is just as important in determining our feelings of satisfaction. The comparison frame reflects the impact of alternative options, past benchmarks, and general expectations. You'll feel good about a purchase if it is better than what your friends have, better than your old bike, or surprisingly better than expected. The more that you understand how a choice is framed, the more you can see where your feelings of satisfaction come from.[7]

So *Lesson from Research #3* is: Go for the top of the product line. In my bicycle purchase, I was thinking about some research conducted by Vicki Medvec, a psychologist working at Northwestern's Kellogg School of Business, and so my immediate instinct was to buy the bike at the top of the product line, the gleaming silver X75. What did Medvec find? Back in Chapter 1, we reviewed her study of Olympic medalists, with the surprising finding that bronze medalists were happier than silver medalists. The reason for this is that medalists were keenly aware of category boundaries. For the silver medalist, the salient boundary was just one step upward: winner versus all the rest. The silver medalist focused on an upward counterfactual which, as we have seen many times, tends to reduce satisfaction. For the bronze medalist, a different category cutoff was most salient: medalist versus nonmedalist. So these individuals instead focused on downward counterfactuals: *Lucky I'm on the medal stand at all*. Medvec, in follow-up research with Ken Savitsky, found that students who have objectively better grades can be more disappointed than those with worse grades if they are near a category cutoff. If 80% is the cutoff for an A grade, a student with 79 is less satisfied than a student who has 77. By the same token, a student narrowly exceeding the cutoff with 81 will be happier than another student with 83. In this case, the comparison frame overshadowed the intrinsic features in determining these students' satisfaction with their grades.[8]

If you want to minimize regret and maximize satisfaction, you need either a 77 or an 81. In purchasing decisions, what this really boils down to is being aware of product lines and their boundaries. The following three cases show how.

Case 1: Fat Boundaries. Let's stick with bicycles, and focus again on the midrange line of bikes I sketched out earlier. Now, let's say the low-end bikes are *really* low-end. This means that there is a big gap, or a really fat boundary, separating the low end from the midrange. The X30, the lowest rung of the midrange, is $350 more than the top of the low end, which is the pathetic little C19. Similarly, there is a big gap separating the midrange from the high end. The amazingly wonderful P9000 is $1,000 more than the top of the midrange, the X75.

You can think of the fat boundaries as psychological insulation—they tend to keep the focus of comparisons within, or inside, the midrange line. So if you focus on the X30, you tend not to think about the low end . . . it's just too low and you'd never in a million years think to lower yourself way down there. So a downward counterfactual that makes the X30 attractive by contrast tends not to come to mind. Similarly, if you buy the X75, you tend not to think of going any higher. The next model up is so high up, so impossibly excessive in expense, that you just know you're never going there. As a result of the fat boundaries, counterfactuals that come to mind will center on comparisons *within* the product line. And remember, your goal is to maximize downward comparisons and minimize upward comparisons. The X75, being the top of the line, is the only model that provides you with nothing but downward comparisons. For each of the others, there's always another, slightly better model just within your reach. If you buy the X30, you'll dream of how the X45 is better and could have been yours with just a bit more money. Or if you buy the X45, you'll be thinking of the X60; and if you buy the X60, you'll be dreaming of that shiny X75. With this understanding that satisfaction depends not just on intrinsic features but also on frames of comparison, the rule is simple: With fat product line boundaries, buy at the top of the product line.

Case 2: Only One Line. Some brands, like Nike, offer a huge variety of products, with multiple product lines to suit every budget. But other, smaller brands aim for a single market segment with a very restricted range of models. Naim is a company that makes high-end stereo components like amplifiers and CD players, and their product line is extremely small. They make nothing at the low end and nothing midrange; everything they do is insanely great and, yes, fantastically expensive. If you have several thousand dollars to spend on a CD player, you can pick between the Naim CDX2 and the Naim CDS3. Both offer stellar performance, but the CDS3 is the more powerful flagship model. If you settle for the CDX2, you'll be kicking yourself later for not going that extra mile to reach the CDS3. When a company makes but one level of product line, the buying strategy that maximizes satisfaction is the same as when there are fat boundaries between multiple lines. Again, the focus of comparison will be entirely within the line, and so again, the way to minimize upward comparisons is to go for the top. Buy the best.

Case 3: Thin Boundaries. At some point you may have been thinking, the message from Medvec's research was that the Olympic bronze medalists were happier, so why isn't there advice to emulate them? After all, bronze ain't the top of the product line. True enough, but although this wasn't emphasized in the Medvec research, mainly because it is so obvious, gold medalists are happiest of all, and the advice so far has been to emulate them, to go for the gold.

The situation in which bronze is the ideal buying strategy comes when the boundaries between product lines are thin, when the gaps are so small that the lines tend to merge in your head. Wine is a good example. You can go to a wine store and see bottles ranging from $5 to $5,000, with a wide variety between those two price extremes. But there are no hard or well-defined categories separating types of wines into distinct quality groups. Wine shoppers instead might invent their own category boundary ("Anything over $20 is too extravagant for me"), but there will be many bottles that are close in price, both above and below ($19 versus $21). In this case, going for the best within the category doesn't help, because there isn't any insulation to prevent the upward comparison to the next-best bottle of wine on the other side of the thin category boundary ("That $21 bottle might have been really great").

When product lines have thin boundaries, "being bronze" is most likely to pay off. Or in terms of the Medvec and Savitsky research on students' reactions to grades, the trick is to get the 81 percent rather than the 79 percent, which in essence means barely exceeding the thin category boundary. The goal then is to locate or even invent a lower-level boundary for yourself. "I cannot bring myself to drink a bottle worth less than $10," you might think. Then buy an $11 bottle. The upper category boundary ($20) is nowhere in sight, and so suggests few upward counterfactuals. But the lower boundary is now salient, and with the resulting downward possibilities etched in your mind, you feel pleasantly relieved that you did not settle for the cheapest of the cheap.

You might see from this last example that a key to managing satisfaction is the recognition of the different ways of defining product lines and category cutoffs. Very obviously, retailers and marketers are already at work on this, and they in many cases have keen instincts for setting prices and defining product lines in psychologically skillful ways that maximize sales. Williams-Sonoma is a retailer that has very successfully implemented a strategy for minimizing upward counterfactuals in customers. For each kind of kitchen appliance, for example, they often offer just one product (one kind of blender, one kind of waffle iron) and each one is a top-line item. Customers enjoy shopping at Williams-Sonoma because opportunities for regretting not buying something better are effectively foreclosed. Notice also how effective it can be to reduce, rather than increase, the range of choice offered to customers!

Only since the 1990s has there been concerted research into the connection of counterfactual thinking to marketing and consumer decision-making. These research efforts are probably about to mushroom. In the next twenty years or so, marketers will become ever more skilled in their attempts to sway purchasing by way of subtle alteration of frames of comparison. Your best protection is to have the same knowledge.

Overswitching: Biased Investment Decisions

You buy something (a car, a bicycle, a Ginsu steak knife) and it breaks. You think to yourself, *I shouldn't have bought it.* Next time, you buy a different brand. This is an entirely sensible sequence of events. It is emblematic of the core sequence of normal decision-making, normal improvement from mishap, and of course, that normal usefulness of counterfactual thinking in spelling out how things might have been better and therefore how things may yet improve in the future. This is a core effect noted in numerous studies. For example, one study showed how regrets about service providers (cabs, hotels, restaurants) corresponded directly to subsequent switching to new service providers.[9]

This is a perfectly smart thing to do in most circumstances. The danger, however, is in too much changing, too much switching, as a result of too much counterfactual thinking. The stock market has been around for a long time, but it is only in the last decade that investors could watch prices updated *every minute.* Each change in a stock price offers new opportunities for regret. Each jump up in price is cause for rejoicing, each drop spells fresh regret. When this information cycles over minutes rather than weeks, regret may become the investor's worst enemy.

Sometimes these regrets are futile, as when there is clearly nothing left to be done. I remember when a friend sold some stock in an airline to raise money for the down payment on his new house. For weeks after the sale he compulsively checked the stock prices on the Internet to see whether they went up or down—to see whether he would have made even more money had he delayed his sale.

If only I had sold my Enron stock earlier! is a counterfactual that filled the minds of many people in 2002. This regret is not so much futile as simply tragic, representative as it was of a degree of deception and corruption in corporate America that had not been foreseen in the boom years of the 1990s. But with the stock market deteriorating over the first years of the new millennium, many investors became obsessed with what they might have done differently to save themselves huge amounts of now-lost money. For stock investors, fueled by Internet-enabled instant access to current prices, the biggest danger is constant price revisions, some of which inevitably result in regret.

Overswitching is the result of too large a counterfactual reaction to minor or nondiagnostic feedback information. A novice investor, realizing that better profits might have been made elsewhere, might sell off stock, but this overactive tendency to change course will likely bring suboptimal results (i.e., financial experts argue that novice investors switch their investments too often). The overactive tendency to "switch," or to undo a previous investment decision repeatedly and rapidly, can produce no gain in profit while wasting money needlessly on brokerage fees.[10]

This is an all-too-easy mistake to make, as the rises and falls in financial markets *seem* meaningful, at least until you step back and look at a graph of their performance over several years. Then what you see is perhaps a big overall trend upward (as in the late 1990s) or downward (as in the early 2000s), along with a whole lot of random variation, a whole lot of meaningless up and down blips. A blip on one day is not useful feedback, and decisions based solely on that one blip are uninformed decisions. Further fueling this bad decision-making is the tendency of financial news analysts not only to comment on these blips, but also to interpret them. It doesn't take a scientist to notice that the interpretations can be nothing more than wild guesses, there being an utter absence of direct evidence to support them. Here are two that I pulled at random from the Internet:

"Signs of weakness in the economy pushed stocks lower Friday."[11]

"Investors pushed stocks higher after the reports came out, apparently focusing on the unemployment rate and pieces of the report such as the workweek figure."[12]

For these to be valid assertions, the commentator would need a sample of investors to complete questionnaires on a nearly daily basis, asking them directly what it is that is pushing their decisions to buy or sell. Even if this were done, social psychologists are well aware that what people say is not necessarily the real cause of their behavior—many times people lie or are simply unaware of the true reasons for their actions. But such surveys are not even attempted in the first place, and so daily interpretations of market movement amount to no more than informed conjecture.

Michael Morris, a psychologist who works at Columbia University's graduate school of business, has conducted a series of studies showing that, in part due to these exaggerated media interpretations, the average investor perceives the stock market in terms of a living, breathing entity, ascribing essentially random up and down movements to humanlike motives and actions, like chasing, hiding, climbing, and rejoicing. Stepping back and viewing this tendency from a distance, it becomes obviously silly.[13]

Overswitching is a problem best remedied with better awareness and fuller background preparation prior to making the first decision, coupled with a keen understanding of when to back off from your own counterfactuals. Jim Sherman and Allen McConnell offered the following wise words back in 1995:

> Given people's tendency to focus on the outcomes of decisions, however, they will sometimes change good decision rules to bad ones on the basis of the counterfactuals that they generate. In fact, changing judgment strategies based on upward counterfactual generation ought to be most beneficial for poor decision-makers, but most dysfunctional for good decision-makers. It may make people feel hopeful that they can ensure success in the future simply by changing to a strategy that would have had a positive outcome for a specific instance in the past, but this is far from rational decision-making. Good decision-making requires an analysis of the conditions under which a decision was made rather than a focus on the outcome of that decision and on the counterfactual worlds that could have emerged under different judgments for the specific instance at hand.[14]

So here then is *Lesson from Research #4*, which is *Beware Faux Feedback*. Be cautious about information that isn't really informative or progress reports that are not really meaningful with regard to long-term growth prospects. Be wary of the impulse to fix, change, or switch strategies because of the momentary sting of regret. Be sure that the basis for switching is a sound one.

Just Can't Stop: Counterfactuals and Gambling

So you're in Vegas, and you're at the blackjack table, and you're going to lose. I'm not a fortune-teller, but I can make that prediction fairly accurately. At least on average, over time, you're going to lose. Casino gambling is rigged against players. The odds are set ahead of time so that on average, the house wins and players come up short. Casinos collect over $25 billion in revenue per year in the U.S. from the pockets of ordinary players.

We've seen how uninformative feedback can create counterfactual thoughts that push people into making overly frequent changes, particularly in financial decision-making. Other research has shown that counterfactual thoughts are one of several ingredients that keep people gambling even in the face of obvious loss.

Tom Gilovich's research showed how gamblers can talk themselves into continued obsessive gambling even after a series of failures by reinterpreting those failures so that they seem more like "near-wins." Gilovich found a group of knowledgeable football fans, then asked them to place hypothetical bets on already-played NFL games. The games were quite old (from 1965) and so none of these fans had direct knowledge of them. Later, after the bets were settled, he asked these fans to explain their wins and losses into a tape recorder. Listening back over these explanations, it was clear that fans were quick to accept wins at face value, but offered counterfactual excuses for losses, pointing out in precise detail why they *nearly* won. Losers were especially likely to seize upon "flukes" in the game, like a fumbled punt followed closely by a fumbled pass, arguing that were it not for these events a victory would have been assured. Fans who latched onto these flukes were likelier to bet again on the same team in a rematch, predict a larger point spread in that rematch, and express greater confidence in victory compared to those who hadn't heard about any flukes.[15]

It is not only feelings of nearly winning that can make people gamble more. Michael Wohl and Michael Enzle, social psychologists working out of the University of Alberta, demonstrated that when gamblers came close to a big loss but narrowly avoided it, it made them feel lucky. Armed with this short-term glow of luckiness, these gamblers were emboldened to bet even more, as fast as possible, before their luck ran out![16]

Casino and lottery operators seem to have an intuitive grasp of how best to manipulate counterfactuals so as to encourage more gambling. At the racetrack, photo finish replays are shown so as to reveal just how close losers were to winning. Keno is a casino game in which players guess the numbers on randomly drawn balls. Winning numbers light up on keno boards located throughout the casino, but the lights also extend to some surrounding numbers, drawing attention to numbers that *nearly* won.[17] And state-run lotteries in their advertising play upon people's counterfactual musings of having almost hit it big, as in this lottery ad jingle sung to the tune of "It Had to Be You":

> It could have been you;
> It could have been you.
> Counting the dough
> Ready to go
> On that three-month cruise . . .

The idea behind this strategy is that people will play the lottery, buy more tickets, if they are motivated to avoid future regret as they realize how much they'd kick themselves if their "favorite numbers" won and they hadn't even bought a ticket. The song continues:

But what can I say?
You didn't play
It could have been you![18]

Possibly the most extreme case of lottery regret on record was a man from Liverpool who committed suicide after his favorite numbers came up to win a $12.8 million jackpot, yet he had forgotten to bet them![19]

If casino managers and lottery advertisers are good at manipulating counterfactuals, then without a doubt the master manipulator is the hustler. The prototypical hustler in American mythology is the pool hustler, like Paul Newman or Tom Cruise in two great pool movies, cool and lean, smoking an upturned cigarette, dispassionately survey-ing the balls before slyly sinking the winning ball.[20] Stringing along a sucker, encouraging him to keep coming back for more is a fine art; the hustler's skill is formidable, but his first trick is to conceal just how for-midable he truly is. He must, in other words, be a skilled creator of counterfactuals in the minds of his victims; he must be a cunning ar-chitect of close games, near misses, and feelings of almostness. Each game that the victim loses must be a close game, a game he nearly won, making him believe that he has a fighting chance of winning the next game. A fluke, a lucky last shot, a one-in-a-million move that allows the hustler to win, just barely, is the time-honored trick in drawing the sucker into the next game, and the next defeat.

I know someone who has spent a bit of time hustling darts, and he told me how he uses this same strategy. An experienced dart player can "waste" a dart or two in each round and still beat a mediocre player. Those spare darts can be deployed skillfully to create the impression that the hustler is shooting wildly, that the hustler's win is just a mat-ter of dumb luck, and that the sucker has a decent chance of winning the next round. My friend told me, "A triple-20 looks a lot luckier when it is surrounded by a single-12 and single-18 than by a single-20 and triple-1, so if the sucker attributes the triple-20 to luck rather than skill, then he'll see this bit of luck as having just as easily worked in his favor." And so off the sucker enthusiastically sails into yet another losing round.

A very similar bit of psychology underlies some of the compulsive marathon playing well-known to video gamers. Playing on game boxes plugged into a television, and especially playing on home computers, gamers can get so involved in the immersive game experience that they can play for hours, even days on end. In the previous chapter we encountered the idea of the reloaded saved-game, the trick programmed into a video game that allows a gamer to work over and over again at a difficult point in the game, slaying the nastiest dragon or defeating the wiliest ninjas. On each attempt the gamer might learn something or develop her skill further, so that when she reloads, she has a better chance of succeeding. Eventually she does. Video games have always embodied tasks of escalating difficulty—they get harder and harder as you go along—and so players must learn and develop new skills to continue onward. Today's video games are sophisticated pieces of software designed to shift the difficulty level on the fly so that it precisely matches the player's skill level at that exact moment. What a fantastic ploy to keep players playing! A game that is too easy is boring, a game that is too difficult is also boring, but a game with a steady flow of challenges that are just right, just barely conquered, is incredibly fun.

Even the earliest video games tapped into the psychology of counterfactuals. I remember that dinosaur era of the late 1970s and early 1980s quite well, having myself spent uncountable teenage hours in video arcades mastering such games as *Asteroids* and *Ms. Pac Man* (my favorite was *Gravitar*). Back around that time, possibly the first psychological analysis of video games appeared, and it is just as relevant and true today as it was back then:

> Often when playing a video game, the game ends because you've made a mistake, and you immediately know exactly what you've done wrong. *If only I hadn't eaten the energizer*

before trying to grab that cherry, you say to yourself. *I knew it was the wrong thing to do, and I did it anyway.* But now you don't have to just sit there being annoyed and frustrated. Instead you can play the game again and correct the mistake. So in goes another quarter. But in the process of playing again, you make another mistake. And spend another quarter to correct *it*. And so it goes.[21]

Gambling and video gaming are similar in that persistence at both can be explained in part, although not completely, by the skillful manipulation of counterfactual thinking in the mind of the player. It is essential to realize that counterfactual thinking is not the sole contributor to excesses at either pursuit; many other psychological forces are at play as well. The simplest is that they give pleasure. Gambling in Vegas is fun, flying a computer-simulated fighter into battle is a hoot. In moderation, they are simple entertainment, but in excess they are dangerous, and psychologists are learning more and more about how basic thought processes feed into behaviors of excess as well as moderation.

Anticipated Regret

The examples we've seen have shown how counterfactual thinking affects your satisfaction with the outcome of a decision. This satisfaction may then feed into a subsequent decision. But what if people get wise to the effect of counterfactual thinking on their own feelings of satisfaction? What if people foresee their own regret experience, decide they'd prefer to avoid that bit of emotional pain, thank you very much, and thus make a decision specifically so as to avoid feeling that later regret? This process involves anticipated regret.

Sometimes we expect to find out exactly what would have happened had we chosen the other way. Investing in the stock market is a perfect example: If I have only so much to invest and select IBM over Microsoft,

I can expect to check anytime over the near future on the performance of Microsoft, and so I can expect to learn exactly what would have happened had I selected Microsoft. In other words, I can see my counterfactual play out in vivid, concrete detail. For other decisions, however, what might have been is left completely to the imagination. Marrying one person over another means that you get detailed information only about the person you marry, and only the most fleeting of gossip about the person you might have married. True, you can imagine the marriage that might have been, but there is no hard, clear, concrete verification that the counterfactual is in any way accurate. You can never know for sure. Anticipated regret is a more common input to decisions in the first than the second case. Anticipated regret jumps out at us when we expect to get detailed future feedback on what might have been.[22]

Sometimes people go out of their way to avoid knowing for sure if it holds a real chance of unleashing later regret. Sometimes people will take a riskier path just to avoid that possibility of regret. Say you're considering buying a used car, and only two models fit the bill at this point. Car A is reliable but more expensive, whereas Car B is more affordable but has a history of mechanical problems. You are leaning toward Car A when your friend Nathalie comes by and informs you that if you don't buy Car B, she will. She has just put you in a bind, because if she buys the car you were considering but passed up, and if it turns out to be a solidly reliable used car purchase, you'll know this, you'll be haunted by it, you'll kick yourself repeatedly every time Nathalie gives you a ride home. So you buy Car B, the riskier choice, even though you were leaning toward Car A initially.[23]

People sometimes pay a premium to avoid later regret. Itamar Simonson, a decision theorist at Stanford's graduate school of business, examined whether consumers would prefer to pay a bigger price for a well-known name brand rather than take a chance on an unknown name brand. The participants of this study made mock buying decisions about pairs of home electronics products, like CD players. The products presented in the study were selected so that the basic features and quality of each pair of products were the same, differing only in how well known the brands were. On average, participants were split: 50 percent of the time they chose the well-known brand. But another group of participants got some more news, designed specifically to get them thinking about the regret they might feel in the future. They were told that later, at the end of the study, they would see summaries from *Consumer Reports* magazine that would inform them exactly which products were the better ones. In other words, these participants expected to get information that might (or might not) tell them that they had chosen wisely. With this inducement to anticipate regret, these participants moved to the more expensive option—67 percent of them chose the well-known but more expensive brand.[24]

Risky choice is not the inevitable result of anticipating regret. Sometimes people will become more cautious. For example, most will refuse to sell an unplayed lottery ticket, even if a buyer offers them more money than they originally paid for the ticket, simply because the regret that they'd feel should that ticket win big is too intense to contemplate risking. *I'd feel like a complete and total moron if MY old ticket made someone else rich,* is the typical reaction. Negotiation offers another example. Negotiators who foresaw future regret became more conservative, harder bargainers, which in turn made a final agreement less likely. And people are more likely to buy insurance when the threat of future regret is salient. *(If we have a fire and there's no house insurance, I'll be furious with myself!)*[25]

People are especially susceptible to the effects of anticipated regret when buying items that may later go on sale. "What if I find it cheaper somewhere else?" goes this anticipated regret. "Then I'll really be kicking myself later." To a large extent the ability to return goods for full refunds, an option most retailers offer, helps dispel the effects of this anticipated regret. Another successful sales strategy is to use price guarantees: If the customer finds the item advertised elsewhere at a cheaper price, the retailer will refund the difference. This sales trick works particularly well, as one recent study showed, at inoculating people against the anticipated regrets that otherwise produce hesitation that reduces sales. For the wary consumer, warning bells should go off inside her head when price guarantees are offered: *I need to be careful with my credit card, as some clever marketer is trying to influence my anticipated regret.* . . . What makes this tactic so interesting from a psychological standpoint is that most advertising aims to put new thoughts into people's heads (I never thought of it before, but I really could use a new doughnut-maker!). But a price guarantee is a bit of advertising aimed at keeping thoughts (anticipated regrets) *out* of mind.[26]

People can become either more cautious or more daring in response to anticipated regret. Basically, people will move their decision strategy in whichever direction provides them the most refuge, the most protection, from the anticipated pain of future regret.[27] Anticipated regret produces, overall, a weaker impact on decision-making than actual regret. One study estimated that of the various kinds of regret mentioned by consumers, only 28 percent involved anticipated regret whereas 72 percent involved the more typical after-the-purchase regret and counterfactual thinking that is the main focus of this book. Even so, it may save you at least a little bit of money to be more aware of the effects of anticipating your own future regret.[28]

On the brighter side, it is not just advertisers and marketers who can manipulate anticipated regret in order to change people's behavior. Health care professionals can use the same strategy in promoting healthier behaviors. In one research project, students watched a videotape dramatization of the extreme regret an individual felt after contracting a sexually transmitted disease. That individual's risky sexual practices were easily preventable, and the students who watched the video vividly saw the regret that they themselves might feel if they were in that individual's place. As a result of this anticipated regret, those students expressed greater intentions to adopt safer sex practices compared to other students who had seen no such video. Research demonstrations such as this hold out the hope that healthier behaviors, from sex to eating to exercising, might be promoted through the skillful manipulation of anticipated regret.[29]

When Earnings Exceed Expectations: Manipulating Counterfactuals to Look Good

Thresholds, boundaries, and categories matter a great deal when it comes to consumer choice and satisfaction. Nearly getting something great, which evokes an upward counterfactual, can make you feel bad. But by the same token, just barely avoiding something bad (which suggests a downward counterfactual) heightens satisfaction.

We've already seen how boundaries may be set by product categories. Expectations can also set important boundaries. Expecting great success means that accomplishing modest success will feel unsatisfactory, even though it is a perfectly reasonable success. Knowing this, many individuals actively manipulate the relation of outcome and expectation so as to evoke downward but not upward counterfactuals. Those downward counterfactuals make them look good.

One way to do this is by manipulating expectations. Just before the 2000 presidential election debates, George Bush's handlers tried to spin low expectations for his performance. This way, virtually any performance by Bush would exceed expectations and thus enhance voter satisfaction via downward counterfactual comparisons. *Wow, I expected Bush would have done a lot worse, but he was actually pretty good,* went the hoped-for reaction. "Lowering the bar" is a time-tested strategy for public relations experts.

The CEO of a large, publicly traded corporation on the other hand has less room to manipulate expectations for earnings performance. After all, the company is monitored by numerous independent analysts, all of whom release their own reports of expected earnings. The trick for the savvy manager then is to manipulate the announced earnings themselves. It turns out that managers often enjoy remarkable flexibility in shifting these earnings estimates, for example, by taking into account sales not yet shipped or finalized, or deferring maintenance costs, or not allowing for bad debt. The last thing a manager wants to do is report earnings that just barely fall beneath expectations, because this typically invites upward counterfactuals of the sort, *With this or that managerial decision made differently, the company might well have met its goal.* Missing the expectation by a wide margin doesn't invite these same counterfactuals so aggressively—it's just harder to visualize all those things that would have to have been done to make up so large a gap. The sweet spot, the place where managers most want to land, is just barely exceeding the expectation. This evokes the downward counterfactual that *things would have been worse for the company but for its skilled management.* That sweet little counterfactual enhances the reputation of the manager.

In a now classic analysis of the earnings estimates and reported earnings of thousands of American companies from 1976 to 1994, economists David Burgstahler and Ilia Dichev found substantial evidence for the savvy manipulation of counterfactuals by corporate managers. These authors found that cases in which companies barely missed a benchmark (set by the company's own past performance) were vastly rarer than what would be expected by chance alone. By contrast, cases in which companies just barely exceeded performance benchmarks were vastly more common than would be expected by chance. Clearly then, managers willfully tinker with earnings reports so as to land in that sweet spot of salient downward counterfactuals.[30]

Next we turn to one of the most challenging aspects of buying, the give-and-take of negotiation. There, too, recent research reveals counterfactual thinking to be at work.

Negotiation

Negotiation is the process of striking a deal, of finding the right balance of cost and benefit between two people so that a mutually advantageous exchange can take place. Many Americans negotiate to reach the best price on a car or a house. They negotiate salary and benefits for new jobs. And beyond these financial exchanges, people negotiate informally with friends and family on a nearly daily basis. You're going to a movie with friends tonight? One of you prefers the new romantic comedy that just won rave reviews, but another friend desires something more suspenseful, and the lot of you must negotiate this outcome, perhaps trading off against future movie nights (you'd rather see something with action, but you agree to see the romantic comedy with the understanding that next time you get to decide). Only the most recent of research has revealed how important counterfactual thinking is to negotiation. Harnessing counterfactual thinking in your negotiation can get you a better deal.

It is important to keep in mind that negotiation behavior is ongoing. Although negotiation might strike you as a brief isolated encounter—buying a new car, agreeing on a salary for a new job, deciding who gets the aisle seat on the flight to Miami—the constant element across these examples is you, the negotiator. Memory from one isolated encounter silently influences the next isolated encounter. Bad habits picked up buying cars carry over to interactions with clients. Even one's overall stance going into the negotiation, risky or cautious, can be influenced by whether a similar stance worked or failed in the past. Counterfactual thoughts have a powerful impact on the satisfaction felt after the negotiation is concluded. The sinking feeling of *I could have done better* can make a person take bigger risks next time, or make unnecessary adjustments to an already-winning formula. To see how this all works, we'll first examine the interconnections between counterfactual thinking, satisfaction, and making the first offer.

Lesson from Research #5: Make the first move. It pays to make the first offer. The person who strikes first, puts the first offer on the table, sets the agenda for the rest of the negotiation. If the first offer is $5,000 for a used car, the other person must now respond to this initial starting point. Psychologists think of starting points as *anchors*. The same way that a ship can be anchored at sea, free to bob a bit to and fro but not too far from its anchor line, negotiations can anchor around a specific amount of money, with back-and-forth movement never shifting too far from that anchor. The *Kelley Blue Book*, a standard listing of values of automobiles of different model years, is a good example in that it often sets the anchor for negotiations for used car purchases. When I sold my white 1993 Toyota Tercel a few years back, both the buyer and I knew the blue book value beforehand, and this value set the stage for the haggling that followed.

Adam Galinsky and his colleagues at Northwestern's Kellogg School of Business ran a series of studies in which they were the ones to determine who made the first offer. Galinsky discovered that whoever made the first offer got the better deal. In these studies, research participants (MBA students taking a course on the art of negotiation) engaged in numerous mock negotiation exercises based on real business problems. For example, one mock negotiation was conducted by e-mail and its goal was to settle a signing bonus for a job candidate in a consulting firm. Some students played the role of job candidate, others played the role of recruiter. When job candidates made the first offer, the final negotiated amount was in the job candidates' favor (an average bonus of $17,843), but when recruiters made the first offer, the amount was in the recruiter's favor (average bonus of $12,887).[31]

So it pays to make the first offer. When all else is equal, being able to set the agenda up front gives the negotiator an edge. But there are some times when making the first offer can backfire. Consider this situation: You are walking down the street and an Oriental rug in a store window catches your eye. You go inside and look over the rug. You like the rug but it has no price tag. The store owner comes from the back of the store and you ask the price. The store owner tells you to make an offer. You offer $500. He quickly says the rug is yours.

If you are like the participants in Galinsky's follow-up research, you are less than thrilled by this bargain. True, objectively speaking you have negotiated quite successfully, having reached a selling price that is close to your ideal, probably less than you initially expected to be feasible.

The typical unfolding of the negotiation is for the seller to then ask a higher price, but he didn't, so your deal is objectively a good one. But if an offer is so rapidly accepted, it makes you wonder. *Could I have gotten the rug for even less? Did I offer too much and does that explain this guy's haste to close the deal?*

Galinsky created several test situations in which negotiators had their first offer accepted immediately, or after a delay during which their opponent hemmed, hawed, and consulted with associates, or after three separate rounds of negotiation. Having the first offer accepted immediately resulted in substantially less satisfaction with the *exact same* negotiated outcome, relative to experiences involving a delay or three rounds of negotiation. Galinsky also measured the amount of upward counterfactual thinking, the aching feeling that *I could have gotten a better price.* The amount of counterfactual thinking corresponded closely to how much satisfaction people expressed: More thoughts of the better deal that "might have been" spelled less satisfaction. It made no difference whether it was a buyer's or seller's first offer that was accepted; both experienced equivalent regret and loss of satisfaction next to other negotiators who either waited or negotiated further. Galinsky commented, "We may be much more satisfied paying $25,000 for a new car after a lengthy negotiation than we would be if our initial offer of $25,000— or even $23,000—had been accepted."[32]

Negotiation for isolated episodes can influence subsequent negotiations. A negotiation that produced more upward counterfactual thinking and less satisfaction led participants to prepare better for a second negotiation. But at the same time, the more counterfactual thoughts they had, the less likely they were to make a first offer again. These participants wanted to avoid being disappointed again, so they played it safe. As we've already seen, making the first offer gives a person the edge. Galinsky points out how to come out ahead: "It is in situations when the negotiator is well prepared with some knowledge of the bargaining zone that making a first offer is most advantageous." The key then is to ride the natural wave of counterfactual thinking that invigorates effort, confidence, and mastery of available information, but then to actively resist that counterfactual-induced caution that impedes moving ahead to the next negotiation with an aggressive first move.[33]

How Many Issues to Negotiate? A standard rule in the art of negotiation is that it is better to bring many rather than few separate issues to the table. This opens opportunities to "logroll," to trade off one issue against another. If you are an automotive executive negotiating with a subcontractor who is to develop a new high-performance tire, you might negotiate simply on the total price of the development contract. But you could also break it down into cost for different design aspects (say, development of the new synthetic rubber versus computer-aided design of the shape of the tire). You could ensure that the most important component for your overall marketing plan is completed under the tightest deadline and the lowest cost while yielding on other components, allowing the subcontractor to come out ahead on those.

Charles Naquin, a professor in the Notre Dame college of business, reported research showing that having more issues to negotiate is not necessarily a good thing. MBA students in a negotiation class participated in the research as part of a course assignment. They negotiated essentially the same deal, but some were given four separate issues to negotiate while others were given eight. After the negotiation, participants were asked to what degree they imagined that their outcome might have been better. Those assigned to negotiate eight issues reported more of these upward counterfactual imaginings than those assigned to negotiate four issues. What's more, whatever amount of counterfactual thinking they engaged in directly accounted for the satisfaction they experienced with the deal they'd made. Earlier in the chapter, we saw that having more buying options is not necessarily a good thing for the consumer. For nearly the same reason, more issues for negotiation is not necessarily a good thing for the negotiator.[34]

Lesson from Research #6:
Burn Some Bridges

Returning purchased goods for a full refund is a staple of American retail. A lot of people enjoy the luxury of making whim decisions, even dangerously ill-considered decisions, because they can be undone. My wife regularly buys kids' clothing knowing that most will be returned: Sometimes she buys multiple sizes of the same item of clothing, knowing that all but one will go back. Other times she buys *just to try it out*. Most Americans, it would seem, not only appreciate but rely on the option of going back on a purchase decision. Without that option, maybe they'd be a lot less happy with their decisions.

New research shows that this assumption is wrong. We are *less*, not more, satisfied with decisions that are changeable, as revealed by Harvard social psychologists Dan Gilbert and Jane Ebert. The reason why, they argued, is that the very experience of being stuck with something, of being unable to change it, is one of several ignition keys for the psychological immune system. Recognizing that it's a "done deal" gears up those hidden mechanisms of rationalization, soon making us happier with the deal that cannot be undone. But when a decision is undoable, when there is still a chance to go back and switch things later, the psychological immune system remains dormant. The end result is that we are usually happier with decisions that are final compared to those that are changeable.[35]

Gilbert and Ebert created a photography class for students at Harvard, teaching both camera work and darkroom developing as a pretext for studying the effects of choices that are either reversible or irreversible. These photography students shot twelve images, then developed two of them. The key choice was which of the two prints they would keep for themselves (their favorite of the two) versus which would be donated for the photography teachers to keep on file. Half of the participants were told that they could change their mind later, that they could come back and exchange their donated photo for the photo they'd decided to keep. But the other half were given no such option; their decision was final. Nine days after the choice was made, students with the chance to change their minds said they liked their kept photo *less* than those who'd had no opportunity to switch.

This research suggests a powerful lesson, that it is sometimes a good idea to burn your bridges. This is military jargon meaning that if an army crosses a bridge, then burns it behind them, they have made an irrevocable commitment to advance forward. With the bridge burned, there's no turning back. Burning bridges means making a firm commitment to pushing ahead and eliminating the opportunity to reverse a decision once made.

As we've seen again and again, regret is useful. Regret that comes quickly, reveals a sharp insight, then makes a classy exit is a perfectly normal part of the usual operation of the human brain. Lingering regret, however, is emotionally damaging. Much of the time our psychological immune system shuts down this lingering regret, but open-ended decisions do not initiate the psychological immune system, leaving the door open for continuing, obsessive counterfactual thinking and regret. Easy-to-undo decisions, like buying a new shirt, are not much of a problem, precisely because they are easy to undo, and so people go ahead and undo them. The shirt is returned. A more dangerous trap resides in the range of relatively large life decisions that might be expected to be changeable in the abstract, but in practical terms their reversal involves huge hassles and headaches.

I know someone who bought a new car with a no-hassle return policy. He had a month to return it, and during that entire month he was a nervous wreck as he continually debated whether to keep the car, whether it was good enough, whether it constituted *just the right* driving experience. He decided to return it, but it turned out after all that a return *was* a significant hassle, and faced with this unexpected headache he changed his mind *again* and kept the car. From this point forward he was happy with his purchase. You can see the psychological immune system at work here—it didn't kick in at all for the first month, so he did not enjoy that biased glow of postpurchase joy, that feeling that "my car is best and all the rest are crap" that is the essence of the "honeymoon" period of any ownership. Not until the decision became irrevocable did this feeling sink in.

Most new jobs that people take are irrevocable. You quit the old one, take the new one, and that's that. Even if the job isn't so hot, you might find yourself saying, "Well, at least it's not as bad as so-and-so's job"—a consoling downward counterfactual created by the psychological immune system. When I quit my job at Northwestern in 2000, I was initially pleased by the fact that my decision was open, that I had the rare freedom to change even as I started the new job at Simon Fraser University. I can see now that this feeling of "keeping options open" helped to prevent my wife and me from settling happily in our new home in Vancouver, Canada. The decision was fluid and could so easily be changed, in that I was soon after recruited by several other schools and, with these concrete options, I became deeply anxious about making *just the right choice*. With big decisions, be they life changes or expensive purchases, the consequences may taste all the sweeter when there's no turning back.

～

Choice is good. Choice is an essential ingredient of American society, and understanding some of its psychological underpinnings can go a long way to making life more pleasant. Some of the newest research makes us see choice in a different light, but it is important not to exaggerate these implications. If new research shows that too much choice is a problem, or too much negotiating room is a problem, this by no means suggests that choice should be eradicated or negotiation avoided. As with most things in life, moderation is the key. There is a happy middle ground for just the right amount of choice, or just the right number of issues to negotiate. This middle ground is unique for each individual, being a product of that individual's unique life experiences. Over the course of life, people adapt to what they have, and if they get more, they adapt to that too, resulting in a steady hunger for a bit more. A person raised with little choice is happy with a moderate amount of choice; a person raised with lots of choice is satisfied only with a very large number of things from which to choose, but both will eventually want a little more. Just a little, not too much, because too much choice is as aversive as too little choice. There is no simple formula for determining an individual's ideal amount of choice, and no simple answer that a book can provide or a marketer can discover.

Is choice real? For centuries, philosophers have debated free will versus determinism, which boils down to whether individuals have the power to make their own individual choices that determine their own future, or whether the laws of physics have already preordained all that is yet to be. Harvard social psychologist Dan Wegner in his book *The Illusion of Conscious Will* argued that brain chemistry, and therefore the self in its truest sense, indeed dictates behavior. What we call conscious experience, and the feeling of willing an action or intentionally doing something, is an illusion. Wegner's experiments reveal a disconnect between behavior and the conscious feeling of choice and control. People can be fooled into believing that they control something that is entirely out of their hands. And the feeling of having made a conscious choice can spring to mind well *after* behavior favoring that choice has started (you feel like you want Pepsi a fraction of a second after your arm starts reaching for the Pepsi). For Wegner, making choices is certainly something that brains do, and so we are all ultimately responsible for our actions. But the special *feeling* of deciding may well be a subsequent, secondhand attempt of our conscious mind to explain what the deeper recesses of our brain have already chosen. Whether choice is an illusion or real will remain the stuff of impassioned debate for many years to come.[36]

The *belief* in choice, illusory or otherwise, constitutes a feeling that many psychologists recognize as an essential ingredient to a satisfied life. Freedom itself, if only an idea in mind, carries with it the psychologically nourishing notion of hope. Back in 1944, the respected free market economist Friedrich von Hayek, commenting on the peoples living under the dictatorships of those days in Germany and in the Soviet Union, wrote these words that resonate still today:

> Nothing makes conditions more unbearable than the knowledge that no effort of ours can change them; and even if we should never have the strength of mind to make the necessary sacrifice, the knowledge that we could escape if only we strove hard enough makes many otherwise intolerable positions bearable.[37]

Chapter 6

Let Me Entertain You

George Bailey stands on a snow-covered bridge, eyes dazed with despair. A business error threatens him with immediate bankruptcy. And what then? With no money, his kids might go hungry, he might lose the house, and perhaps most important, he'd lose his self-respect. George already feels unfulfilled—his dreams of going to college and traveling the world were given up long ago—and with his job gone as well he faces utter devastation. George looks at the frigid river below and ponders whether to jump.

It's a Wonderful Life

If you are like millions of other Americans, you know that George's jump is interrupted. In this pivotal scene in the much-loved 1946 film *It's a Wonderful Life*, George's intention to take his own life is cut short by the appearance of a kindly old man, an angel, sent from above to offer George an incredible vision. The vision is a counterfactual. The counterfactual is the world as it might have been had George never been born.

Of course, few of us make such a difference that the entire world would be noticeably different if we'd never been born. But on a smaller scale, in just one small corner of the globe, a village or a neighborhood, many of us can indeed make a difference in the lives of others. This is the essential, uplifting message of *It's a Wonderful Life*, that every life can make a difference, that every life can have meaning by way of its positive causal effects on the lives of others. It's a message that feels good to hear because we often fail to appreciate it.

Whisked away to the counterfactual stream of events in George's hometown that might have been had George never been born, George sees a depressing vision, a vision of poverty and malaise that is decidedly worse than the town he actually knows. George also gets a privileged glimpse into other people's lives, lives that would have been far worse had George never been around. George's wife, Mary, for example, does not marry and lives a life of empty loneliness. George's brother drowns as a child because George is not there to save him. And of course George's three children do not exist at all.

The power of the film, rerun on television year after year at Christmastime, owes much to the vivid realization of a downward counterfactual. As we know, downward counterfactuals tend to evoke positive emotions, such as relief and gratitude that a worse world was avoided and thus has not come to be. The film draws heavily on flashbacks, scenes set earlier in time than the main action, as when we see scenes from George's childhood. The flashback is a narrative device well known to any film lover. The counterfactual is also a narrative device, and although it is every bit as important, effective, and widely used as the flashback, it is not commonly known as such. Film critics will often make casual reference to a cinematic flashback, but never is there casual reference to a cinematic counterfactual. This chapter is all about the many ways that counterfactuals make drama more dramatic, be it in film, theater, literature, or any other kind of storytelling. In this chapter we'll see many examples of counterfactuals in storytelling, and try to understand what underlying psychological principles account for their popularity. And I'll go out on a limb when I say that counterfactuals are the essence of effective drama.

To be dramatic, a story *needs* counterfactuals.

Counterfactuals make any tale more entertaining, more enjoyable, for the simple reason that we have seen repeatedly in this book: counterfactuals influence emotions. Upward counterfactuals create negative emotions; downward counterfactuals create positive emotions. By skillfully injecting a story with counterfactuals, a storyteller is able to manipulate the emotions of her audience with subtlety and aplomb.

There are two ways to do this. The film *It's a Wonderful Life* works its magic by wrapping its entire plot around a counterfactual. In other words, there is elaborate action and adventure within a counterfactual world, and the plot depends heavily on spelling out a stream of events that never were but might have been. These sorts of stories are *counterfactual plots*. They come across vividly in no small part because of their rarity. Counterfactual plots are used only infrequently in cinema and literature.

The other way that counterfactuals can create drama is vastly more common, even ubiquitous. These are the *close-call moments*. They are smaller counterfactuals, sometimes mere hints or suggestions inserted at strategic points within a narrative stream that juice up the audience's emotions. A close call means that something nearly happened, and that something might be bad (nearly fell into the pit of snakes) or good (nearly bumped into a long-lost lover in the supermarket), and in a moment we'll see just how common, and necessary, a tool these close-call moments are for effective storytelling.

Sliding Doors

Helen Quilley is having a terrible day. First she is fired from her job as a public relations consultant. Then she misses the last subway train before a breakdown paralyzes the subway system, forcing her to waste money on a cab. While trying to get a cab, she is attacked and injured by a mugger. After a visit to the hospital, she finally makes it home, utterly drained. Looking back on the day, she mentions to her boyfriend, Gerry, that "I just couldn't help thinking . . . If only I had just caught that bloody train it would never have happened. I'd have been home ages ago." Gerry is dismissive: "You don't want to go wondering about things like that. . . . 'If only' this . . . 'what if' that. It's *done* now," he says.

But what if she had caught the train? How might her life have been different? This is the starting point for the 1998 film *Sliding Doors*, featuring Gwyneth Paltrow as Helen. Most counterfactual thoughts are examples of backward thinking, in that we start with something gone wrong, then work our way backward to alternative actions that would have allowed us to bypass that thing gone wrong. But we can also move mentally forward in time, start with some little action or occurrence, and then imagine the flow of events from that point onward, from that fork in the road. This is the basis of the plot of *Sliding Doors*: the fork in the road is whether the doors on the subway train slide shut to leave Helen behind, or slide back open to let her in. With a tinkle of "mystical" background music, it all turns on whether a little girl on the stairs to the subway platform blocks Helen's descent (causing her to miss the train) or is tugged aside by her mother (allowing Helen to make the train). The deeper meaning of the story is that many big events in life hinge on such small, apparently meaningless random turns.

As the film unfolds, the audience sees what might have happened had she caught the train. But which time line is real, and which is counterfactual? Both proceed side by side. In the first time line, Helen is injured by a mugger, is unable to find new work in her chosen profession and so toils as a waitress, and fails to realize that Gerry is cheating on her behind her back. In the second time line, Helen is not delayed and arrives home that first day to discover Gerry in bed with another woman, and immediately breaks up with him. Helen then strikes up a friendship with John, and romance seems to bloom, albeit slowly. This second version of Helen soon gets a much better hairstyle (a clever trick to allow us to differentiate the two Helens!) and then brazenly launches her own public relations business, which enjoys immediate success. As the romance with the obviously more charming John grows, it seems clear that this time line is the better one, the upward one of the two: her job is better, her love life is better, and her hair is better!

Near the end, the audience learns which of the time lines is real and which is the counterfactual. The second (upward) Helen dies after a freak car accident. The other Helen, the Helen of the first time line, finally realizes that Gerry has been cheating on her, finally breaks up with him, and as we watch this one remaining Helen move on with her life, she meets John (again? . . . no! . . . for the first time in this time line), they seem to hit it off, romance blooms (again, yes), and we are left with a pleasantly uncanny summary of the average person's conception of fate and reality.

Which is this:

Many of the events of life turn on minor incidents and random circumstances, like catching (or not catching) a train, eating at one restaurant instead of the one across the street, or meandering into a used bookstore rather than walking straight home. Most of the time we barely notice these minor twists of routine, but sometimes they enlarge to enormous significance if we connect them to a defining moment, like finding true love. Yet, in *Sliding Doors* both versions of Helen eventually meet John and fall in love with him. It was fate, as the old saying goes, and so one way or another, Helen ends up together with John, and the delight of the film is that it reveals both ways, side by side, by which Helen finds the love she was fated to find. In the next chapter we'll explore the psychology of fate and how it fits with counterfactual thinking, but for now it's worth pointing out that fate and counterfactuals connect together easily in most people's minds.

The film *Sliding Doors* uses a counterfactual plot to dramatize how important events can turn on seemingly inconsequential, random occurrences. The film *It's a Wonderful Life* uses a counterfactual plot to emphasize how one person's life, the sum of all actions and choices, can make a difference in the world. But what about individual choice? How much of a difference can a single decision, or a single action, make? As we saw in Chapter 5, choice and counterfactuals are intimately mixed, and so it should come as no surprise that a particularly effective counterfactual plot line is one that dramatizes the psychological power of a single choice.

The City on the Edge of Forever

Difficult choices breed painful counterfactuals, and there can be no more difficult choices than those involving love and death. Most dramatic of all then is the choice *between* love and death. A golden moment in television storytelling presented just such a choice, wrapped inside a counterfactual version of reality in which Nazi Germany won the Second World War.

Of all the various sequels and offshoots of the *Star Trek* franchise, the 1967 television episode entitled "The City on the Edge of Forever" remains the all-time favorite. In poll after poll it is named the best episode of the original television series, and it ranked number 68 in *TV Guide*'s 1996 list of the "Most Memorable Moments in TV History" (the 1969 moon landing ranked number one).[1] I have long thought that the episode's counterfactual plot structure contributed essentially to its continuing popularity, to its "gee whiz" atmosphere of awe and wonderment. It is television magic spun from counterfactuals.

Star Trek is science fiction; it takes place aboard a spaceship zipping about deep space some two hundred years in the future. In this particular episode the crew of the spaceship discovers a time machine on a distant planet. The normally competent Dr. McCoy accidentally injects himself with medication that makes him psychotic, and in a crazed state he jumps into the time machine and transports himself back to the 1930s, to Depression-era New York City. We don't know at first what he does when he arrives in the 1930s—all we see is McCoy disappearing into the time machine, but in the wink of an eye all is different. History has been changed. Dr. McCoy has done something to alter the course of history, to actualize a counterfactual. What might this counterfactual be? It's a mystery, one that the other two principal characters, Kirk and Spock, must unravel.

Kirk and Spock use the time machine themselves to travel back to the 1930s in an attempt to repair the course of time, to set history back onto its "correct" track. Bit by bit they learn how history had been altered. Spock explains to Kirk: "In the late 1930s, a growing pacifist movement delayed the United States' entry into the Second World War. While peace negotiations dragged on, Germany had time to complete its heavy water experiments, letting them develop the A-bomb first. With the A-bomb, and with their V2 rockets to carry them, Germany captured the world." McCoy triggered this cascade of events by preventing a young woman named Edith Keeler from dying in a traffic accident. Saved from this death, she later goes on to become a leader of the pacifist movement. To set history back on its proper course, Edith Keeler must die. The big problem, however, is that Kirk has fallen in love with Edith Keeler.

And so this counterfactual story begins with a random accident that throws history into its counterfactual variant. But then it falls to human choice, one man's choice, as to whether history will be brought back to its correct course. Kirk faces a staggeringly difficult choice. If he sets history "straight again," the woman he loves dies. If he saves the woman he loves, history remains off course, and "millions will die who did not die before."

In the end, Kirk decides to set history back on its normal course and return to the history and the future he knows. And Edith Keeler dies. The pain of making the choice, the extreme regret that ineluctably follows from either option, and the vivid play upon counterfactual ruminations made this one of television's most riveting moments.

Close-Call Moments

Any sports fan can tell you: A game in which the outcome is never in doubt is a dull game. When one team is heavily favored to win and plays the entire game far ahead of the opponent to an easy victory, yawning prevails. But a win following a series of tight scores, reversals, and most of all a string of key plays that *could easily have turned out otherwise* is the very recipe for excitement. The perception of alternatives, of opportunities missed and disasters avoided, *of counterfactuals*, is the single most essential ingredient for effective drama, be it in sports, theater, literature, or any other narrative form of entertainment. Counterfactuals of the moment, those that embody close calls in which something else would have happened but for some key play, move, or action, make stories fun.

A close-call moment is a brief instance in which a counterfactual becomes vividly clear. In Chapter 3 we saw how our brains seem particularly attuned to noticing almostness in everyday life. The feeling that something bad almost happened creates a momentary tension, followed rapidly by a release of positive emotion when it becomes clear that this something bad did not happen. Winning a race, scoring a big promotion, getting the girl are all positive story outcomes, satisfying endings that leave audiences pleased. But a race won that was nearly lost, a promotion that was nearly a termination, and a girl who came so very close to falling in love with some other guy are all story endings with dramatic flair born of that feeling of almostness, and they leave the audience all the more satisfied.

Creating situations in which something else almost happens is a staple of good storytelling. As a plot unfolds, forks in the road, surprising twists, and the overall recognition of multiple possibilities breathe life into the story. Devices that the author can plant to emphasize the almostness, the palpable alternative that nearly happened, create dramatic tension. Recently a friend told me this story by e-mail:

> So I'm driving down I-57 from Chicago today, spacing out, and suddenly realize that I'm on empty. Not NEAR empty, mind you, but on empty. It's been at least 10 miles since the last gas station, so I slow down to 65 to conserve gas and hope for the best. Seven nervous miles later, I see a sign for gas at the next exit. I begin up the off ramp, and just as I crest it the car dies. Just dies. I tried to swerve back and forth real quick like race car drivers do, but nothing. I lose my power steering, but the steering wheel doesn't lock so I just try to make it over the crest. BUT GET THIS! The gas station is right there, and down an incline. So I just steer toward it and pull the emergency brake (lost power brakes, you see), and voilà! *Had the car died 20 feet earlier, I wouldn't have made it.*

You can probably see that there are two ways to tell this (or any) story, a bad way and a good way. The bad way is simply to say, "I wasn't paying attention and my car ran out of gas but I managed to coast to a station, where I filled up without difficulty." The bad way neglects the use of counterfactuals to stress that feeling of almostness, that feeling that something terrible was just around the corner. The good way, which is the way my friend told it, is to take every opportunity to stress how *close* the downward counterfactual—being stuck on the road without gas—was to becoming a reality.

Moviemakers employ a variety of tricks to emphasize close calls. Some are blatant, as when an action hero's sidekick suffers a gruesome death (eaten by an alligator, melted in a vat of acid), a fate spelled out in vivid detail so as to drive home the counterfactual that the very same fate *nearly* befell the hero. Some are only a little less blatant, as when the fate is not directly portrayed but rather hinted at: a vat of boiling acid or a pit of snakes is shown, the hero nearly falls in, but doesn't. We see the acid or snakes, but we are left to imagine on our own how awful it would have been to fall into such places. These are sharp and quick close-call moments, and even a slow-moving story is sure to have a dozen of them.

Sometimes the close call is drawn out, elongated and elaborated for dramatic effect. My favorite example is the classic cliché of the ticking time bomb. It surely will go off unless the hero deactivates it. The climactic scene of the 1964 James Bond film *Goldfinger* uses this cliché to great effect. Bond must defuse an atomic bomb rigged to go off at Fort Knox, but it is no simple job, and Bond fiddles and pokes at the tricky wiring while a conveniently readable digital clock ticks down the remaining seconds to detonation. At the last possible moment, a bomb expert appears at Bond's side, sticks his arm in, and stops the clock. And here we feel sharp relief, satisfied pleasure, that such a terrible thing came so very close to happening, then was thwarted *just in time*. It was a happy ending, yet its happiness is magnified many times over by the counterfactual realization that the atomic bomb nearly went off in Bond's face.

Other times, the close call is subtler still, with more of its details left to the imagination, even though we feel the steady march of time pressure toward a dreaded downward alternative. The prospect of losing out on true love was the big close call in the 1967 film *The Graduate*. Benjamin Braddock (played by Dustin Hoffman) must stop the woman he loves, Elaine Robinson, from marrying that other guy. Trouble is, he only just found out about it, and the wedding is *today*! He speeds off in his red Alfa Romeo roadster, driving like a madman, desperate to reach the church before the fateful "I do's" are uttered. The clock is ticking. His car runs out of gas, so he gets out and runs, arrives panting at the church, and there follows one of the classic scenes of cinema history. Standing behind a mezzanine glass wall, Benjamin looks down on the wedding ceremony and howls, "Elaine!" The "I do's" have been said, and Elaine's mother even says "It's too late!" but Elaine counters, "Not for me!" Elaine and Benjamin run away, leaving the wedding party behind. They escape just in time, presumably to live happily ever after.

To make a happy ending happier, the skillful use of downward counterfactuals is called for, as in *Goldfinger* and *The Graduate*. But to make tragedy poignant, the skillful use of upward counterfactuals is absolutely necessary. The 1997 film *Titanic*, at the time of writing the top-grossing film of all time, presents a case in point. We all know how the film ends (the ship sinks!), but the inevitability of the plot by way of our historical knowledge in no way diminishes the dramatic impact of the film. Indeed, at several key points along the way we glimpse how the disaster might easily have been averted. The captain orders full steam ahead, and we feel a tingle because we know icebergs lurk in the North Atlantic waters. *If only the captain and his corporate superiors weren't in such a rush, the* Titanic *might have been traveling slowly enough to dodge that fateful iceberg.* Later, a passionate kiss between the stars Leonardo DiCaprio and Kate Winslet distracts two seamen lookouts posted high up on a ship's mast. They are supposed to be keeping a steady watch for icebergs along the path ahead, and *if only they had been minding their job instead of ogling the young lovers, they might have given a few extra seconds' warning to the bridge crew, who might then have steered the* Titanic *away from the iceberg with a few inches to spare.* Even if we know a disaster is coming, suspense can nevertheless be evoked via skillful reminders of how the disaster might have been averted.

As screenwriters manipulate these various close calls, narrow escapes, and tight shaves, they are always aiming to nail the same psychological principle, which is to emphasize a counterfactual, which in turn creates emotional reactions in the audience. If it is a downward counterfactual, then something bad nearly happened, and this emphasizes emotions of joy, relief, and the release of anxious tension. If it is an upward counterfactual, then something wonderful nearly happened (or some tragedy was nearly averted), which in turn emphasizes emotions such as disappointment, regret, or poignant sadness. Next time you see a story unfold, pay attention to the number of counterfactuals that appear, either explicitly revealed or quietly hinted, and how each is intended to manipulate your emotions. When the story is done, your satisfaction is enhanced by the realization of how close something else (either good or bad) came to happening.

Alternate History

This blurb appears on the back cover of a paperback collection of short stories:

> Alternate history: The what-if fiction that has finally come into its own! Shedding light on the past by exploring what could have happened, this bold genre tantalizes your imagination and challenges your perceptions with thrilling reinventions of humanity's most climactic events. Enter worlds that are at once fanciful and familiar, where fact and fiction meld in a provocative landscape of infinite possibilities. . . . [2]

Hyperbolic, yes, yet this blurb conveys the essential excitement of the genre called "alternate history." These novels and short stories are often sold alongside science fiction, and there is certainly a natural connection. Both alternate history and science fiction emphasize imaginative places that do not exist. In science fiction, it might exist in the future; in alternate history, it never existed, but might have.

The blurb is insightful, moreover, in that it touches on two psychological reasons why counterfactual stories are entertaining. First, counterfactual stories play with the interconnection of theme and variation, combining in intriguing ways the "fanciful and familiar." Second, counterfactual stories are cognigenic, meaning that they spur further creative thought, which is to say that they "tantalize your imagination."

Each year brings the publication of numerous new alternate history novels and short stories. The website Uchronia.net has been faithfully cataloging these for the last decade and at last count had tabulated over twenty-three hundred separate works. My hunch is that the most popular topic, the most intriguing point of departure from reality, is the Second World War. What if the Germans had won the Second World War? Just ahead, we'll see how this premise was used in the bestselling novel *Fatherland*. But there is a very good reason why stories of the Second World War are so common.

The principles that explain counterfactual thinking in everyday life also explain which sorts of counterfactuals appeal to us as the most intriguing and thought-provoking. We saw in Chapter 3 that situations that are negative and that contain a feeling of almostness are those most likely to evoke counterfactual thinking. The worse the event, and the closer it came to a clear and plausible alternative, the more vivid is the resulting counterfactual thinking. The cause of 45 million deaths, the Second World War is clearly among the most horrific events of recent history. And the story of the Second World War contains many twists and turns, many forks in the road, many ways that history might have gone differently. What if the British had not successfully evacuated at Dunkirk? What if the Japanese had defeated the American navy at Midway? What if the Germans were victorious at Stalingrad? There were so many close calls that storytellers have a very easy time launching their plots into alternatives, and the gravity of the events, the multitude of lives held in the balance, conspires to make the resulting story riveting. Indeed, the same focal points in history that draw the scholarly attention of historians and political scientists are the same ones that inspire the creative energies of fictional storytellers.

Many historical events have been seized for such counterfactual stories. What if the South had won the Civil War? MacKinlay Kantor, author of the popular Civil War novel *Andersonville*, explored this idea in a novella that first appeared in *Look* magazine in 1960. In Kantor's counterfactual vision, Gen. Ulysses S. Grant is killed after being thrown from his horse in May 1863. Then, a Confederate victory at Gettysburg results in the formation of three independent American nations (Texas is the third one), but the common bond among the citizens of these three nations in the years ahead means that they nevertheless remain close allies in both world wars and in the Cold War, and eventually re-unify into the single nation that we all know today as reality. Kantor's point: America was inevitable.[3]

A daunting challenge posed by alternate history is that it demands on the part of the reader no small bit of historical expertise. It's no fun reading a story about what might have happened if Babe Ruth hadn't been traded by the Boston Red Sox to the New York Yankees if you didn't know in the first place that Ruth really did play baseball for the Red Sox. Or if you've never even heard of Babe Ruth! Alternate history requires a basic knowledge of history for it to come truly alive. In *Almost America,* author Steve Tally came up with a clever solution. For each of his twenty-eight fanciful short stories (like, what if President Nixon had decided to fight impeachment rather than resign in the summer of 1974?), he begins with an engaging summary of history as it actually was, bringing the reader up to speed on the relevant information, before launching into his "what if" scenario.[4]

What other underlying psychological principles can explain the success of what-if scenarios? Let's find out.

Theme and Variation

My daughter Emma loves stories. She especially loves the children's storybook series called *Angelina Ballerina*, written by Katharine Holabird. I'd been reading the first book of the series to Emma, over and over, for quite some time. One day, I surprised Emma with a gift, another book from the same series. The new book has the same style of art, the same cover design, the same text font, and so immediately there was visual recognition. "It's the *same*," Emma squealed in delight. "But . . . it's *different!*" The joy Emma experienced is the same joy many of us feel as a result of the most basic psychological mechanism by which art influences emotion. *It's the same but it's different*—it sounds oxymoronic at first, but we all know what Emma means, it makes perfect sense. It is the pleasure of recognition, of seeing an old friend, coupled simultaneously with the mild surprise of something wonderfully yet nonthreateningly new. The first *Angelina Ballerina* book that we'd read many times established a theme, and the new book in the series represented a variation on that original theme.

The counterpoint of "theme and variation" is the basis of much great art. And it is also one of the reasons why counterfactual stories can be so much fun. Reality is the theme. Counterfactual is the variation. From the juxtaposition of the two, a combination of the joy of recognition with surprise at something new, comes a variety of emotions and insights. Back in 1985, Douglas Hofstadter argued that "the crux of creativity resides in the ability to manufacture variations on a theme." He went on further to link the way ordinary people easily and naturally think counterfactual thoughts to the effortless, creative, imaginative capacity locked within every human brain. In a sense then, artists who use variations on a theme as the basis of art are mimicking the natural way the human brain sees the world. Brains comprehend reality by generating benchmarks built of past experience. Often these benchmarks match what the brain sees (here is a tree, and it reminds me of similar trees I've seen in the past). But when the brain sees something surprising, the experience of surprise itself comes from the mental benchmarks that pop to mind and reveal how things could have been. Our brains are continuously producing creative variations (i.e., counterfactual elaborations of alternatives to current experiences) as we experience the flow of events in our lives.[5]

The basic structure of theme and variation pervades nearly all art enterprises, from painting to film to literature, but it finds an especially happy home in music. A melody is heard, and then a revised or altered form of that melody is offered. The first melody establishes a context, and the second is a sort of wandering figure, a central character, that moves against the backdrop of the context. A great melody is meant for variation. Sometimes a melodic theme comes from one composer, only to be varied by another composer, the best-known example being Brahms' *Variations on a Theme by Haydn*. Or consider the simple melody at the heart of "Twinkle, Twinkle Little Star." It seems a ridiculously simple set of musical notes, yet at the hands of Mozart, it was spun into innumerable variations, each adding successively more detail, flourish, and ornamentation. A variation on a simple melody can grow quickly into a work of majesty and complexity.[6]

This is no less true of music today than it was in Mozart's day. Pop albums often inspire follow-up "remix" or "dub" albums, in which new artists (like DJs) take the original recordings, strip them to their rhythm elements, alter the beat, then layer on new sound effects. In 2001 a British band called The Faint released an album called *Danse Macabre*, a catchy collection of synth-driven songs. Two years later *Danse Macabre Remixes* appeared, an album containing new, twisted, strangely remixed versions of the tracks on the original release. Each new track was remixed by a different DJ, each a respected artist in his or her own right, like Photek and Junior Sanchez. The fun of the remix album resides in that same pleasant feeling of "it's the same but it's different."

To become truly great art, theme and variation need a third companion, *resolution*. In a three-act play, three distinct sections correspond to establishing the setting, introducing a problem, and then presenting a solution to the problem. The three parts create a satisfying feeling of plot development and resolution. Like the three-act play, a plot counterfactual embraces this triplet structure but on a grander stage. With a plot counterfactual, the theme is reality as we know it. The variation is the counterfactual, and contained in the counterfactual is some problem that confronts the main characters. The resolution is an ending that reveals to us some truth about the actual workings of reality that might otherwise have gone unrecognized.

Thomas Harris' 1992 novel *Fatherland* was an international bestseller, becoming perhaps the most widely read version of the premise that the Germans might have won the Second World War. Built of simple sentences and rapid pacing, it makes for a grippingly quick read. It is a mystery story that follows the actions of a detective named Xavier March. As a counterfactual novel, it is a perfect example of how theme and variation interact to create repeated surprises and repeated delight in the recognition of familiar items turned sideways . . . or completely upside-down.

Xavier March is a sympathetic figure. He cares about his son even though they have grown apart since a painful divorce. He cares about his job and wants to do his best at it. These are features that normally create the sympathy a reader might feel for a fictional character, but in this case, there is a jarring wedge driven into the sympathy that might have been—March is a Nazi, a member of the SS, a detective working for the state police in a German Reich that is alive and kicking in the year 1964. In reality the SS were the chief engineers of mass murder during the Second World War, but like the rest of the Nazi regime, they were defeated in 1945. And so it is rather difficult to sympathize completely with March. Yet little by little his antipathy toward the Nazi regime is revealed, and we grow to like him . . . a little.

Another jarring variation occurs when we learn that Kennedy is president of the United States. Well, it's 1964, and so our first reaction is that wow, Kennedy survived the assassination attempt of 1963 in this alternative version of history. The theme of Kennedy's assassination establishes a background set of assumptions for what comes next. In this counterfactual 1964, the U.S. had successfully defeated Japan in the Second World War but is now locked in a different sort of Cold War, not the one with the Soviet Union that is part of our factual history, but a Cold War with the victorious German Empire that spans Europe and Asia. But Harris throws us for a loop: it is not John F. Kennedy who is president, it is his father, Joseph P. Kennedy. In reality, the elder Kennedy played an active role in sculpting his son's political career but was silenced by a massive stroke not long after the younger Kennedy was elected to the presidency. That the elder Kennedy was, in the years preceding World War II, avidly pro-German adds to the jarring effect this bit of president-switching has on the reader.

The primary theme-variation pairing of the novel is the Holocaust. In this alternative version of history, Nazi Germany completes its Final Solution, eradicating the Jewish population of Europe. But the crime is completed behind an iron curtain, hidden from the world. What is common knowledge to the reader is the central mystery for the main characters. What happened to the Jews of Europe? March stumbles on a clue, a photograph lost inside the woodwork of his apartment, apparently left behind by former tenants. The photograph depicts a family, but March doesn't recognize them. He confides his obsession with the photograph to Charlotte Maguire, an American journalist who gradually becomes his partner in searching for the truth: "I found [the photograph] tucked behind the wallpaper in the bedroom. I tell you, I took that place to pieces, but that was all there was. Their surname was Weiss. But who are they? Where are they now? What happened to them?"[7] March and Maguire eventually discover the secrets of the Holocaust, and the novel ends as the world too is about to discover the truth. As the variation comes to a conclusion, the resolution is left for readers to ponder. Could a government cover up and keep secret so huge a mass murder as the Holocaust for so long a period of time? And if yes, what contemporary atrocities remain hidden to this day, perhaps for future generations to discover?

A key restriction on the plot counterfactual is the degree of variation, or the amount of alteration to reality, that should be used for maximum entertainment. In a nutshell, there must be recognizable alteration, but it must not be too extreme. You might call this a basic law of art, and I'll call it *Berlyne's Law* in celebration of the psychologist

Daniel Berlyne, who several decades ago first applied the tools of experimental psychology to an understanding of how art influences emotion. His insight was to demonstrate experimentally that what strikes us as good art is usually a slight deviation from our expectations. Art that perfectly fits our expectations is boring (been there, done that); art that is too large a departure from what we already know strikes us as bizarre and repugnant (too "out there"). Somewhere in between the extremes of the boring and the bizarre lays a sweet zone of recognition coupled with mild surprise. What most people, on average, consider to be great art more often than not represents a modest (but not large) change from the status quo.[8]

Berlyne's Law applies to counterfactuals as well, whether they are used by artists to influence an audience's emotions or as persuasive arguments to convince someone of a particular point of view. A persuasively compelling counterfactual, one that convinces you that some alternative might well have happened, must follow what Phil Tetlock has termed a minimal rewrite rule. Small, minor changes to reality are fine; big changes leave the audience baffled. The regrets with which we kick ourselves on a regular basis also follow this minimal rewrite rule. We usually focus on just one single action to alter within the counterfactual. For example, *"I should have had an apple for dessert rather than that chocolate cheesecake."* All other aspects of reality—the main dish, the restaurant location, the weather, and the state of the global economy remain within the counterfactual exactly as they truly are. And so again we see how the best art mirrors the workings of our own brains. In the best stories of the alternate history genre, there are a few key differences between the story and reality, but also innumerable similarities: the laws of physics remain the same (objects never fall up rather than down), the weather remains the same (a sunny day is a sunny day), and the essential nature of human beings is held constant (human beings have two arms, two legs, and an assortment of conflicting cravings that land them in all manner of trouble). Plot counterfactuals that follow this minimal rewrite rule are the most compelling.[9]

Of course, rules were made to be broken. As I conclude my case for counterfactuals as the very essence of drama, I will point to yet another way to entertain with counterfactuals, which might be called the "maximal rewrite" approach. By pushing the envelope of plausibility, counterfactuals can be pleasingly whimsical. I'll close with the words of the expert on whimsy, the children's author who went by the name of Dr. Seuss:

> If we didn't have birthdays, you wouldn't be you.
> If you'd never been born, well then what would you do?
> If you'd never been born, well then what would you be?
> You might be a fish! Or a toad in a tree!
> You might a doorknob! Or three baked potatoes!
> You might be a bag full of hard green tomatoes.
> Or worse than all that . . . You might be a WASN'T!
> A Wasn't has no fun at all. No, he doesn't.
> A Wasn't just isn't. He just isn't present.
> But you . . . You are YOU! And, now isn't that pleasant.
> —*Dr. Seuss, 1959*[10]

Chapter 7

Making Meaning

≈

When Tereza leaves, Tomas is devastated. He hadn't quite realized how much he loved her. They are an expatriate Czech couple living in Switzerland, and Tereza has left to return to Prague. Complicating matters is the fact that the year is 1968, the fateful year in which the Czech movement toward democracy is brutally crushed by an occupying army of the Soviet Union. In these years, the Soviets are intent upon keeping Czechoslovakia and the rest of Eastern Europe firmly inside their communist sphere of influence.

Tomas decides to give up his new life in Switzerland to track down Tereza. Soon they are reunited in Prague, and as he lies in bed with her pondering the mystery of love, he contemplates a counterfactual proffered by Tereza long ago. She'd said, "If I hadn't met you, I'd certainly have fallen in love with him," the "him" referring to a close friend of Tomas. In a nutshell, Tereza does not believe she was destined to love Tomas—she could as easily have spent her life with someone else, so she thinks. This example reveals how tightly connected are counterfactual thoughts and beliefs in fate. At first glance it seems as though the connection is one of opposites. The more you believe that the present could easily be otherwise, the less you believe in fate. Fate means that there is no other way the present could have turned out. But it turns out that for many Americans, these beliefs are much more complicated than simple opposites.[1]

People spontaneously think about what might have been, and this process is intimately connected to seeking answers and finding meaning for life's events, both big and small. As people make meaning of the events in their lives, they sometimes fall prey to bias driven by counterfactual thinking. In this chapter we'll see three ways that counterfactual thoughts shape people's attempts to find meaning. We'll begin with fate, the idea that what happens was meant to happen. Then we'll turn to superstition, in which people come to believe things that are not true. Finally, we'll examine survivor's guilt, which is the agonizing belief after escaping a mass tragedy that one not only could have but also *should have* been killed along with the other victims. Survivor's guilt, rooted to downward counterfactual thinking, is an extreme case that involves a breakdown in people's ability to make sense of an experience. These three examples of sensemaking reveal that it would be virtually impossible for you to reach a deeper understanding of the vagaries of life without making reference to counterfactual possibilities.[2]

≈

As Tomas obsesses further over his own experience of love, he assumes that most people believe love is a product of heavy fate: "We all reject out of hand the idea that the love of our life may be something light or weightless; we presume our love is what must be, that without it our life would no longer be the same." But his own experience seems more accidental, even improbable. He too could as easily have fallen in love with someone else. He expresses this feeling of lightness in terms of a string of improbable coincidences that conspired to bring him and Tereza together:

> Seven years earlier, a complex neurological case *happened*
> to have been discovered at the hospital in Tereza's town. They

called in the chief surgeon of Tomas's hospital in Prague for consultation, but the chief surgeon *happened* to be suffering from sciatica, and because he could not move he sent Tomas to the provincial hospital in his place. The town had several hotels, but Tomas *happened* to be given a room in the one where Tereza was employed. He *happened* to have had enough free time before his train left to stop at the hotel restaurant. Tereza *happened* to be on duty, and *happened* to be serving Tomas's table. It had taken six chance happenings to push Tomas towards Tereza.

Each of these improbable events that just happened to have occurred seem, in Tomas's mind, to combine to indicate just how improbable, how "fortuitous" their love is, "a love that would not even have existed had it not been for the chief surgeon's sciatica."[3]

Fate is a curious word that people use in many different ways. It harkens back to the debate between determinism versus free will, for if everything is determined by fate, there must be little free will. And if there is little free will, choice is merely an illusion. And if choice is an illusion, so too is the counterfactual belief that you could have done it differently, because fate had long ago determined what *had to* happen. And so one way people use the word "fate" is to say that there was nothing you could have done to have altered what happened—in other words, that it was meant to be. Milan Kundera, a novelist, sketches a view of fate in which most people believe in a sort of fate defined by a complete heaviness of predetermination, but some small minority of people, poets and dreamers and idealists and the like, see the world very differently, in terms of the *lightness* of possibility. Kundera assumes that fate and free choice are opposites, that a person must believe in either one or the other.

Recent research shows that people often believe in a mix of both fate and counterfactual possibility. Some situations and experiences are seen as fated (say, meeting your true love), whereas other experiences are due to personal initiative (say, dieting) and hence could have gone one way or another depending on the effort put into them. New research conducted at the University of Illinois suggests that college students believe that about one-quarter of their experiences are due to fate and three-quarters are determined by their own personal initiative. This perspective was very much evident in one young person I spoke to. She told me that the choices she made (and made freely), along with the fate for her determined by her God, were a matter of continual back-and-forth negotiation. She'd do something of her own free will, and large segments of her life (such as where she lived, where she worked, who were her friends) would be utterly dependent on her own choice, but these choices would in turn influence the fate that was in store for her. Other aspects of her life (such as her overall "good work" in life) were very much determined by fate, and in particular by the God she believed in, but the exact form and timing of that fate would depend further on her own choices. In other words, she saw fate not as writing set in stone, but more like chalk on a blackboard, open to continuing erasure and revision.[4]

The results of this research argue against the conception in Kundera's novel *The Unbearable Lightness of Being*. It is not that people see the world as *either* heavy or light, as *either* ruled by fate or by counterfactuals reflective of personal choice. People see both, and they fit together quite nicely. This view also raises the possibility that there is more than one kind of fate. In the next section we'll see how new research has identified two distinct kinds of belief in fate.

Beliefs in Fate Across Two Cultures

Whether our beliefs focus on a fate that is fixed or changing was the centerpiece of a new analysis of fate by psychologists Maia Young of Stanford University and Michael Morris of Columbia University. They argued that the idea of fate is actually two distinct ideas, or two kinds of fate, which they call *Deity Control* and *Destiny Control*. Deity Control refers to the sort of fate controlled by God—that is, by an active decision-maker who considers events, changes His mind, and therefore can modify fate to reward or punish. Deity Control is not fixed, not set in stone. People who express a strong belief in Deity Control have little difficulty seeing how their own personal actions combine and intertwine with the motives of God to determine the future. With Deity Control, there is no contradiction at all between counterfactual thoughts about past actions and belief in fate.[5]

Destiny Control refers also to fate, but one that is unchanging over time because it is fixed by cosmic or physical forces. Astrological beliefs are a good example of Destiny Control. In astrology, a complicated set of interactions between planetary forces is seen by adherents to dictate human affairs. Those trained in astrological readings, they believe, can attain a privileged glimpse into future events.

Young and Morris used these ideas of two kinds of fate to explore cultural and religious differences in destiny and counterfactual thinking. In Chapter 3 we saw that there are few differences in counterfactual thinking across cultures, but the cultures studied thus far have been extremely limited, touching only on North America, some parts of Europe, and some parts of east Asia. But the moment we begin to talk about how the past might have been different or how the future might be predestined, one of the most obvious places to look for cultural variation is on the Indian subcontinent, where many believers in the Hindu faith embrace beliefs in reincarnation and destiny. The concept of *karma* refers to a type of destiny in which the good and bad actions by an individual in previous lives get added to a cosmic ledger, which then determines experiences in the current life. Karma embodies Destiny Control. And karma is the form of fate that might well constrain perceptions of counterfactual versions of the past. If karma long ago determined that a certain mishap had to happen to you, then there was nothing you could have done to prevent it.

In their pioneering cross-cultural research, Young and Morris examined the beliefs in fate of Americans (all steeped in the Judeo-Christian religious tradition) and Indians (all Hindus living in northern India and Nepal). They used a questionnaire designed to provide estimates of the strength of belief in the power of personal action, and also beliefs in both Deity Control and Destiny Control.

In both the American and Indian groups, a remarkable similarity was immediately apparent: Americans and Indians both expressed their strongest beliefs in the ability of individuals, independent of fate, to control their own destiny! As Young and Morris point out, many Americans assume that Hindus minimize the importance of personal action in favor of beliefs in karmic fate, but this assumption turns out to be inaccurate. Americans and Indians also shared similar beliefs in Deity Control. That is, both cultural groups believed that God controls the lives of human beings to a similar degree. The big difference between the two cultures, however, hinged on Destiny Control. Indians indeed expressed a stronger belief in the idea that impersonal machinations of cosmic forces *also* control human affairs.

It is this extra belief in Destiny Control that helps explain the cultural differences in counterfactual thinking uncovered by this research. For example, research participants rated their agreement with this counterfactual statement: "I often think about what might have been if I had made different choices in my life." Americans expressed much more agreement with this statement than did Indians. Similarly, Americans claimed more difficulty in making lifestyle choices, and in feeling regret over the way past decisions turned out. Although on average Americans voice greater counterfactuals and regret than Indians, it is essential to remember that this is simply a relative difference. Hindus also expressed regret, just not as much as Americans.

Despite these interesting examples of cultural variation, the overall lesson of this research is the same as in Chapter 3—that even with all the tremendous differences that separate the cultures of the world, the core psychological dynamics of counterfactual thinking appear to be universal. Like Americans, Indians see life as a complicated blend of experiences born of personal initiative, acts of God, and an impersonal fate. Fate is a multifaceted belief. As we've seen, it often springs from religious beliefs, but in the next section we'll see how it may also emerge from the simple experience of surprise.

Making Sense of Surprise

Surprise demands explanation. This is a very basic observation from the psychology of causal explanation. When something peculiar, strange, or unusual happens, we demand to know why, and our brains work overtime to locate the reason. The ordinary, the mundane, the typical, these all melt into the background of our minds without a second glance. As the old adage goes, dog bites man isn't news; man bites dog . . . now that's news! News reports focus on things that are surprising, which is to say new, and so it goes without saying that news reports nearly always contain explanations, analyses, and background insights to help the audience reach a state of understanding of what has newly occurred.

Not only is it the case that surprise demands explanation, but the bigger the surprise, the more powerful an explanation is demanded. A single person dies of a stroke, and we are satisfied to learn that smoking and poor diet were contributing factors. But if a thousand people die of a stroke all on the same day in the same neighborhood, then a vastly more comprehensive explanation is expected. A terrorist plot? A new epidemic involving an unknown virus? The mind works overtime to provide an explanation big enough and comprehensive enough to match the magnitude of the event itself.

Small events demand small explanations, and big events demand big explanations. Little wonder then that the Warren Commission report on President Kennedy's assassination, with its conclusion that a single lone gunman committed the crime, seemed so unsatisfying to so many. How could the course of history be thrown off into a new direction by the actions of a single man? An event like the assassination of President Kennedy, so huge in its impact and implications, demands a correspondingly huge explanation. An explanation involving a vast conspiracy, with participants ranging from the Mafia, evil politicians, Cuban and Soviet communists, and disgruntled military leaders much better satisfies the thirst for a huge explanation than a gunman acting alone. Most of the time this rule of thumb—big explanations for big events—works quite well and we hardly notice it. After all, most of the time, big effects do depend on big causes and small effects do depend on small causes. But every once in a while, this rule of thumb just doesn't work.[6]

I heard a story about a young man who got lucky playing blackjack in Vegas. He won a lot of money in a short time, was surprised and awed, and arrived at an explanation for his sudden fortune that most people would find utterly silly—he attributed his success to the "lucky" silk shirt he had been wearing. The next day he lost all the money he'd won, and then lost some more, because he believed that his lucky shirt would at any moment "kick in" and shower him with new riches. It never happened, and it is an obvious reminder of how incorrect causal explanations can bring disastrous mistakes in decision-making.

Journalist Thomas Friedman offered the same interpretation, the same underlying psychology, for events on a much grander scale. In the Six-Day War of 1967, Israel decisively defeated the armies of Egypt, Syria, and Jordan and captured the Sinai Peninsula, the Gaza Strip, and the West Bank. In the weeks preceding the war, Israelis were pessimistic, grimly expecting another Holocaust, even digging extra graves in expectation of devastating carnage. When victory came swiftly and at little cost in June 1967, many believed it was a miracle. *It could have been so much worse,* many thought. Victory was unexpected, spellbinding, but above all it was surprising. A surprise of such magnitude demanded a correspondingly enormous explanation, and indeed many interpreted it "providentially and messianically." People believed the victory was preordained, that it was meant to happen by some sort of divine intervention or cosmic plan. And so rather than recognizing the hard work and meticulous planning of various branches of the military and the civilian government, many chose a more cosmic explanation for the 1967 victory. The downside of an explanation that tends toward the cosmic rather than the mundane, as Friedman argued, is arrogance. If careful planning weren't the main reason for the victory, then it need not be emphasized in the future. If cosmic forces conspired to create events, then mere human beings need not be proactive. Friedman suggested that the newfound confidence of the Israeli leadership contributed to a carelessness that left Israel unprepared for the 1973 Yom Kippur War. Caught off guard, the Israeli army initially lost ground, but even as they turned the tide to achieve a military victory, many Israelis considered the Yom Kippur War a political failure.[7]

Could the 1973 war have been averted? Was the 1967 victory for Israel something truly providential? Or might it be that the very improbability of the 1967 victory contributed to perceptions that it was fated to occur? Social psychologists, drawing on years of laboratory research, tend to prefer the latter explanation. And intriguingly, if we push this line of reasoning full circle back to the topic of love, the topic with which this chapter began, we see the intimation that the more surprising or improbable the romantic union, the more that the two lovers will see providential or cosmic explanations as the reasons behind their union. To return to the example of Tomas and Tereza, lightness (meaning improbable or chance encounters) can paradoxically lay the seeds for a subsequent belief in heaviness, that the love was meant to be.

Lessons from Research. Enjoy the ride. Some people, having read Kundera as well as any of numerous other novelists and poets, might assume that love is the work of fate and true love is destined to be. This can place a heavy burden on the individual: a feeling that he or she must find that one perfect love that they were fated to find and meant to be with.

Research in social psychology offers two distinct reasons to back off from this often impossible objective. First, people are fabulously adept at *creating their own meaning*, and they are flexibly competent at this sensemaking within a wide range of circumstances. Indeed, because surprise accelerates the processes of sensemaking, it may well be the case that those for whom love seems improbable and least predestined are the most satisfied. Second, in reality there is probably little fate to any romance, at least not in the cosmic sense. It turns out that a big predictor of romance and marriage is simple physical proximity. You are much more likely to marry someone who lives near you than far away, someone who works near you rather than on the other side of town, who frequents the same shops or commutes using the same bus or train. Of all the billions of potential partners on the planet Earth, the fantastically small fraction of human beings living in your immediate vicinity are the ones most likely to be a part of your life.[8] And so the lesson from research is simply to relax and enjoy the ride, which is to say, enjoy the meaning, cosmic or otherwise, that your brain works overtime to create.

Superstition

Beliefs in fate, whether they focus on deity or destiny, are often matters of faith, part of established religious teachings that hold truth for some but not others. Superstition is also a matter of faith, but superstition is generally taken to mean something that stands apart from religion.

Superstition can be defined as ritualistic beliefs that are at odds with what most would accept as reality. The *Catholic Encyclopedia* defines "superstition" as an excess of religious fervor involving inappropriate idolatry and vain observances, with black magic and the occult given as examples.[9] Perhaps the most common understanding of superstition focuses on mundane behaviors we are ritualistically warned to avoid, like walking underneath ladders, spilling salt, or stepping on sidewalk cracks. According to a 1996 Gallup poll, 78 percent of Americans confessed to being at least a little bit superstitious, and 72 percent said they owned at least one good luck charm.[10]

Where do superstitious beliefs come from? Many people recognize their irrational nature, yet abide by them just the same. A friend told me yes, his superstitious beliefs were probably baseless, and no bad luck would ever come his way regardless of ladders, salt, or sidewalk cracks, yet even so he felt there was no harm going along with these superstitions, *just in case* they turn out to be true.

Some superstitions are harmless. Veering out of the path of a black cat is unlikely to cause any major changes to one's life as a whole, it takes only a moment to do it, so what does it matter? As we'll see, recent research illuminates at least a few cases where harm *can* come from superstition. Moreover, it is fascinating to consider the underlying reasons why superstitions can feel so right even when they are so demonstrably wrong. Careful experimentation reveals the psychological mechanisms that conspire to create both the feeling of rightness along with that objective wrongness. In recent years, counterfactual thinking has been fingered as one such mechanism responsible for creating superstitious beliefs.

Here's my favorite example. Have you ever had the experience of waiting in one of several busy checkout lines at a supermarket, then considering switching to a new line, hoping to get through quicker? (This example also works perfectly well for freeway commuters: your lane seems to move slower, so maybe you should change lanes to go faster.) Many people believe superstitiously that you shouldn't switch lines (or lanes), because your new line will then slow down and your old line will turn out to have progressed the quickest. A friend told me, "That's no superstition. It's true!" To a scientist, of course, it seems decidedly unlikely that one individual's single decision, and their tiny bit of line-switching or lane-changing, has the power in and of itself to influence the speed with which cashiers work or drivers drive. More likely, there is some deeper psychological explanation that accounts for why we believe it does.

In research conducted by social psychologists Dale Miller and Brian Taylor at Princeton University, the interplay between memory and counterfactual thinking was shown to contribute to this checkout line misperception and to the development of superstitious beliefs in general. The starting point of their analysis was the question of regrets of action versus inaction (Chapter 2): For long-term regrets, people are more likely to focus on failures to act, on things they should have done differently. But for recent regrets, people instead focus on actions, that is, on things they should NOT have done. Miller and Taylor pointed out that staying in line when you could have switched is an example of inaction. But switching, actually moving out of your old line into a new line, is an example of action. Regrets will be more intense, therefore, for the long wait suffered after switching than if you had stayed put.[11]

If switching instead of staying is more likely to bring a counterfactual thought to mind *(If only I had stayed put!)*, then a line-switching counterfactual will be more solidly stored in memory than a counterfactual about staying put. And this means that later on, while reviewing from memory your experiences when shopping and driving, painful regrets centering on switching will be more vivid than those centering on staying. If someone asks you whether switching results in longer waits, your brain rapidly and automatically compiles relevant instances—past experiences at supermarket lines, freeway traffic jams, and the like—and arrives at an answer that summarizes these. With memories of action regrets (switching) more memorable in the short term than inaction regrets (staying), your overall judgment will overemphasize the action regrets, leading you to the biased conclusion that line-switching produces worse results than line-staying, even when in reality switching and staying probably involve the same waiting times.

Whether you hold to this superstition or not, you are unlikely to suffer more than a few moments of inconvenience. The next section focuses on some real problems that can come of such superstitions.

Everyday Superstitions: Test-Taking

In recent years Americans have increasingly found themselves at the mercy of standardized tests. For decades college admissions have been determined in part by performance on aptitude tests like the SAT. Private corporations, public institutions, and the U.S. military all to varying degrees rely on tests of aptitude and ability to assign workers to specific tasks. At this very moment, numerous school boards, state panels, parents, and teachers are debating the appropriateness of using standardized tests to decide whether students should advance to the next level of grade school. Some decry the rise of standardized testing because it underemphasizes other important aspects of education; others applaud its use as a way of improving educational standards across school districts; but whichever opinions hold sway, the fact is that success at test-taking is now a central hurdle along the way to success in our society.

There are many test-taking skills. Some are simple rules of thumb, either learned through experience, passed on from others, or enshrined in the thousands of "how-to" books designed to improve study skills. Might some of these popular rules of thumb be the result of superstition?

Justin Kruger, a colleague of mine at the University of Illinois, suspected so. His research throws a spotlight on a core aspect of the test experience—the uncertainty that accompanies the moment of answering one specific test question. The test-taker might mark down an answer, a gut hunch based on a first impression, but recognize the feeling of uncertainty and decide to return to that question later to reassess the gut hunch. And then later, the test-taker indeed might think a different answer is the correct one. And there's the problem. It comes down to a choice. Stick with the original answer, or change the answer to what now seems to be the best answer. What would you do?

There is a rule of thumb that a lot of students hear, which is to stick to your first answer. Stay with your first instinct. This rule of thumb is even enshrined in the advice given by the Kaplan people, a company that specializes in preparing students for standardized tests like the SAT or GMAT. "Exercise great caution if you decide to change an answer," goes the advice from one of their books. "Experience indicates that many students who change answers change to the wrong answer." In surveys of college students, about three out of four students say they agree with this advice.[12]

This rule of thumb and this piece of advice are utterly wrong. So wrong that we can call this another *Lesson from Research*, which is: When taking a test, feel free to change your answer at any time.

When taking a test and deciding whether to keep your original answer, your second thoughts are probably more accurate than your first thoughts. Educational research from numerous sources and spanning seventy years is nearly unanimous in showing that it is better to switch than to stick with your first instinct. Most answer changes go from incorrect to correct, and people who change their answers usually improve their test scores. And it doesn't matter at all whether the test is structured in multiple-choice format versus some other format, whether it is administered with or without time limits, or whether it is completed on paper versus on a computer. Whichever kind of test is used, it pays to change answers.[13]

But this begs the question of why in the first place so many people mistakenly believe that it is best to cling to a first instinct. Kruger and his colleagues found that counterfactual thinking stealthily contributes to the formation of this *First Instinct Fallacy*. Kruger found among University of Illinois undergraduates a pervasive belief in sticking to first instincts, and also that this belief was inaccurate. By examining each student's midterm exam for markings left from an eraser, they were able to count up all the instances in which students changed their answers, which also allowed them to see whether these changes made their overall score better or worse. More than three-quarters of exams showed evidence of at least one erasure. Of all the erasures, 54 percent were changes that helped (wrong answer changed to right answer) and only 19 percent were changes that hurt (right changed to wrong). The rest of the changes were from one wrong answer to another wrong answer.[14]

Like switching lines in a supermarket, the mere act of switching answers makes a subsequent poor result more regrettable. Because counterfactual thoughts centering on action are more vivid in mind in the short term, they are more likely to be stored away in memory and thus more likely to be recalled later. And what is more likely to be recalled later will feed into the rules of thumb, right or wrong, that people intuitively invent to summarize their past experiences. In other words, mentally kicking yourself after changing an answer from right to wrong is just more likely to sit and fester in your memory than kicking yourself after neglecting to change an answer from the wrong one to the correct one. In one of their studies, Kruger found that several weeks after taking a version of the SAT exam, students misrecalled the consequences of switching answers and sticking to their original answers. Students mistakenly remembered that switching answers was worse for their exam performance than it actually was, and that sticking to the original answer was better for their exam performance than it actually was.

Kruger put all of these elements into a direct test, a grand experiment modeled after the popular television game show *Who Wants to Be a Millionaire*. Hosted by Regis Philbin, the game requires contestants to answer a sequence of questions. Each correct answer brings a big jump in prize money, and if the contestant answers fifteen questions correctly in a row, she or he wins that full million dollars. Along the way, contestants may use any of three "lifelines." For example, the contestant can poll the audience as to the correct answer or phone a friend for advice. Chapter 6 showed how counterfactuals can be skillfully manipulated to heighten dramatic tension, and the makers of *Who Wants to Be a Millionaire* clearly recognized this. When a contestant is uncertain, Regis encourages her to tell us her first instinct. Say the question is: In what year did the Beatles first appear on the *Ed Sullivan Show*? "Hmm," the contestant says, "I'm not sure but I wanna say 1965." She then phones her friend Sue, who tells her, "No, it was 1964." The dramatic tension is now sharpened: Should she stick with her initial gut hunch or go with Sue's advice? The tension becomes even more unbearable if she asks the audience for advice, and the majority of them say 1966! Now what is the poor contestant to do? (In case you're wondering, the Beatles first appeared on the *Ed Sullivan Show* on February 9, 1964.)

In Kruger's laboratory version of the *Millionaire* game show, there was no million-dollar prize—actually, there was no prize at all. The research participants simply watched a videotaped version of *Who Wants to Be a Millionaire* (created by Kruger and his team specifically for the research project) and then shared their reactions to the show. They watched contestants answer forty questions. Kruger edited the videotape to create several versions with varying numbers of times when the contestant switched when she should have stuck (that is, followed the advice of the lifeline rather than sticking with her first instinct, which turned out to be right) and stuck when she should have switched. Research participants used scoring sheets to record the outcome of each question (whether right or wrong) and, more important, how foolish they thought the contestant had been.

Research participants thought that the contestant was more foolish for missing questions when she switched when she should have stuck, compared to when she stuck when she should have switched. To take an example, in all the edited versions of the videotape, the contestant got the answer wrong to the question "Where is Karl Marx buried?" (The answer is London.) In one version of the video, the contestant's first instinct was correct but she switched her answer, and in the other version the contestant stuck with her incorrect answer, but the lifeline's suggestion turned out to be correct. The research participants found the contestant to be more foolish when she switched than when she stuck, even though in both cases she was wrong. Another group of research participants was asked one week after watching the game show video to recall what they had seen. In the minds of these game show observers, the contestant's experience of missing an answer after switching was indeed more memorable than the experience of missing an answer by sticking to one's first instinct.

The belief that it is bad to make changes on a test is clearly a bit of bad advice, as it is demonstrably clear from oodles of research evidence that making changes pays off in the form of better test scores. The reason is that going through an entire exam often dislodges various bits of knowledge from memory, knowledge that can prove useful in revising answers made previously. Sometimes a later test question contains a solid hint for an earlier test question, and you can only capitalize on the hint if you go back and make a change. Yet many people persist in the belief that it is bad to make a change.

What makes this kind of superstitious belief particularly fascinating is that it gets bigger even in the face of mounting personal evidence to the contrary. The more experience people have with taking tests, the more biased memories that pile up in support of superstitions, and so the more likely people are to believe that changing answers is bad. Becoming more aware of the silent influence of counterfactual thinking on everyday thinking may help you counter this memory bias.

If we step back and look at superstitions in general, one curious aspect seems more understandable in light of these latest findings. Isn't it interesting that the majority of superstitions focus on actions rather than inactions—on things you should be careful to avoid doing as opposed to things you should remember to do? Superstitions mostly focus on *don'ts* rather than *dos*. DON'T let a black cat cross your path, goes the superstition. In other words, be sure to avoid this particular action of having one cross your path. If you can't avoid it, and bad luck follows, the regret of action will be more intense, will linger longer in memory, and result in the superstitious belief that a black cat crossing your path is bad. By contrast, avoiding an inaction (a DO rather than a DON'T), such as remembering to stroke the fur of a white cat, is less likely to become a superstition, as the regret of inaction that follows from forgetting to stroke that white fur is less memorable over time. The same logic may well apply to the numerous other superstitions that take the form of DON'Ts, such as don't walk under a ladder, don't step on a crack, don't use the number thirteen. How many of the personal, unique, idiosyncratic superstitions of your own life take the form of DON'Ts rather than DOs?

Survivor's Guilt

People use counterfactuals to make sense of events both big and small, from true love to taking exams. Surprises and problems are especially likely to spur thoughts of what might have been, and these thoughts then contribute to a coherent understanding of the flow of events. Put differently, people try to write their own mental stories that weave together the events of their lives into a satisfying whole. The sheer ease of doing so is one reason we tend not to notice how much we do this. But sometimes, in the most tragic of circumstances, the process of making meaning is no longer easy but impossible. The pain of survivor's guilt is a reaction to tragedy that thwarts attempts at finding meaning. Survivor's guilt comes from downward counterfactual thinking.

Harry Waizer is a tax lawyer who worked for Cantor Fitzgerald, a securities brokerage firm. Its head office had been atop the World Trade Center, tower number one, the first to be hit by a terrorist-hijacked airliner on September 11, 2001. Of the thousand or so Cantor Fitzgerald employees based in New York, 658 lost their lives as a result of the terrorist attack. In short, much of the company perished, and it nearly went bankrupt as a result. Harry Waizer was at work that morning at the World Trade Center, yet he lived. Everyone else who worked at those offices, located eight floors above the airliner's impact, died.

Harry survived because he just happened to be in an elevator when the airliner struck.

The fireball of exploding jet fuel engulfed the elevator and Harry was badly burned. "I burnt my hands fighting the flame, my fingertips up to my elbow," he recalled later. "My legs burned above the knees, six inches or eight inches up. And my face was burnt. I remember the elevator plummeting, the screech of metal on metal. There were sparks shooting all over from the car braking or hitting the shaft, and then all of a sudden it caught itself and glided to the 78th floor."[15]

Other elevators simply fell and were utterly destroyed, but the elevator Harry was in stopped intact, allowing him to get off and walk down seventy-eight flights of stairs to safety. Halfway down he nearly collapsed, but an emergency worker on his way up found him and helped him the rest of the way back down. He was in a coma for a month. Upon waking, his family slowly revealed to him the extent of the terrorist attacks and just how many of his fellow Cantor Fitzgerald coworkers had perished. For Harry Waizer, that's when the feeling of survivor's guilt set in.

"It took a whole month before I could even call the families of my friends," Harry explained. "I'd pick up the phone, then couldn't think of what to say. I worried that when we talked they'd think *Why you? Why were you and Karen* [his wife] *the lucky ones?* I realize how lucky I was. A few seconds earlier and I would have been above the fire line and unable to escape. And even though they'd never ask me those questions, it was impossible to ignore the thought process."[16]

The feelings Harry conveyed were shared by many other survivors of the September 11 terrorist attacks. The experience of survivor's guilt is one of anguished self-blame at the realization that you could have died as easily as someone else, maybe even *should have* died instead of someone else. The inescapable question is "Why me?" *Why was I the one to survive rather than the person next to me, or the people who worked alongside me?* The "why" question is a search for explanation and meaning, but it comes up short. The automatic brain mechanisms responsible for sensemaking sputter to a stop. There is no good reason why.

As we've seen from the research detailed in this book, people spontaneously think about what might have been, and this process is intimately connected to seeking answers and finding meaning for life's events, both big and small. Most counterfactual thoughts focus on personal action. People can't help it—these thoughts spring automatically to mind: *I should have been more careful; I could have gone the other way; I might have been quicker.* For small and minor everyday life events, focusing on personal actions allows people to see how they can improve next time, and they benefit from a feeling of control, of being in command of their fate.

But with survivor's guilt, the same basic brain processes are short-circuited, so to speak. As with mundane life events, the counterfactuals that spring effortlessly to mind center on one's own actions of a relatively minor, ordinary nature. And the smallness of these actions, which each might have spelled the difference between life and death, are obviously and utterly wrong as deep explanations for why something so terrible has occurred. Another Cantor Fitzgerald survivor just happened to delay arriving at work to ask about a new gym opening nearby. If he had left his questions about the gym for another day, he would have died. This is a counterfactual, the sort that springs easily to mind, but it is certainly not an explanation that makes sense of why this employee lived when so many others died. Counterfactuals usually convey meaning, help us make sense of events, but this counterfactual does nothing of the sort. It is a counterfactual that shoots blanks. And so survivor's guilt is a particularly clear case of how under the most extreme stress, counterfactual thinking can get in the way of successful coping by conjuring phantom explanations and phony sensemaking or simply by failing to provide resolution and understanding.

Matt McMullen and Keith Markman were the first to describe how downward counterfactuals, which usually produce consolation, can occasionally produce feelings of anxiety and panic. Most of the time, they argue, counterfactual thinking is a comparison, meaning that people mentally view their current circumstances alongside a counterfactual alternative, emphasizing the differences between what is and what might have been. In this *comparison mode*, downward counterfactuals make current circumstances feel, in contrast, better. But sometimes a counterfactual vision is an experience in and of itself. In this *experiential mode*, people "get inside" the counterfactual, living and breathing it as though it were real. Survivor's guilt is a grim example of how people can get inside a downward counterfactual, focusing on its contours and details so intently that they actually feel the anxiety and horror that this negative outcome would have entailed.[17]

Survivor's guilt is very much a social experience. To feel survivor's guilt is to realize your link to the experiences of others, to see a connection to their suffering. Anthony Lin, a New Yorker, wrote the following passage about September 11 in an online journal:

> The feeling of guilt guided me to Union Square the following Saturday. At one point I caught a "missing person" sign posted on a tree with the picture of a father, his baby son in his arms. The missing person was Antonio Javier Alvarez, his birth date, May 12, 1978. He and I shared a similar first name and the same birthday, only he was two years younger. His tragic story struck my heart, the first time it had been struck so intimately since Tuesday. Given the common threads that joined me and Antonio, I thought for a brief moment, why him and not me? He did not deserve that fate more than I do. So why him? It may have only been a momentary thought, but to wish for one's own death is rare, if not insane. Without an answer, I resorted to an empty feeling of guilt.[18]

In previous chapters we saw various instances of a psychological immune system in action—an automatic, silent set of brain mechanisms that keep our emotions in balance by shifting our interpretation of the world around us. Self-serving beliefs, blame laid at the feet of others rather than oneself, and a selective pleasure at the misfortune of others are examples of the psychological immune system at work. Standard operating procedure for the psychological immune system is emphasizing and exaggerating the differences between oneself and another person, particularly a victim of misfortune. To blame a victim for their own tragedy involves emphasizing something different about the victim from you yourself—he was not too bright; her judgment was off; he just didn't have the right stuff. And to see a difference between you and that poor victim invokes a buffer separating you from the prospect of suffering a similar fate. But survivor's guilt constitutes the failure of the psychological immune system to grapple with tragedy of great magnitude. Like an infection that overwhelms the body's immune system, survivor's guilt overwhelms the psychological immune system. Instead of exaggerating the difference between oneself and a victim, the similarity is what strikes people as most obvious. *That poor guy was no different from me; it could just as well have been me instead of him.* With survivor's guilt, the differences between oneself and another person shrink, and so too do the differences between what actually happened and what could have happened.

As with a bad infection, the best recourse is medical treatment. Survivor's guilt can be insidious in that it may take months to build to a crescendo of anguish diagnosable as post-traumatic stress disorder (PTSD). Symptoms of PTSD include (a) continued intrusive thoughts about the traumatic event, including flashbacks and nightmares, (b) withdrawal from social life along with use of alcohol and drugs as a means of escape, and (c) an overall level of anxiety that makes normal work and social activities difficult. Sufferers of survivor's guilt should see a trained mental health professional. There are no simple tricks, no simple lessons that can possibly be conveyed in a book such as this that could effectively counter its effects.

What is life all about? What sense can we make of the events that befall us? At every instance, our brains work overtime to provide us with answers, with causal explanations that create a feeling of meaning, of knowing and understanding. This brain work proceeds automatically, unconsciously, and as we ponder the reasons why things happen, from the blissful joy of true love to the nightmarish horror of a terrorist attack, the answers seem merely to pop into our heads, for we cannot glimpse the hidden mental machinations that produced them. In recent years psychologists have begun to unlock the mysteries of those unseen mental processes. As people make meaning of the events in their lives, they sometimes fall prey to predictable biases, as in the case of whether to follow your first gut hunch. Yet even with such biases recognized, it is worth pausing to marvel at the majesty of the ability to make meaning that is a core component of each and every human brain.

Chapter 8

Harnessing Regret

~

If this book were distilled into one message, it would be this: Regret is good. Regret helps. Regret serves a necessary psychological purpose. Regret is the most visible and obvious form of counterfactual thinking, and counterfactual thinking is a key component of a silently effective brain system by which people comprehend reality, learn from mistakes, move forward, and achieve a bettering of their life circumstances.

You might hear a lot about avoiding regret, to live life with no regrets, to never admit regret because to do so is to admit failure. You might hear that the ideal in life is to have zero regrets. These ideas are wrong. Regret is as necessary for healthy living as eating. But like eating, problems arise from both excess and shortfall. It is true that you can suffer too many regrets, making it important to leave the past behind and move on with your life. But so too can you have too few regrets. Neglecting the messages of your own emotions can mean persisting in counterproductive behaviors and missing unique opportunities for growth and renewal. There seems to be an ideal amount of regret, a moderate middle ground of optimal counterfactual thinking, neither too much nor too little, that best describes the mentally healthy individual.

In the chapter ahead, I will summarize six main lessons drawn from recent research. These lessons each connect to a simple insight, that the human brain is already marvelously and powerfully effective in its ability to fix problems, cope with misfortune, and set us on an emotionally stable path. Like a skilled sailor who uses knowledge of wind and sea to travel faster and farther, the individual who grasps the workings of counterfactual thinking can harness these thought processes for even more effective travel through life's turbulent times. The central theme of this chapter is to ride the regret. Let the brain do its natural work, enhance and facilitate that work where possible, but most of all do nothing to inadvertently thwart that work. The first rule of stormy sailing is that when waves swell high, turn into the wave, go straight up the wave and straight down the back side. Ride each wave while steering a straight course. And so too with negative emotions and counterfactual thinking, hold on and ride the regret to positive life changes.

Riding the Regret: My Own Story

A few years ago I had an opportunity of a lifetime: the chance to move back to my hometown, a beautiful, friendly place where I had longed to live for years. I had chosen a career path, college professor, that doesn't give you much choice as to where you live. It's a bit like being in the military—you move where the work is. With so very few academic jobs open at any given moment across North America, young professors can wind up working and living virtually anywhere across the continent. I had been living in Chicago for a few years, but I originally had moved there only because Northwestern University just happened to offer me a job when I got out of graduate school.

Then out of the blue came a great job opportunity in my hometown of Vancouver, Canada, and with it a chance to move near again to my extended family and old friends and familiar hangouts. True, this opportunity meant leaving behind my job at Northwestern, a job that

I had grown to love. Even so, it was an easy decision, and so I moved with my wife and baby daughter several thousand miles from Chicago to Vancouver to begin a new life, and a new job at Simon Fraser University. It was supposed to have been a wonderful, fabulous new chapter of our lives.

It didn't take more than a couple of months for the regret to set in. I felt, quite simply, that I had ruined my life. Once the dust settled, the decision to move from Chicago to Vancouver felt like the worst decision I had ever made. I missed my old job, my old colleagues and students at Northwestern, my friends in Chicago. And I missed living in the U.S. The daily experience of severe regret for me took the form of an obsessive review of my recent past. I'd awaken at three in the morning with cold sweats, immediately recall that I had ruined my life, then spend the next few sleepless hours going over each day, each week, each month of the previous year of my life in a madly fruitless search for the exact moment at which I had begun the sequence of events that had led to this disaster.

Regret feels bad, yes, but it also forces the individual to look inward, to reassess the assumptions and patterns of the past. I came to realize that there were large parts of my old life that I had simply taken for granted, yet had depended upon so essentially that when they were gone, I was shattered. I missed the United States. . . . I longed for the action, the energy, the competition at top American universities. It had been a personal triumph for me, growing up in a small Canadian town, to be able to compete and succeed in the frenzied world of American academia, and in giving it all up, I realized that I'd lost an important piece of myself.

And so I decided to reverse my earlier decision, decided to return to the U.S. This time, however, I'd take what I'd learned and make things even better. At first, this new decision made me feel even worse, because it meant turning my back on my relatives who lived in Vancouver, my mother especially, all of whom had been so excited to see us living nearby. And it meant turning my back on the great new colleagues I'd met at Simon Fraser University, folks who'd bent over backward to make me feel welcome. I felt ill about even considering making another move. Yet after two months of severe regret, I took action and started working the phones to see about a new job back in the Midwest. With a second baby on the way, my wife and I decided that a small college town, quiet and affordable, suited us best. The hiring process in academia is long and convoluted, but I eventually accepted a job offer from the University of Illinois, located in the small college town of Champaign-Urbana. A year later my family and I moved to Champaign and started yet another new life.

I tell this story because it illustrates the power of riding the regret, of harnessing regret to new action rather than suppressing it. It shows the value of experiencing regret deeply, listening to what these emotions tell you, what they reveal about your deepest wishes, then acting quickly on these newfound insights.

The First Juncture: Change Your Situation or Change Your Mind

You've probably come across this prayer:

God grant me the serenity to accept the things I cannot change . . . the courage to change the things I can . . . and the wisdom to know the difference.

It appears on first glance to be a well-worn cliché, yet it stands as a profound comment on the interplay between psychology and contemporary life. The brain indeed appears to be rigged with two standard responses to problematic situations. One: change the situation, and two: change your mind about the situation. Changing the situation is the first response. If the change is successful, end of story. But if unsuccessful, the brain's next response is to fire up the psychological immune system, which involves a wide range of mental tricks for seeing the situation differently, seeing it in a more positive light, which in turn creates more positive emotions. Changing the way you see things is part of the brain mechanism responsible for regulating, or calming down, emotional fluctuation. And so we see that the first juncture point in the experience of regret, the first tangible decision made by the brain, is the decision as to whether a situation is fixable. As the old prayer says, this requires wisdom, which is to say that it is not always easy to recognize when things can or cannot be fixed.

In regretting my move from Chicago to Vancouver, I recognized immediately that my job situation was changeable. The job market was active, I had a solid track record behind me, and so from the start I was hopeful about the opportunities I still had. That recognition was both boon and curse. Boon because I managed to fix the situation; curse because the very recognition prevented me from feeling better, prevented my psychological immune system from kicking in. As you'll recall from the discussion of "burning bridges" in Chapter 5, the very act of realizing that things are fixable creates a psychological obligation to go and fix them, and without the fix, regret deepens. (*Why didn't I fix it?!*) By contrast, research shows that when people see situations as unchangeable, the psychological immune system kicks in faster and people grow quickly to *like* their unchangeable situation. In other words, the quicker people realize that they cannot change the situation, the quicker they reach the serenity of not just accepting it, but liking it, too.[1]

The biggest pitfall is the situation that is definitely not fixable, yet the individual continues to act as though it is fixable by reviewing regret after regret, counterfactual after counterfactual, that cannot possibly be implemented to improve matters. Regrets over the death of a loved one exemplify this pitfall. "I was thousands of miles away and never able to say good-bye," said one middle-aged woman about the suicide of her mother. "I had moved away to Utah. Had I been with her . . . had she been able to talk to me . . ." But death is final, it cannot be changed, and no amount of wishful regret can bring a loved one back. And this means that the kind of counterfactual thinking that can result in learning and channeling new insights into future behavior is impossible. This regret is like the wheels of a truck mired in mud, spinning round and round yet getting nowhere. This is a classic example of the problem of an excess of counterfactual thinking.[2]

Counterfactuals for Betterment: Six Strategies

If counterfactuals are for betterment, how can you harness them for your own benefit? Our psychology is built out of trade-offs. Brains do many things very well, but they do not necessarily do all of them well at the same time. When the brain does one thing, it may trade off against something else. Upward counterfactual thinking can enhance learning and bring improvement in performance, but these thoughts come at the expense of unpleasant emotions. You can make yourself feel better by emphasizing downward counterfactuals, but then you miss out on the performance benefits brought by upward counterfactuals.

The key is balance, an ideal middle zone of optimal counterfactual thinking, a sweet spot of moderation, with neither too much nor too little of upward and downward counterfactuals. With this in mind, here are six strategies gleaned from recent research, refined from insights revealed throughout this book, that aim to keep you in that ideal middle zone of optimal counterfactual thinking.

Strategy #1: Spring Back Fast

V. runs his own company that creates computer software for automated data collection, report-building, and databasing. Just before he was about to send some new custom software to a client, he discovered a bug. A nearly fatal bug that would render his software, which took months to develop, useless under some circumstances. It was an error that he should have caught, should have seen, should have corrected long ago. But he'd missed it. His reaction was instant. The regret he felt was intense and all-encompassing. "For two days, I couldn't eat," he said. "In my mind I was reviewing each day of product development, obsessively wondering why I hadn't spotted the bug sooner."

But after two days that searing regret was gone. In the blink of an eye, V. had put the regret behind him and was back at work, fixing the original bug but, more important, implementing new company policy that would prevent the recurrence of such a bug in the future. "When you run your own company," he told me, "you've got to move fast. It's your money on the line, and waiting around will cost even more, so I need to have the fix in a hurry."

V. is an entrepreneur, a person who puts his wealth on the line to invest in new projects, some very risky but that nevertheless hold the tantalizing hope for a big future payoff. Recent research shows that successful entrepreneurs as a group use counterfactual thinking with striking effectiveness. How? First, they are above average in the intensity of their regret experience. They kick themselves *hard* after mistakes. Second, they get over it fast. And third, they use their regret as a springboard to further action, hurling themselves toward thorough fixes and rapidly implemented solutions. If there is a lesson to be learned from the entrepreneurial spirit, it is that experiencing regret deeply can be extremely useful so long as you spring back fast and ride the wave of regret as rapidly as possible to further action.[3]

Strategy #2: Look Further

Ordinarily, our first reaction to a mishap is a single upward counterfactual that specifies how things might have been better if only a different action had been taken. This one counterfactual privileges a single explanation as the best or only reason why something happened. But many events in life are multiply determined, meaning that there is more than one reason why the event in question happened. If you rely on the first counterfactual that comes to mind, you may be ignoring other valid explanations that may be harnessed for future improvement.

Let's say a friend doesn't call back, even after you've left several messages. You might quickly believe that she might have called you already if only you'd remembered her birthday last fall. The ease with which this counterfactual springs to mind might make it feel particularly valid, but it's remarkable how rarely we stop to think further about the myriad *other* reasons why someone might act as they do. In this simple little example, there are many potential reasons why a friend might neglect to return a phone call—a hectic week at work, a plumbing disaster, a bout of food poisoning. And there's no reason why several of these might not combine together to make phoning back especially unlikely.

Looking further means considering the fuller range of past possibilities, past actions that might have been taken. Maybe you forgot her birthday, but was there something else you did, or failed to do, that might also explain the event in question? As first mentioned in Chapter 4, a good strategy is to force yourself to think of additional reasons why someone behaved as they did. Maybe there's a better explanation right around the corner. A side benefit is that thinking about these additional counterfactuals can feed into an increased feeling of personal control, which can promote optimism and fortified persistence. Overall, looking further means reframing the regret experience itself so as to recognize the hidden possibilities for learning.[4]

Strategy #3: Think Downward

Downward counterfactuals, those thoughts about how things might have turned out worse, spring to mind only very rarely. But they have the benefit of making you feel better, so why not take the time to ponder them more often?

In a 2003 *Time* magazine cover story about the job market, an

employee named Tod gave a good example of how downward counterfactuals may round out the deck of reactions to a problem to foster a
more balanced response. As the Internet boom fizzled in the early
2000s, Tod's pay at an electronics firm was cut repeatedly. When he was
down to an annual salary of $70,000, the most natural counterfactual
to come to mind centered on the salary he used to make—which was
$115,000—and how much better life would be if he had that level of
salary back again. He was thinking this, to be sure, and yet he also said
that he was "grateful just to have a regular paycheck," the implication
being that with the economy in such poor shape and many others out
of work, matters could be worse, and the fact that things *weren't* worse
for him brought some measure of relief.[5]

The downward counterfactual produces two main benefits. First, it
feels good. Research confirms that downward counterfactual thinking
can bring a momentary burst of positive emotion. Second, it helps keep
things in perspective. Recognizing that things can always be worse and
taking note of the most plausible way a recent bad experience might
have come out even worse gives you a soberingly balanced view of your
life as a whole.

Together, strategies #2 and 3 might be taken as a form of "stacking
the deck," of adding a few extra counterfactual cards to your deck of
thoughts to achieve behavioral and emotional benefit. An extra two or
three counterfactual thoughts help us round out the range of past possibilities under consideration. But don't *force* yourself to think of *too
many* extra counterfactuals, for therein lurks another danger. This is the
danger of overthinking.

Strategy #4: Don't Overthink

After a setback, it's easy to think of things you might have done differently, up to a point. Then it becomes difficult. The more effort you
need to put into thinking of counterfactual actions, the more likely it

is that you'll get a boomerang effect that makes you feel less, not more, in control of your life. As we saw in Chapter 4, it's generally a good thing to feel in control of your life.

When a skinny person successfully lifts a heavy barbell, an observer might conclude "he's stronger than he looks." But obviously, the observer will want to check to see just how heavy that barbell is. If it turns out to be light, then the observer will no longer be impressed by the strength of that skinny person. This kind of "correction" takes place constantly in the beliefs and judgments we form in everyday life. In particular, if something is easy or difficult to think of, we take this into account (usually without realizing it). In one research experiment, people described themselves (on average) as fairly assertive after giving six examples of their own assertive behavior. But when they were asked to write down twelve examples of times that they had been assertive, they described themselves as *less* assertive.[6]

Just think about that for a moment: These people came up with *more* examples of being assertive, and this very act caused them to believe they were in fact *less* assertive. It seems strange at first, but the reason why this happened is that their brains silently took account of how easy or difficult it was to come up with those examples. Coming up with twelve examples is *harder* than coming up with six, and so without any realization on the part of these research participants, their brains automatically corrected their estimate of assertiveness, reducing the estimate simply because it was difficult to generate so many examples of assertiveness.

By the very same process, thinking of too many counterfactuals can make people feel less in control of their lives. Thinking of just one, two, or three ways that you might have done something differently emphasizes for you the power of your own actions to change things. Doing this actually makes you feel more in control, in tighter command of your life. But the more you *force* yourself to think of these counterfactual actions, and the more difficult it becomes to do so, the more you might feel, paradoxically, less in control of your life. This was the finding in an

experiment conducted at the University of Illinois. In that study, everyone was asked first to focus on a recent negative experience, and then to
write some details about it. Then everyone was asked to list some ways
that the negative experience might have been avoided. Some people
were asked to write down two ways it could have been avoided, but others were asked to write down twelve ways. Although both groups enjoyed a boost in their perceptions of the ability to control and therefore
correct the *specific situation* they'd been focusing on, those who had
written down twelve counterfactuals actually felt *less in control* of their
lives as a whole. In other words, too many counterfactuals evoked feelings of powerlessness.[7]

The lesson is clear. Don't overthink. You can push yourself to think
of a couple more counterfactual thoughts, but more than five puts you
in the danger zone. Once again, try to ride the wave of regret without
tinkering too much with mother nature.

Strategy #5: Write It Down (The Surprising Value of Blogging)

In recent years, blogging has become a popular pastime. "Blogging"
is short for "web logging," recording a diary and then posting it on the
Internet for all to see. Blogs can be extensive, detailed like a novel, or
simply brief notes on the day's personal events. The best-known blogs
are those of people living through extraordinary circumstances—a citi-
zen of Baghdad in April 2003, say, or a Manhattanite in September
2001—yet blogs are commonly written by regular folks of all ages and
backgrounds. A common first reaction to the phenomenon of blogging
is surprise: Surprise first at how many people seem happy to reveal their
personal lives to others, and further surprise that those others would actually care! But beyond their entertainment value, you may be further
surprised to learn that blogging may be good for your health.

A lot of advice on dealing with regret emphasizes controlling it, holding it back, keeping it in check. But trying too hard to suppress a thought can lead to a boomerang effect. Trying to clamp any thought can work in the short term, but later on, particularly when you become distracted, that thought may return with even greater urgency.[8] In Chapter 2, I first mentioned the groundbreaking research of James Pennebaker of the University of Texas, whose program of research revealed that the mere act of telling others about your troubles is good for you. Telling others can improve health, reduce doctor visits, fortify your immune system, and increase life satisfaction.[9] Further research has revealed that it is not so much the act of telling others, but simply expressing emotions, even simply by writing them down on paper, that can have positive health consequences.[10]

If you start blogging, or writing any sort of personal journal, you don't need to post it on the Internet for it to have positive life consequences. Other people need never see it. I have been keeping my own journal for about five years, and I never show it to anyone, and I hope quite frankly that no one *ever* sees it. Into my journal I type the most foolish, childish, and emotionally primitive thoughts that occur to me. I expel them from my mind without editing, without self-censorship, and the result is a largely unreadable mess. I can't personally tell from experience whether this does me any good because I cannot know for sure what I would have been like had I not been keeping a journal these last years. From experiments published over the last decade, it is fairly clear that my silly little journal has done me at least a little bit of good.

How best to blog? Keeping a blog can be as simple as keeping an old-fashioned diary, which when I was a kid meant a small leather-bound book sealed with a tiny lock and key, tucked away in a safe place where others never see it. The essential goal is simply to write something down. As long as you go into emotional detail, probe your feelings in depth, the sting of recent regret can be substantially reduced. And what do you write about? It could be problems, it could be regrets, but the main focus should be the emotional experiences of recent days. Don't focus too much on boring, day-to-day routine. Emphasize the peaks and valleys of your emotional life, your highs and lows, and be sure to include lots of detail about the circumstances leading up to emotionally charged events.

Pennebaker suggests a few further tips. Set aside at least fifteen minutes to write things down nearly every day. Once you begin, write continuously and don't worry about the spelling or grammar, just keep plugging away. If you run out of things to say, feel free to repeat anything over again. The key point is to keep thinking, keep writing, keep getting something onto the paper (or computer monitor).[11] Why does blogging work so well? Social psychologist Laura King suggests that it boils down to self-awareness. Writing offers the chance to learn more about oneself. Writing, she argues, "may serve to integrate life experiences into a larger, more sensible framework." This is an intriguing observation that refines some ideas touched on earlier. Recasting personal events into a redemption story is the best formula for realizing the positive benefits of diaries and journals. But the most recent research suggests that the redemption story format is not necessary to reach those positive effects. Rather, it is merely the act of looking back in detail—reviewing and integrating—that is the most basic ingredient underlying the value of blogging.[12]

Strategy #6: Eye on the Big Picture

We all have a tendency to focus on the immediate situation, on the small aspects of a problem without seeing the larger context. Reminding yourself what the big picture is all about can help channel regrets into renewed action.

The successful moon landing of July 1969 has become a national fable, a tale of great victory won through insurmountable odds by way of raw human daring. It's a great story precisely because of all the counterfactuals hidden inside it, the close calls and narrow escapes, but it also contains within it the centerpiece of this chapter, the idea that from intensely remorseful regret can come rebirth, renewal, and victory.[13]

The disaster that very nearly ruined the American moon program was the Apollo 1 fire of January 1967. Three astronauts died when a fire raged inside their spacecraft during a routine test on the ground. Progress toward the moon landing stopped as despairing engineers picked through the burnt wreckage of the Apollo 1 capsule in search of the cause of the fire. And all during this time, the feeling of survivor's guilt pervaded the NASA workforce. Few probably felt it as severely as Joe Shea, a key Apollo project manager. His feeling was that "the people on the ground [had] to live with [the] knowledge that they *might have done things differently*. This could be more painful than dying. . . ."[14] Shea was haunted by a particularly vivid counterfactual, that he was very nearly inside the capsule at the time of the fire. He intended to monitor the tests directly alongside the astronauts, but a problem with his communication headset had delayed his appearance inside the space capsule. Many times he wished he had been in the spacecraft with the astronauts. Maybe he would have died, too, which would be fine with him—a classic expression of survivor's guilt. But he also believed that if he had been in the spacecraft, huddled beneath the astronauts' couches, he would have been near to where the fire started and might actually have had time to smother it with his bare hands![15]

As deeply as NASA was scarred by the tragedy of the Apollo 1 fire, its response was a textbook example of riding the regret. The pain and anguish of failure was felt keenly and deeply, but it did not hold up new progress. Quite the contrary, it rejuvenated that progress. Faced with a clear problem to fix, the engineers attacked it with a vengeance, tearing apart the old Apollo capsule and finding the cause of the problem (bad wiring) as well as a host of other problems that would have spelled disaster in space had they not been found. These problems were fixed. And with a new spirit of determination, the moon program surged forward with spectacular success. Human beings first walked on the surface of the moon on July 20, 1969.

The human brain has a natural tendency to narrow its focus of attention when disaster strikes, to focus intently on the causes of that disaster and ignore all else. This is the focalism bias discussed in Chapter 4.[16] Problems are inevitable, and so when they do come along, it helps to remind yourself of the big picture. What are the overall goals, for you personally, for your family, or for your organization? After the Apollo 1 fire, there wasn't any long-term narrowing of attention merely to the specific cause of the fire and the fire alone. Rather, there was an urgent emphasis on the big picture, the number-one goal of meeting President Kennedy's challenge of landing a human being on the moon before the decade was over. This was the big-picture goal, the clock was ticking, and a key ingredient to the success of the Apollo moon program was an emphasis on all aspects of the program, not just the Apollo 1 fire problems, that needed to be perfect to meet that big-picture goal.

It might seem perverse that some NASA workers believed the Apollo 1 fire had a silver lining. But Charles Murray and Catherine Cox discovered precisely this "overarching irony" in interviews conducted for their book, *Apollo:* "Might it not, after all, have been a good thing for Apollo that the fire occurred? Many in NASA thought so." Joe Shea believed that the fire was a "unifying force." It brought the NASA teams closer together, inspiring their shared commitment. Another engineer said that the fire "really woke people up," made them focus on numerous minor design issues that had simply been put aside for later. Those challenges were then met full on.[17]

The lesson here is that regret works best in the service of the big picture. By riding the wave of regret, harnessing it to catalyze further creative, innovative action, regret can be brought forward to its highest degree of usefulness. In riding the regret to ultimate victory, NASA engineers never lost sight of the big picture.

Doing It

Just Do It was the first *Lesson from Research* in Chapter 2, and it emphasized how regrets from action are quicker to be killed off by the psychological immune system than regrets of inaction. If you go out and do something that ends badly, it probably won't still be haunting you a decade down the road. You'll reframe the failure, explain it away, move on, and forget it. But with inaction, the regret centering on what might have been had you taken the initiative is much longer lasting. And so when looking back on their lives as a whole, most people are haunted by things left undone—romantic opportunities untried, career changes unexplored, friendships neglected.

There is a further reason to emphasize action, and that is its power to move the individual beyond the nightmare of severe regret stemming from an unchangeable life situation. Earlier we saw the example of a woman gripped by regret over the suicide death of her mother. Maybe she could have done something to prevent that death. But this regret accomplishes nothing, for no new useful future action can come of this regret—her mother will never again be alive. So what can this person do? The answer is: Anything, as long as it is a deliberate, direct action, as long as it gets her mind off the past. This advice is a centerpiece of contemporary cognitive psychotherapy. The advice is simply to get out and do something different. Start new projects, find fresh challenges, develop new skills, and enjoy new pastimes, but overall, reorient your focus of attention to the future rather than the past.

Generativity is a form of direct action that may be especially nourishing, psychologically speaking. Generativity involves giving back to the community, with a special emphasis on nurturing a younger generation. It is mentoring and teaching, with a unique passion for creating a lasting legacy of personal contribution. The word "generativity" goes back to the writings of the great psychoanalytic theorist Erik Erikson, but finds new relevance in the contemporary research by Northwestern's

Dan McAdams. In studying the behavior and mental health of older adults, McAdams has discovered that generativity is a particularly effective antidote to tragedy and loss, and that a turn toward generativity is associated with improved mental health, particularly a boost in satisfaction with life as a whole.[18]

Diana was a participant in a 1997 study published by McAdams and his colleagues, and her story is emblematic of the power of embracing generativity to defeat regret. Diana, 49, was a teacher and mother of three grown children. As a child she felt lucky to be a member of a devout and tightly knit community in rural Iowa. Her father was a Methodist minister, and she lived her early years immersed in the social life of her father's congregation. Not long after her family moved to Chicago when she was eight years old, a tragic event befell her that echoed through the rest of her life. She was outside, playing and watching over her younger brother. It was her responsibility to keep track of her brother. In one horrifying instant, her little brother ran into the street and was hit by a car, dying soon after at a local hospital. You can see the kind of ferocious regret a child would feel after seeing her own brother, left in *her* care, suddenly die. And yet as severe as this regret and guilt were, it marked the beginning of a life dedicated to the care, encouragement, and nurturance of others. Diana's decision to make teaching her life's work was no accident, as "giving something back" was long a key goal for her. In her interview with McAdams' research team, she emphasized that her most important value in life was "to grow and help others grow."[19]

Diana's story illuminates the pattern by which many people are able to respond to tragedy by turning their life focus outward, by reaching out to help others. Moving on, turning thoughts into real action, and "just doing it" in a way that nurtures and guides a new generation of youngsters is a particularly effective response to severe regret.

An emphasis on "doing it" also pays off when it comes to decisions as to where to spend your leisure money. My mother used to tell me that if you have a choice between spending money on an object (like clothing or a television set) versus an experience (like going on a vacation or hearing a concert), it's better to pick the experience. My mother felt that although the pleasures of experiences and material possessions might be similar in the short term, experiences last longer in memory. You'll fondly recall a vacation of long ago, she said, but never a television set you owned long ago. It's been twenty years since I heard her say those things, so I asked her again recently whether she felt the same way. "Absolutely," she said. "My favorite memories are of you kids when you were small. And I also love to remember the trips on the train I took with my father when I was a child. But except for my first car, I can't much remember things I bought over the years."

Sometimes mothers know best, but other times they get it wrong, and social psychologists run experiments to reveal which bits of mother's wisdom we should take to heart. Social psychologists Leaf van Boven and Tom Gilovich put the idea to the test, and their research showed it to be essentially right. One of their studies, published in 2003, surveyed a nationwide cross-section of Americans to ask them about purchasing decisions. The survey respondents consistently declared greater pleasure and happiness resulting from money spent on experiences (like attending a concert) than on material objects (like buying new clothing). If new experiences are more rewarding than new material objects, then it goes without saying that faced with a choice between the two, picking an experience will produce less regret in the future than deciding to buy a new object. Van Boven and Gilovich point out that people quickly grow accustomed to their purchases, but enjoy the experience of remembering great old times. As one survey respondent explained: "Material possessions, they sort of become part of the background; experiences just get better with time."[20] Ed Diener, my colleague at the University of Illinois, quipped, "Materialism is toxic for happiness."[21]

If you have some money set aside and can spend it either on a vacation to Florida or a big-screen TV, pick the vacation to Florida. Don't forget to bring the camera!

Epilogue

⬥

You see things; and you say "Why?"

But I dream things that never were, and say "Why not?"

These words appeared in George Bernard Shaw's play *Back to Methuselah*, published in 1922. Robert Kennedy used them in his presidential campaign speeches in the spring of 1968. After his assassination, his brother Edward Kennedy, voice breaking with emotion, closed his eulogy for his slain brother Robert with the same words. It is an irony of history that words that speak of the counterfactual launchpad for hope, used in a political campaign back in an era much in need of hope, should later come to symbolize a life that might have been. Had he not been killed on June 5, 1968, Robert Kennedy might have been nominated as the Democratic candidate for president, might have beaten Richard Nixon in the fall 1968 election, might have taken the reins of power and steered a course for America that bypassed the widening of the Vietnam War into Cambodia and averted the tragedy of the Watergate scandal.[1]

This is a hopeful counterfactual. It is upward, which usually makes people feel bad, but this one doesn't have that emotional effect. If anything it is uplifting, because it suggests that political change can happen, that big events hold the possibility of modifying society for the better, and that individual initiative may well be meaningful and impactive.[2] This is one last counterfactual benefit that we have scarcely touched on so far, the power to see hope in possibility. Linguist George Steiner had this to say about it: "Language is the main instrument of man's refusal to accept the world as it is. Without that refusal, without the unceasing generation by the mind of counter-worlds, . . . we would turn forever on the treadmill of the present. Reality would be . . . 'all that is the case' and nothing more. Ours is the ability, the need, to gainsay or 'unsay' the world, to image and speak it otherwise."[3]

How interesting it is then that the first round of psychological research aimed at counterfactual thinking took the general perspective that such thoughts are dangerous. This work, extending through the 1980s, had a vaguely pessimistic tone, revealing in study after study how upward counterfactual thinking and regret were common sources of negative emotions and biased decision-making. Further studies suggested that counterfactual thinking interfered with coping and thus extended the heartache people suffer following traumatic events. Still other studies suggested that counterfactuals might be a precursor to depression.

It was not until the early 1990s that this view began to change, that a more balanced, even optimistic, description of the overall psychological significance of counterfactual thinking took hold. According to this new view, counterfactual thinking is deeply intertwined with the normal workings of emotion and behavior control. Working on a job, dining with friends, conversing with acquaintances, studying for exams, mapping out the financing of childrens' educations . . . all these everyday life behaviors require planning, management, organization, and frequent course corrections. Problems are inevitable. Accidents happen, glitches arise, and people struggle to fix what has blocked the road to their desires. Emotions are part of the basic brain system of behavior control, in that negative emotions signal to us when, and by how much, to make adjustments in ongoing behaviors, while positive emotions tell us that things are running smoothly. Emotions are guides to course corrections.

Counterfactual thinking helps us stay on course. Throughout this book I have tried to show that counterfactuals are for betterment. And in explaining six strategies for harnessing counterfactual thinking for personal betterment, I emphasized the theme of riding the wave of regret. Which is to say: Don't try too hard to unmake your thought processes and emotions. Rather, grab them and hold on, steer just a little bit, and ride them to success.

It can be an enormously liberating feeling to realize that no matter which way you decide things, no matter whether you respond to regret with big life changes or with big mental changes, you'll end up similarly satisfied in the end. But that is how our brains work, at least for most people, most of the time.

Regret is good. Thinking about what might have been is a normal component of the brain's attempt to make sense of the world, and of the human quest for betterment. Henry David Thoreau said it best:

> Make the most of your regrets; never smother your sorrow, but tend and cherish it till it comes to have a separate and integral interest. To regret deeply is to live afresh.[4]

Notes

≈

Introduction

1. Norman Rush, *Mating* (New York: Vintage Books, 1991), 108.
2. Philosophers were discussing the logical basis of counterfactual reasoning long before psychologists began to study their use in everyday thinking. The first major scholarly treatment of counterfactuals by a philosopher was N. Goodman, "The Problem of Counterfactual Conditionals," *Journal of Philosophy* 44 (1947): 113–28.
3. N. J. Roese, "The Functional Basis of Counterfactual Thinking," *Journal of Personality and Social Psychology* 66 (1994): 805–18; N. J. Roese and J. M. Olson, "Functions of Counterfactual Thinking," in N. J. Roese and J. M. Olson, eds., *What Might Have Been: The Social Psychology of Counterfactual Thinking* (Mahwah, NJ: Erlbaum, 1995), 169–97.

Chapter One

1. N. J. Roese, L. J. Sanna, and A. D. Galinsky, "The Mechanics of Imagination: Automaticity and Control in Counterfactual Thinking," in R. Hassin, J. S. Uleman, and J. A. Bargh, eds., *The New Unconscious* (New York: Oxford University Press, 2004), 138–70; E. P. Seelau, S. M. Seelau, G. L. Wells, and P. D. Windschitl, "Counterfactual Constraints," in N. J. Roese and J. M. Olson, *What Might Have Been,* 57–79.
2. The connection of causation to counterfactuals is one that has intrigued many thinkers, from philosophers to psychologists. For more on the philosophical debate about whether counterfactuals define causation, see David Lewis, *Counterfactuals* (Cambridge, MA: Harvard University Press, 1973); and John Collins, Ned Hall, and L. A. Paul, eds., *Causation*

and Counterfactuals (New York: Bradford Books, 2004). For a recent discussion of the psychological connection between counterfactuals and causation, see B. A. Spellman and D. R. Mandel, "When Possibility Informs Reality: Counterfactual Thinking as a Cue to Causality," *Current Directions in Psychological Science* 8 (1999): 120–23.

3. Even so, these improvements in safety could not alter the fact that these planes were just too expensive to operate. Concorde service ended in October 2003.

4. N. J. Roese, "Counterfactual Thinking," *Psychological Bulletin* 121 (1997): 133–48; N. J. Roese, "Counterfactual Thinking and Decision Making," *Psychonomic Bulletin and Review* 6 (1999): 570–78; N. J. Roese and J. M. Olson, "Counterfactual Thinking: The Intersection of Affect and Function," in M. P. Zanna, ed., *Advances in Experimental Social Psychology*, vol. 29 (San Diego: Academic Press, 1997), 1–59.

5. For a more detailed portrait of how optimists and pessimists differ in their thoughts of the future and past, see L. J. Sanna, "Defensive Pessimism, Optimism, and Simulating Alternatives: Some Ups and Downs of Prefactual and Counterfactual Thinking," *Journal of Personality and Social Psychology* 71 (1996): 1020–36; and L. J. Sanna, "Mental Simulation, Affect, and Personality: A Conceptual Framework," *Current Directions in Psychological Science* 9 (2000): 168–73.

6. Roese and Olson, "Counterfactual Thinking: The Intersection of Affect and Function."

7. V. H. Medvec, S. F. Madey, and T. Gilovich, "When Less Is More: Counterfactual Thinking and Satisfaction among Olympic Athletes," *Journal of Personality and Social Psychology* 69 (1995): 603–610. Jerry Seinfeld probably was the first to notice the plight of the silver medalist, or as he put it, "the number one loser." A part of his early standup comedy routine, Seinfeld's observations on silver versus bronze medalists can be heard on his 1998 concert recording, *I'm Telling You for the Last Time.*

8. Timothy Wilson, *Strangers to Ourselves: Discovering the Adaptive Unconscious* (Cambridge, MA: Harvard University Press, 2002), 6–7.

9. The complete transcript of pop-up balloons for this song appears on the Internet: http://www.geocities.com/Broadway/Balcony/8682/titanic bubble.html

10. D. Kahneman and D. T. Miller, "Norm Theory: Comparing Reality to Its Alternatives," *Psychological Review* 93 (1986): 136–53. A discussion

of some similar ideas (the "implicosphere") appeared in Douglas R. Hofstadter, *Metamagical Themas* (New York: Ballantine, 1985).

11. Roese et al., "The Mechanics of Imagination."

12. K. D. Markman and M. N. McMullen, "A Reflection and Evaluation Model of Comparative Thinking," *Personality and Social Psychology Review* 7 (2003): 244–67; J. M. Olson and N. J. Roese, "Comparing Comparisons: An Integrative Perspective on Social Comparison and Counterfactual Thinking," in J. Suls and L. Wheeler, eds., *Handbook of Social Comparison: Theory and Research* (New York: Plenum Press, 2000), 379–98.

13. A. E. Wilson and M. Ross, "The Frequency of Temporal-Self and Social Comparisons in People's Personal Appraisals," *Journal of Personality and Social Psychology* 78 (2000): 928–42; A. E. Wilson and M. Ross, "From Chump to Champ: People's Appraisals of Their Earlier and Present Selves," *Journal of Personality and Social Psychology* 80 (2001): 572–84.

14. These ideas have appeared in numerous sources, but one of the earliest and most influential was written by P. Brickman and J. R. Bulman, "Pleasure and Pain in Social Comparison," in J. M. Suls and R. L. Miller, eds., *Social Comparison Processes: Theoretical and Empirical Perspectives* (Washington, DC: Hemisphere, 1977), 149–86; also see T. A. Wills, "Downward Comparison Principles in Social Psychology," *Psychological Bulletin* 90 (1981): 245–71.

15. K. D. Markman, I. Gavanski, S. J. Sherman, and M. N. McMullen, "The Mental Simulation of Better and Worse Possible Worlds," *Journal of Experimental Social Psychology* 29 (1993): 87–109; see also Roese, "Functional Basis" and "Counterfactual Thinking."

16. Roese and Olson, "Counterfactual Thinking"; Wilson and Ross, "The Frequency of Temporal-Self and Social Comparisons."

17. D. T. Gilbert, E. C. Pinel, T. D. Wilson, S. J. Blumberg, and T. Wheatley, "Immune Neglect: A Source of Durability Bias in Affective Forecasting," *Journal of Personality and Social Psychology* 75 (1998): 617–38; D. T. Gilbert and T. D. Wilson, "Miswanting: Some Problems in the Forecasting of Future Affective States," in J. Forgas, ed., *Feeling and Thinking: The Role of Affect in Social Cognition* (New York: Cambridge University Press, 2000), 178–97.

18. D. P. McAdams et al., "When Bad Things Turn Good and Good Things Turn Bad: Sequences of Redemption and Contamination in

Life Narrative and Their Relation to Psychosocial Adaptation in Midlife Adults and in Students," *Personality and Social Psychology Bulletin* 27 (2001): 474–85, 474.

19. Douglas R. Hofstadter, *Gödel, Escher, Bach: An Eternal Golden Braid* (New York: Vintage Books, 1979), 643.

20. Roese, "Functional Basis."

Chapter Two

1. Gustave Flaubert, *Madame Bovary,* trans. A. Russell (1857; reprint, London: Penguin, 1950), 57.

2. S. B. Shimanoff, "Commonly Named Emotions in Everyday Conversations," *Perceptual and Motor Skills* 58 (1984): 514.

3. Roese, "Functional Basis"; L. J. Kray and A. D. Galinsky, "The Debiasing Effect of Counterfactual Mind-Sets: Increasing the Search for Disconfirmatory Information in Group Decisions," *Organizational Behavior and Human Decision Processes* 91 (2003): 69–81; M. W. Morris and P. C. Moore, "The Lessons We (Don't) Learn: Counterfactual Thinking and Organizational Accountability After a Close Call," *Administrative Science Quarterly* 45 (2000): 737–65; J. A. Stewart and E. A. Vandewater, "'If I Had It to Do Over Again . . .': Midlife Review, Midcourse Corrections, and Women's Well-Being in Midlife," *Journal of Personality and Social Psychology* 76 (1999): 270–83.

4. S. A. Nasco and K. L. Marsh, "Gaining Control through Counterfactual Thinking," *Personality and Social Psychology Bulletin* 25 (1999): 556–68.

5. The nine articles (containing eleven studies total) that present rankings of life regrets are:
M. K. DeGenova, "If You Had Your Life to Live Over Again: What Would You Do Differently?" *International Journal of Aging and Human Development* 34 (1992): 135–43; T. Gilovich and V. H. Medvec, "The Temporal Pattern to the Experience of Regret," *Journal of Personality and Social Psychology* 67 (1994): 357–65; N. Hattiangadi, V. H. Medvec, and T. Gilovich, "Failing to Act: Regrets of Terman's Geniuses," *International Journal of Human Development* 40 (1995): 175–85; M. Jokisaari, "Regret Appraisals, Age, and Subjective Well-Being," *Journal of Research in Personality* 37 (2003): 487–503; R. T. Kinnier and A. T. Metha, "Regrets and Priorities at Three Stages of Life," *Counseling and Values* 33 (1989): 182–93; J. Landman and J. D. Manis, "What Might

Have Been: Counterfactual Thought Concerning Personal Decision,"
British Journal of Psychology 83 (1992): 473–77; J. Landman, E. A. Vandewater, A. J. Stewart, and J. E. Malley, "Missed Opportunities: Psychological Ramifications of Counterfactual Thought in Midlife
Women," *Journal of Adult Development* 2 (1995): 87–97; L. Lecci, M.
A. Okun, and P. Karoly, "Life Regrets and Current Goals as Predictors
of Psychological Adjustment," *Journal of Personality and Social Psychology* 66 (1994): 731–41; C. Wrosch and J. Heckhausen, "Perceived Control of Life Regrets: Good for Young and Bad for Old Adults,"
Psychology and Aging 17 (2002): 340–50.

6. M. Elias, "Psychologists Now Know What Makes People Happy—It's
Not Great Riches, but Friends and Forgiveness," *USA Today,* Decem-
ber 9, 2002, p. 11D; E. Diener and C. Diener, "Most People Are
Happy," *Psychological Science* 7 (1996): 181–85.

7. Barry Cadish, *Damn!: Reflections on Life's Biggest Regrets* (Kansas City:
Andrews McMeel, 2001), 47.

8. Ibid., 56.

9. Ibid., 99, 53–54.

10. Roese, unpublished survey data, University of Illinois.

11. Ibid.

12. Cadish, *Damn!,* 60.

13. Landman and Manis, "What Might Have Been."

14. Cadish, *Damn!,* 99, 69.

15. Gilovich and Medvec, "The Temporal Pattern"; T. Gilovich and V. H.
Medvec, "The Experience of Regret: What, When, and Why," *Psychological Review* 102 (1995): 379–95.

16. M. J. Zeelenberg, J. van der Pligt, and A. S. R. Manstead, "Undoing
Regret on Dutch Television: Apologizing for Interpersonal Regrets Involving Actions or Inactions," *Personality and Social Psychology Bulletin*
24 (1998): 1113–19, 1115.

17. T. Gilovich, V. H. Medvec, and S. Chen, "Commission, Omission, and
Dissonance Reduction: Coping with the 'Monty Hall' Problem," *Personality and Social Psychology Bulletin* 21 (1995): 182–90.

18. If this explanation still doesn't convince you, think of it in terms of three
concrete prizes, like a can of tuna, a wheelbarrow, and a new car, then
think through each of three possible outcomes hinging on your first
choice. Your first choice is essentially random—you have three identical

doors and they're all the same to you. Let's say you pick (without realizing it) the can of tuna. Monty then MUST eliminate the wheelbarrow in order to preserve the drama of the show by keeping the good prize, the new car, in contention. For the tuna, then, switching wins and staying loses. Next, think about picking the wheelbarrow first. In this case, Monty MUST again eliminate the other poor prize, the tuna, leaving the car as the other choice, and so again switching wins and staying loses. In the third possible choice, you just happen to have picked the car. Monty can eliminate either the tuna or the wheelbarrow, doesn't matter which, and the result in either case is that switching loses and staying wins. So now we have three possibilities depending on three ways that the original random choice might have turned out, and for two of the three, switching wins and staying loses. Two out of three chances of winning by switching is the same as saying that switching compared to staying exactly doubles your chances of winning.

19. Zeigarnik's work is described in Alfred J. Morrow, *The Practical Theorist: The Life and Work of Kurt Lewin* (New York: Basic Books, 1979).

20. K. Savitsky, V. H. Medvec, and T. Gilovich, "Remembering and Regretting: The Zeigarnik Effect and the Cognitive Availability of Regrettable Actions and Inactions," *Personality and Social Psychology Bulletin* 23 (1997): 248–57; G. Sanders, *What Might Have Been* (Don Mills, Ontario, Canada: Harlequin Books, 1994), 14.

21. Hattiangadi et al., "Failing to Act"; T. Gilovich, R. F. Wang, D. Regan, and S. Nishina, "Regrets of Action and Inaction across Cultures," *Journal of Cross-Cultural Psychology* 34 (2003): 61–71.

22. Wrosch and Heckhausen, "Perceived Control of Life Regrets."

23. E. T. Higgins, "Beyond Pleasure and Pain," *American Psychologist* 52 (1997): 1280–1300; N. J. Roese, T. Hur, and G. L. Pennington, "Counterfactual Thinking and Regulatory Focus: Implications for Action versus Inaction and Sufficiency versus Necessity," *Journal of Personality and Social Psychology* 77 (1999): 1109–20.

24. N. J. Roese, G. L. Pennington, J. Coleman, M. Janicki, N. Li, and D. T. Kenrick, "Sex Differences in Regret: All for Love?" (manuscript submitted for publication).

25. Cadish, *Damn!*, 113.

26. Ibid., 84.

27. Roese, unpublished survey data, University of Illinois.

28. Cadish, *Damn!*, 81.

29. Hume, *A Treatise of Human Nature,* ed. with an introduction by Ernest C. Mossner (1739–40; New York: Penguin, 1985), 462.

30. *Seinfeld* (television series), "The Nose Job," episode 26, original air date: November 20, 1991.

31. Antonio R. Damasio, *Descartes' Error: Emotion, Reason, and the Human Brain* (New York: G. P. Putnam, 1994).

32. Arthur Schopenhauer, *Essays and Aphorisms,* trans. R. J. Hollingdale (1851; reprint, London: Penguin Books, 1970), 44–45.

33. James W. Pennebaker, *Opening Up: The Healing Power of Expressing Emotions* (New York: Guilford Press, 1997).

Chapter Three

1. Paul L. Harris, *The Work of the Imagination* (Oxford, UK: Blackwell, 2001), 124, 126.

2. Alfred H. Bloom, *The Linguistic Shaping of Thought: A Study on the Impact of Language on Thinking in China and the West* (Hillsdale, NJ: Erlbaum, 1981).

3. T. K. Au, "Counterfactuals—In Reply to Alfred Bloom," *Cognition* 17 (1984): 289–302. See also A. H. Bloom, "Caution—The Words You Use May Affect What You Say: A Response to Au," *Cognition* 17, 275–87.

4. T. K. Au, "Words, Reasoning, and Presuppositions in Social Cognition," in G. R. Semin and K. Fiedler, eds., *Language, Interaction, and Social Cognition* (London: Sage, 1992), 194–213.

5. A vintage Presto Hot-Dogger from the 1970s can be purchased on eBay for about ten dollars.

6. Nathan McCall, *Makes Me Wanna Holler: A Young Black Man in America* (New York: Vintage Books, 1994), 140–41.

7. N. J. Roese and T. Hur, "Affective Determinants of Counterfactual Thinking," *Social Cognition* 15 (1997): 274–90.

8. T. P. German, "Children's Causal Reasoning: Counterfactual Thinking Occurs for 'Negative' Outcomes Only," *Developmental Science* 2 (1999): 442–47.

9. P. A. Parker, M. S. Middleton, and J. A. Kulik, "Counterfactual Thinking and Quality of Life among Women with Silicone Breast Implants," *Journal of Behavioral Medicine* 25 (2002): 317–35.

10. Philosophers speak about the closeness of a counterfactual alternative,

or "possible" world, as indicators of its acceptability or truthfulness. For example, see David Lewis, *Counterfactuals* (Cambridge, MA: Harvard University Press, 1973).

11. An experiment on physical distance appeared in D. T. Miller and C. McFarland, "Counterfactual Thinking and Victim Compensation: A Test of Norm Theory," *Personality and Social Psychology Bulletin* 12 (1986): 513–19; an experiment on temporal distance appeared in D. Kahneman and A. Tversky, "The Simulation Heuristic," in D. Kahneman, P. Slovic, and A. Tversky, eds., *Judgment under Uncertainty: Heuristics and Biases* (New York: Cambridge University Press, 1982): 201–08.

12. L. J. Sanna, C. D. Parks, S. Meier, E. C. Chang, B. R. Kassin, and T. M. Miyake, "A Game of Inches: Spontaneous Use of Counterfactuals by Broadcasters," *Journal of Applied Social Psychology* 33 (2003): 455–75.

13. O. E. Tykocinski and T. S. Pittman, "The Consequences of Doing Nothing: Inaction Inertia as Avoidance of Anticipated Regret," *Journal of Personality and Social Psychology* 75 (1998): 607–16.

14. R. N. Lebow and J. G. Stein, "Back to the Past: Counterfactuals and the Cuban Missile Crisis," in P. E. Tetlock and A. Belkin, eds., *Counterfactual Thought Experiments in World Politics* (Princeton, NJ: Princeton University Press, 1996).

15. Richard Rhodes, *Dark Sun: The Making of the Hydrogen Bomb* (New York: Touchstone, 1995), 575–76.

16. Len Deighton, *SS-GB: Nazi-Occupied Britain, 1941* (London: Jonathan Cape, 1978); Philip K. Dick, *The Man in the High Castle* (New York: Vintage Books, 1962); Robert Harris, *Fatherland* (London: Arrow Books, 1992).

17. For a short term I imagined I was the first to see the connection of saved/reloaded video games to the natural use of counterfactual thinking. After writing this passage, however, I discovered that psychologists Geoffrey and Elizabeth Loftus made the exact same observation more than twenty years ago: ". . . Since you saved the game, you can go back and create an alternative world, thereby eliminating the regret. So you do. Computer games provide the ultimate chance to eliminate regret; all alternative worlds are available"; Geoffrey R. Loftus and Elizabeth F. Loftus, *Mind at Play: The Psychology of Video Games* (New York: Basic Books, 1983), 32–33.

Chapter Four

1. The line comes from the film *Star Trek: The Motion Picture* (1979).
2. C. N. Macrae, A. B. Milne, and R. J. Griffiths, "Counterfactual Thinking and the Perception of Criminal Behaviour," *British Journal of Psychology* 84 (1993): 221–26.
3. Douglas R. Hofstadter, *Gödel, Escher, Bach*, 641.
4. In the previous chapter, negative outcomes and "almost" outcomes were listed as determinants. Here, agency and abnormality are listed as determinants. For a few years there was some confusion over which factors determine counterfactual thinking, in that these determinants were listed together ambiguously. In previous scholarly writings I argued that there are two key aspects of counterfactual generation: mere activation (whether the person actually begins to think of a counterfactual or not) versus content (what the counterfactual focuses on). Negative outcomes and "almost" outcomes influence mere activation, whereas agency and abnormality influence content. This conceptualization is retained here in a somewhat simplified format. The original conceptualization appeared in Roese, "Counterfactual Thinking Critical Overview" and in N. J. Roese and J. M. Olson, "Counterfactual Thinking: A Critical Overview," Roese and Olson, *What Might Have Been*, 1–59.
5. E. J. Langer, "The Illusion of Control," *Journal of Personality and Social Psychology* 32 (1975): 311–28.
6. E. J. Langer and J. Rodin, "The Effects of Choice and Enhanced Personal Responsibility for the Aged: A Field Experiment in an Institutional Setting," *Journal of Personality and Social Psychology* 34 (1976): 191–98; C. Peterson, "Personal Control and Well-Being," in D. Kahneman, E. Diener, and N. Schwarz, eds., *Well-Being: The Foundations of Hedonic Psychology* (New York: Russell Sage Foundation, 1999), 288–301; R. Schulz, "Effects of Control and Predictability on the Physical and Psychological Well-Being of the Institutionalized Aged," *Journal of Personality and Social Psychology* 33 (1976): 563–73.
7. Nasco and Marsh, "Gaining Control"; M. N. McMullen, K. D. Markman, and I. Gavanski, (1995). "Living in neither the best nor the worst of all possible worlds: Antecedents and consequences of upward and downward counterfactual thinking." In Roese and Olson, *What Might Have Been*, 133–67.
8. Gilovich and Medvec, "The Temporal Pattern"; N. J. Roese and J. M.

Olson, "Outcome Controllability and Counterfactual Thinking," *Personality and Social Psychology Bulletin* 21 (1995): 620–28.

9. K. D. Markman, I. Gavanski, S. J. Sherman, and M. N. McMullen, "The Impact of Perceived Control on the Imagination of Better and Worse Possible Worlds," *Personality and Social Psychology Bulletin* 21 (1995): 588–95.

10. Kahneman and Tversky, "The Simulation Heuristic."

11. Other studies that have demonstrated the role of normality in counterfactual thinking include M. L. Buck and D. T. Miller, "Reactions to Incongruous Negative Life Events," *Social Justice Research* 7 (1994): 29–46; I. Gavanski and G. L. Wells, "Counterfactual Processing of Normal and Exceptional Events," *Journal of Experimental Social Psychology* 25 (1989): 314–25; N. J. Roese and J. M. Olson, "The Structure of Counterfactual Thought," *Personality and Social Psychology Bulletin* 19 (1993): 312–19.

12. Melvin J. Lerner, *The Belief in a Just World: A Fundamental Delusion* (New York: Plenum Press, 1980).

13. K. J. Turley, L. J. Sanna, and R. L. Reiter, "Counterfactual Thinking and Perceptions of Rape," *Basic and Applied Social Psychology* 17 (1995): 285–303. See also N. R. Branscombe, S. Owen, T. Garstka, and J. Coleman, "Rape and Accident Counterfactuals: Who Might Have One Otherwise and Would It Have Changed the Outcome?" *Journal of Applied Social Psychology* 26 (1996): 1042–67.

14. S. D. Goldinger, H. M. Kleider, T. Azuma, and D. R. Beike, "Blaming the Victim under Memory Load," *Psychological Science* 14 (2003): 81–85.

15. C. G. Davis, D. R. Lehman, R. C. Silver, C. B. Wortman, and J. H. Ellard, "Self-Blame Following a Traumatic Event: The Role of Perceived Avoidability," *Personality and Social Psychology Bulletin* 22 (1996): 557–67.

16. C. G. Davis, D. R. Lehman, C. B. Wortman, R. C. Silver, and S. C. Thompson, "The Undoing of Traumatic Life Events," *Personality and Social Psychology Bulletin* 21 (1995): 109–24, 113.

17. See also D. R. Mandel and D. R. Lehman, "Counterfactual Thinking and Ascriptions of Cause and Preventability," *Journal of Personality and Social Psychology* 71 (1996): 450–63.

18. C. G. Davis and D. R. Lehman, "Counterfactual Thinking and

Coping with Traumatic Life Events," in Roese and Olson, *What Might Have Been,* 353–74.

19. R. J. Bulman and C. B. Wortman, "Attributions of Blame and Coping in the 'Real World': Severe Accident Victims React to Their Lot," *Journal of Personality and Social Psychology* 35 (1977): 351–63; D. T. Miller and C. A. Porter, "Self-Blame in Victims of Violence," *Journal of Social Issues* 39 (1983): 139–52.

20. W. K. Campbell and C. Sedikides, "Self-Threat Magnifies the Self-Serving Bias: A Meta-Analytic Integration," *Review of General Psychology* 3 (1999): 23–43.

21. C. O. Fraser, "Was It My Fault? Effects of Counterfactual Mutation Focus and Self-Presentation Strategy," *Journal of Applied Social Psychology* 31 (2001): 1076–95.

22. N. J. Roese and J. M. Olson, "Self-Esteem and Counterfactual Thinking," *Journal of Personality and Social Psychology* 65 (1993): 199–206; S. E. Taylor and J. D. Brown, "Illusion and Well-Being: A Social Psychological Perspective on Mental Health," *Psychological Bulletin* 103 (1988): 193–210.

23. L. Festinger and E. Walster, "Post-Decision Regret and Decision Reversal," in L. Festinger, ed., *Conflict, Decision, and Dissonance* (Stanford, CA: Stanford University Press, 1964), 112–27; Gilbert and Wilson, "Miswanting."

24. Taylor and Brown, "Illusion and Well-Being."

25. R. E. Lucas, A. E. Clark, Y. Georgellis, and E. Diener, "Reexamining Adaptation and the Set Point Model of Happiness: Reactions to Changes in Marital Status," *Journal of Personality and Social Psychology* 84 (2003): 527–39.

26. L. Y. Abramson, G. I. Metalsky, and L. B. Alloy, "Hopelessness Depression: A Theory-Based Subtype of Depression," *Psychological Review* 96 (1989): 358–72.

27. M. R. Monroe, J. R. Skowronski, W. MacDonald, and S. E. Wood, "The Mildly Depressed Experience More Post-Decisional Regret than the Non-Depressed," *Journal of Social and Clinical Psychology* (in press); see also K. D. Markman and G. Weary, "Control Motivation, Depression, and Counterfactual Thought," in M. Kofta, G. Weary, and G. Sedak, eds., *Personal Control in Action: Cognitive and Motivational Mechanisms* (New York: Plenum Press, 1998), 363–90.

28. R. Hastie, D. A. Schkade, and J. W. Payne, "Juror Judgments in Civil Cases: Hindsight Effects on Judgments of Liability for Punitive Damages," *Law and Human Behavior* 23 (1999): 597–614.

29. N. J. Roese and S. D. Maniar, "Perceptions of Purple: Counterfactual and Hindsight Judgments at Northwestern Wildcats Football Games," *Personality and Social Psychology Bulletin* 23 (1997): 1245–53; N. J. Roese and J. M. Olson, "Counterfactuals, Causal Attributions, and the Hindsight Bias: A Conceptual Integration," *Journal of Experimental Social Psychology* 32 (1996): 197–227.

30. J. K. Robbenolt and M. S. Sobus, "An Integration of Hindsight Bias and Counterfactual Thinking: Decision Making and Drug Courier Profiles," *Law and Human Behavior* 22 (1997): 539–60; M. J. Stallard and D. L. Worthington, "Reducing the Hindsight Bias Utilizing Attorney Closing Arguments," *Law and Human Behavior* 22 (1998): 671–83.

31. T. D. Wilson, T. P. Wheatley, J. M. Meyers, D. T. Gilbert, and D. Axsom, "Focalism: A Source of Durability Bias in Affective Forecasting," *Journal of Personality and Social Psychology* 78 (2000): 821–36.

32. D. A. Schkade and D. Kahneman, "Does Living in California Make People Happy? A Focusing Illusion in Judgments of Life Satisfaction," *Psychological Science* 9 (1998): 340–46.

33. H. R. Arkes, D. Faust, T. J. Guilmette, and K. Hart, "Eliminating the Hindsight Bias," *Journal of Applied Psychology* 73 (1988): 305–7; E. R. Hirt and K. D. Markman, "Multiple Explanation: A Consider-an-Alternative Strategy for Debiasing Judgments," *Journal of Personality and Social Psychology* 69 (1995): 1069–86.

Chapter Five

1. This example appears in Eric S. Knowles and Jay A. Linn, *Resistance and Persuasion* (Mahwah, NJ: Erlbaum, 2004).

2. M. Tsiros, "Effect of Regret on Post-Choice Valuation: The Case of More Than Two Alternatives," *Organizational Behavior and Human Decision Processes* 76 (1998): 48–69; S. B. Walchli and J. Landman, "Effects of Counterfactual Thought on Post-Purchase Consumer Affect," *Psychology and Marketing* 20 (2003): 23–46.

3. A. D. J. Cooke, T. Meyvis, and A. Schwartz, "Avoiding Future Regret in Purchase-Timing Decisions," *Journal of Consumer Research* 27 (2001):

447–59; K. A. Taylor, "A Regret Theory Approach to Assessing Consumer Satisfaction," *Marketing Letters* 8 (1997): 229–38; M. Zeelenberg, J. J. Inman, and R. P. G. Pieters, "What Do We Do When Decisions Go Awry: Behavioral Consequences of Experienced Regret," in J. Baron, G. Loomes, and E. Weber, eds., *Conflict and Tradeoffs in Decision Making* (Cambridge: Cambridge University Press, 2001), 136–55.

4. S. S. Iyengar and M. R. Lepper, "When Choice Is Demotivating: Can One Desire Too Much of a Good Thing?" *Journal of Personality and Social Psychology* 79 (2000): 995–1006.

5. S. S. Iyengar, W. Jiang, and G. Huberman, "How Much Choice Is Too Much? Determinants of Individual Contribution in 401(k) Retirement Plans" (unpublished manuscript, Columbia University, 2003); B. Schwartz, "Self-Determination: The Tyranny of Freedom," *American Psychologist* 55 (2002): 79–88.

6. S. M. Nowlis and I. Simonson, "Sales Promotions and the Choice Context as Competing Influences on Consumer Decision Making," *Journal of Consumer Psychology* 9 (2000): 1–16.

7. E. H. Creyer and W. T. Ross, "The Development and Use of a Regret Experience Measure to Examine the Effects of Outcome Feedback on Regret and Subsequent Choice," *Marketing Letters* 10 (1999): 379–92; B. Mellers, A. Schwartz, and I. Ritov, "Emotion-Based Choice," *Journal of Experimental Psychology: General* 128 (1999): 332–45.

8. Medvec et al., "When Less Is More" V. H. Medvec and K. Savitsky, "When Doing Better Means Feeling Worse: A Model of Counterfactual Cutoff Points," *Journal of Personality and Social Psychology* 72 (1997): 1284–96.

9. M. Zeelenberg and R. Pieters, "Comparing Service Delivery to What Might Have Been: Behavioral Responses to Regret and Disappointment," *Journal of Service Research* 2 (1999): 86–97.

10. Roese, "Counterfactual Thinking and Decision Making."

11. Alexandra Twin, "Stocks Edge Lower: But Markets Muster Another 'U' Week," *CNN Money* (website), May 16, 2003.

12. "Blue-Chips Sink; Climax Ahead?" *CNBC Market Dispatches* (website), October 4, 2002.

13. M. W. Morris, O. P. Sheldon, D. R. Ames, and M. Young, "Metaphors for the Market: Price Charts, Physical and Psychological Metaphors, and Biased Forecasts" (unpublished manuscript, Columbia University).

14. S. J. Sherman and A. R. McConnell, "Dysfunctional Implications of Counterfactual Thinking: When Alternatives to Reality Fail Us," in Roese and Olson, *What Might Have Been*, 199–231, 220; M. Zeelenberg, "The Use of Crying over Spilled Milk: A Note on the Rationality and Functionality of Regret," *Philosophical Psychology* 12 (1999): 325–40.

15. T. Gilovich, "Biased Evaluation and Persistence in Gambling," *Journal of Personality and Social Psychology* 44 (1983): 1110–26.

16. M. J. A. Wohl and M. E. Enzle, "The Effects of Near Wins and Near Losses on Self-Perceived Luck and Subsequent Gambling Behavior," *Journal of Experimental Social Psychology* 39 (2003): 184–91.

17. These examples appeared in Sherman and McConnell, "Dysfunctional Implications of Counterfactual Thinking."

18. J. Landman and R. Petty, "It Could Have Been You: How States Exploit Counterfactual Thought to Market Lotteries," *Psychology and Marketing* 17 (2000): 299–321.

19. Anecdote mentioned in Landman and Petty, "It Could Have Been You."

20. Paul Newman starred as Fast Eddie Felson in the 1961 film *The Hustler*. He reprised the role in the 1986 film *The Color of Money*, in which he mentored an up-and-coming pool hustler played by Tom Cruise.

21. Loftus and Loftus, *Mind at Play*, 30

22. Zeelenberg, "The Use of Crying over Spilled Milk."

23. This example comes from ibid., 97.

24. I. Simonson, "The Influence of Anticipated Regret and Responsibility on Purchase Decisions," *Journal of Consumer Research* 19 (1992): 105–18.

25. Lottery tickets: M. Bar-Hillel and E. Neter, "Why Are People Reluctant to Exchange Lottery Tickets?" *Journal of Personality and Social Psychology* 70 (1996): 17–27; Negotiation: R. P. Larrick and T. L. Boles, "Avoiding Regret in Decisions with Feedback: A Negotiation Example," *Organization Behavior and Human Decision Processes* 63 (1995): 87–97; Insurance: J. J. Hetts, D. S. Boninger, D. A. Armor, F. Gleicher, and A. Nathanson, "The Influence of Anticipated Counterfactual Regret on Behavior," *Psychology and Marketing* 17 (2000): 345–68.

26. A. R. McConnell, K. E. Niedermeier, J. M. Leibold, A. G. El-Alayli, P. G. Chin, and N. M. Kuiper, " 'What If I Find It Cheaper Someplace Else?': Role of Prefactual Thinking and Anticipated Regret in Consumer Behavior," *Psychology and Marketing* 17 (2000): 281–98.

27. Zeelenberg, "The Use of Crying over Spilled Milk."

28. McConnell et al., " 'What If I Find It Cheaper?' "

29. F. Gleicher, D. Boninger, A. Strathman, D. Armor, J. Hetts, and M. Ahn, "With an Eye Toward the Future: The Impact of Counterfactual Thinking on Affect, Attitudes, and Behavior," in Roese and Olson, *What Might Have Been,* 283–304.

30. D. Burgstahler and I. Dichev, "Earnings Management to Avoid Earnings Decreases and Losses," *Journal of Accounting and Economics* 24 (1997): 99–126; W. W. van Dijk, M. Zeelenberg, and J. van der Pligt, "Blessed Are Those Who Expect Nothing: Lowering Expectations as a Way of Avoiding Disappointment," *Journal of Economic Psychology* 24 (2003): 505–16. Research on earnings management has not to date drawn on psychological theory of counterfactual thinking. This research, situated within the fields of accounting, finance, and economics, uses different theory and different terminology to explain the findings, yet the underlying logic is clearly rooted to counterfactual thinking. In drawing this connection here for the first time, I am indebted to David Piercey and Shaun Fingland.

31. A. D. Galinsky and T. Mussweiler, "First Offers as Anchors: The Role of Perspective-Taking and Negotiator Focus," *Journal of Personality and Social Psychology* 81 (2001): 657–69.

32. A. D. Galinsky, V. Seiden, P. H. Kim, and V. H. Medvec, "The Dissatisfaction of Having Your First Offer Accepted: The Role of Counterfactual Thinking in Negotiations," *Personality and Social Psychology Bulletin* 28 (2002): 271–83, 273.

33. A similar finding, that negotiators become more conservative, or play it safer, after experiencing regret, appeared in Experiment 3 of Zeelenberg and Beattie. M. Zeelenberg and J. Beattie, "Consequences of Regret Aversion 2: Additional Evidence for the Effects of Feedback on Decision Making," *Organizational Behavior and Human Decision Processes* 72 (1997): 63–78.

34. C. E. Naquin, "The Agony of Opportunity in Negotiation: Number of Negotiable Issues, Counterfactual Thinking, and Feelings of Satisfaction," *Organizational Behavior and Human Decision Processes* 91 (2003): 97–107.

35. D. T. Gilbert and E. J. Ebert, "Decisions and Revisions: The Affective

Forecasting of Changeable Outcomes," *Journal of Personality and Social Psychology* 82 (2002): 503–14.

36. Daniel Wegner, *The Illusion of Conscious Will* (Cambridge, MA: MIT Press, 2002); Daniel C. Dennett, *Freedom Evolves* (New York: Viking, 2003).

37. F. A. Hayek, *The Road to Serfdom* (Chicago: University of Chicago Press, 1944), 104.

Chapter Six

1. Curiously, this very same episode ranked way down at number 92 on *TV Guide*'s list of the "100 Greatest Episodes of All Time," published in June 1997.

2. Gardner Dozois and Stanley Schmidt, eds., *Roads Not Taken: Tales of Alternate History* (New York: Del Rey, 1998).

3. MacKinlay Kantor, *If the South Had Won the Civil War* (New York: Forge, 1960).

4. Steve Tally, *Almost America: From the Colonists to Clinton, A "What If" History of the U.S.* (New York: Avon, 2000).

5. Hofstadter, *Metamagical Themas*, 249.

6. Mozart, *Theme and Twelve Variations on "Ah, Vous Dirais–je Maman"* (KV 265), composed in 1782.

7. Harris, *Fatherland*, 209.

8. D. E. Berlyne, *Studies in the New Experimental Aesthetics: Steps Toward an Objective Psychology of Aesthetic Appreciation* (New York: Taylor & Francis, 1974).

9. Geoffrey Hawthorn, *Plausible Worlds: Possibility and Understanding in History and the Social Sciences* (New York: Cambridge University Press, 1991); R. N. Lebow, "What's So Different About a Counterfactual?" *World Politics* 52 (2000): 550–85; P. E. Tetlock and A. Belkin, "Counterfactual Thought Experiments in World Politics: Logical, Methodological, and Psychological Perspectives," in Tetlock and Belkin, *Counterfactual Thought Experiments in World Politics*, 1–38.

10. T. Geisel and A. S. (Dr. Seuss), *Happy Birthday To You!* (New York: Random House, 1959).

Chapter Seven

1. Milan Kundera, *The Unbearable Lightness of Being* (New York: Harper & Row, 1984), 34.

2. An expanded discussion of this topic appears in A. Galinsky, K. Liljenquist, L. J. Kray, and N. J. Roese, "Finding Meaning in Mutability: Making Sense and Deriving Significance through Counterfactual Thinking," to appear in D. R. Mandel, D. J. Hilton, and P. Catellani, eds., *The Psychology of Counterfactual Thinking* (London: Routledge).

3. Kundera, *The Unbearable Lightness of Being*, 35.

4. J. Burrus and N. J. Roese, "Fate and Counterfactual Thinking" (manuscript in preparation, University of Illinois).

5. M. J. Young and M. W. Morris, "Existential Meanings and Cultural Models: The Interplay of Personal and Supernatural Agency in American and Hindu Ways of Responding to Uncertainty," in J. Greenberg, S. L. Koole, and T. Pyszczynski, eds., *Handbook of Experimental Existential Psychology* (New York: Guilford Press, 2004).

6. Richard Nisbett and Lee Ross, *Human Inference: Strategies and Shortcomings of Social Judgment* (Englewood Cliffs, NJ: Prentice-Hall, 1980). See also D. L. H. Sim and M. W. Morris, "Representativeness in Counterfactual Thinking: The Principle That Outcome and Antecedent Correspond in Magnitude," *Personality and Social Psychology Bulletin* 24 (1998): 595–609.

7. Thomas L. Friedman, *From Beirut to Jerusalem* (New York: Farrar, Straus & Giroux, 1990), 262–63. Friedman's comments paraphrase the writings of Israeli philosopher David Hartman.

8. The role of proximity in attraction is well established by social psychology research and is summarized in detail in this textbook: S. S. Brehm, R. S. Miller, D. Perlman, and S. M. Campbell, *Intimate Relationships* (New York: McGraw-Hill, 2002).

9. http://www.newadvent.org/cathen/

10. Richard Wiseman, "The Luck Factor," *Skeptical Inquirer* (May–June 2003), 26–30.

11. D. T. Miller and B. R. Taylor, "Counterfactual Thought, Regret, and Superstition: How to Avoid Kicking Yourself," in Roese and Olson, *What Might Have Been*, 305–31.

12. Samuel C. Brownstein, Ira K. Wolf, and Sharon Weiner Green, *Barron's*

How to Prepare for the GRE: Graduate Record Examination (Hauppage, NY: Barrons Educational Series, 2000), 6.

13. L. T. Benjamin, T. A. Cavell, and W. R. Shallenberger, "Staying with Initial Answers on Objective Tests: Is It a Myth?" *Teaching of Psychology* 11 (1984): 133–41.

14. J. Kruger, D. Wirtz, and D. T. Miller, "Counterfactual Thinking and the First Instinct Fallacy" (unpublished manuscript, University of Illinois).

15. Tom Barbash, *On Top of the World* (New York: HarperCollins, 2003), 190.

16. Ibid., 192.

17. Markman and McMullen, "A Reflection and Evaluation Model."

18. http://www.inthefray.com/200202/interact/lin11/lin11.html

Chapter Eight

1. Gilbert and Ebert, "Decisions and Revisions."

2. Deborah Layton, *Seductive Poison: A Jonestown Survivor's Story of Life and Death in the People's Temple* (New York: Anchor Books, 1998), 135.

3. R. A. Baron, "Cognitive Mechanisms in Entrepreneurship: Why and When Entrepreneurs Think Differently than Other People," *Journal of Business Venturing* 13 (1998): 275–94; R. A. Baron, "Counterfactual Thinking and Venture Formation: The Potential Effects of Thinking about 'What Might Have Been,'" *Journal of Business Venturing* 15 (1999): 79–91; R. A. Baron, "Psychological Perspectives on Entrepreneurship: Cognitive and Social Factors in Entrepreneurs' Success," *Current Directions in Psychological Science* 9 (2000): 15–18.

4. Kray and Galinsky, "The Debiasing Effect of Counterfactual Mind-Sets"; S. E. Taylor, L. B. Pham, I. D. Rivkin, and D. A. Armor, "Harnessing the Imagination: Mental Simulation, Self-Regulation, and Coping," *American Psychologist* 53 (1997): 429–39.

5. Tod's story appeared in D. Kadlec, "Where Did My Raise Go?" *Time,* May 26, 2003, 44–54.

6. N. Schwarz, "Accessible Content and Accessibility Experiences: The Interplay of Declarative and Experiential Information in Judgment," *Personality and Social Psychology Review* 2 (1998): 87–99.

7. N. J. Roese and J. R. Kuban, "Counterfactual Thinking and Accessibility Experiences" (unpublished manuscript, University of Illinois, 2003).

8. Daniel M. Wegner, *White Bears and Other Unwanted Thoughts: Suppression, Obsession, and the Psychology of Mental Control* (New York: Guilford Press, 1989).

9. Pennebaker, *Opening Up.*

10. L. A. King and K. N. Miner, "Writing about the Perceived Benefits of Traumatic Events: Implications for Physical Health," *Personality and Social Psychology Bulletin* 26 (2000): 220–30.

11. See James Pennebaker's website: http://homepage.psy.utexas.edu/ HomePage/Faculty/Pennebaker/Home2000/WritingandHealth.html

12. L. A. King, "The Health Benefits of Writing about Life Goals," *Personality and Social Psychology Bulletin* 27 (2001): 798–807, 806.

13. The most dramatic close-call moment occurred when the Eagle, the lunar spaceship piloted by Apollo 11 crewmen Neil Armstrong and Buzz Aldrin, was descending for a landing. Armstrong and Aldrin noticed an unexpected field of boulders obstructing their intended landing site. With fuel running low, Armstrong took the controls and flew the Eagle past the boulders. The spacecraft landed on the surface of the moon with only a few seconds of fuel remaining in the tanks. Had Armstrong flown just a bit farther, stayed aloft just a little longer, the fuel would have run out and the Eagle would have crashed onto the lunar surface.

14. Charles Murray and Catherine S. Cox, *Apollo: The Race to the Moon* (New York: Touchstone, 1989), 200–1.

15. Ibid., 223.

16. Schkade and Kahneman, "Does Living in California Make People Happy?"; Wilson et al., "Focalism."

17. Murray and Cox, *Apollo,* 222.

18. Erik H. Erikson, *Childhood and Society* (New York: Norton, 1963); Dan P. McAdams, *The Stories We Live By: Personal Myths and the Making of the Self* (New York: Guilford Press, 1993).

19. D. P. McAdams, A. Diamond, E. D. Aubin, and E. Mansfield, "Stories of Commitment: The Psychosocial Construction of Generative Lives," *Journal of Personality and Social Psychology* 72 (1997): 678–94, 689.

20. L. van Boven and T. Gilovich, "To Do or to Have? That Is the Question," *Journal of Personality and Social Psychology* 85 (2003): 1193–1202.

21. M. Elias, "Psychologists Now Know What Makes People Happy—It's

Not Great Riches, but Friends and Forgiveness," *USA Today,* December 9, 2002.

Epilogue

1. I would not have known the full derivation of this quotation had I not read it in Hofstadter, *Metamagical Themas.*
2. D. S. Boninger, F. Gleicher, and A. Strathman, "Counterfactual Thinking: From What Might Have Been to What May Be," *Journal of Personality and Social Psychology* 67 (1994): 297–307.
3. George Steiner, *After Babel: Aspects of Language and Translation* (New York: Oxford University Press, 1975), 217–18.
4. Entry entitled "Regret" from November 13, 1839, in Henry D. Thoreau, *The Journal of Henry David Thoreau, Volume 1, 1837–1846* (Boston: Houghton Mifflin, 1906), 95.

Index

~

About the Author

~

Neal Roese is Associate Professor of Psychology at the University of Illinois. The author of more than forty scholarly publications, he is one of the leading researchers on counterfactual thinking and regret. His ongoing program of research is supported by grants from the National Institute of Mental Health. His previous book was a co-edited collection of scholarly essays entitled *What Might Have Been: The Social Psychology of Counterfactual Thinking.* He lives with his wife and two children in Champaign, Illinois.